Edward Anthony's earlier works include books on popular culture and information technology. He lives in Sussex.

THY ROD AND STAFF

Edward Anthony

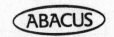

An *Abacus* Book

First published in Great Britain by
Little, Brown and Company 1995
This edition published by Abacus 1996
Reprinted 1997

Copyright © Edward Anthony, 1995

The moral right of the author has been asserted.

A CIP catalogue record for this book
is available from the British Library.

ISBN 0 349 10709 2

Printed and bound in Great Britain by
Clays Ltd, St Ives plc

Abacus
A Division of
Little, Brown and Company (UK)
Brettenham House
Lancaster Place
London WC2E 7EN

For Bill

ACKNOWLEDGEMENTS

The author offers grateful thanks to the following publishers for permission to quote extracts from titles held under copyright: BFI (British Film Institute) Publishing, for generously allowing me to save myself considerable labour by deploying Professor Anne McLintock's clear-headed exegeses, part of the *Dirty Looks: Women, Pornography, Power* collection of essays edited by Pamela Church Gibson and Roma Gibson; Little, Brown, for use of the quoted passages from both *Beauty's Release* by A. N. Roquelaure, and *9½ Weeks* by Elizabeth McNeill; the Alice Kerr-Sutherland Society, for permission to quote from both *The Queen of the Grove* and *Sweet Retribution*; David and Charles, for *War in 2080* by David Langford; Gerald Duckworth & Co., for Ian Gibson's *The English Vice*; Glidrose Publications, for the use of the small but perfectly formed quotation from Ian Fleming's *Dr No*; Hambledon Press, for *The Victorian Governess* by Kathryn Hughes; Katharine Whitehorn and her agents Peters Fraser & Dunlop for permission to reproduce part of *How To Survive Children*; Jay Landesman, for use of the quotation from Gershon Legman which introduces Patrick Kearney's fascinating and invaluable *The Private Case*; Random House UK Ltd for permission to retell the awful story of Beatrice Fry, as originally recounted in Ronald Morris's *The Captain's Lady*; to HarperCollins, for kind permission to quote from the late Arthur Marshall's *Whimpering in the Rhododendrons*; to Villard Books (New York), for allowing me to quote from *Different Loving* by Gloria G. Brame, William D. Brame and Jon Jacobs; and John Bird, for kindly granting me permission to use his evidence about Percy Grainger's remarkable childhood (*Percy Grainger*). Every effort has been made to trace copyright owners of material used in this book. Where acknowledgement has been omitted, the author is happy to make the appropriate acknowledgement in future editions.

I also happily express my gratitude to Peter Farrer for drawing to my attention the various passages in Victorian and Edwardian publications from which I have so freely quoted; to the Alice Kerr-Sutherland Society for generously granting me access to their unparalleled picture archive; to Michael Goss of Delectus Books for many kindnesses and much practical assistance in my literary researches; to Tim Woodward of *Skin Two* magazine for constant encouragement and support; to my editor at Little, Brown, Richard Beswick, who really, honestly only bought the book because he thought it would make a good, commercial volume; to my agent Julian Alexander who sold it to him for – it goes without saying – the same reasons; to those of my friends 'in the know' who urged me to hold nothing back, nothing at all, let it all hang out; and lastly (on this list but in no other sense), my adored wife, who is still not entirely sure about this project but has her own ways of getting even if things should turn out badly.

CONTENTS

ix

PART III FLAGELLATION AND SOCIETY

INTRODUCTION

'And what exactly is your new book *about*?'

Many an author, offered such an opening, would be delighted to take fullest advantage. If his book is still taking shape, it gives him a chance to rehearse his arguments; if newly on sale, an opportunity to promote it. Indeed, the real problem – as many incautious enquirers have discovered – is to stop authors talking about their new books once they've been invited to begin.

It has been rather different during the life of this project.

'And what is your new book about?'

'F . . . ah . . . fl . . .'

'Sorry?'

'Fly fishing.'

Or:

'And what is your new book about?'

'Span . . . sp . . .'

'Yes?'

'Er . . . Spanæmia.'

'Come again?'

'It's a deficiency of the red corpuscles. Induces moral coward-ice. I'm a sufferer.'

During the eighteen months or so in which *Thy Rod and Staff* gradually took shape, it was not lost on me that my own unusual reluctance to reveal, let alone discuss, its subject matter was of no small significance – part of the problem, in fact. Although I had fully intended to come clean the first time the topic naturally arose (though not proposing to go so far as to raise it myself), when the crisis actually arrived I suddenly found myself hesitating at the prospect of raised eyebrows, half-suppressed smirks, 'Oh, *really*?' and the rest of the phenomena that usually greet unwise, indiscreet or tactically disadvantageous admissions. In terms of the trauma it engenders, to declare that one is writing a book about flagellation (there, I've said it!) is rather like admitting to a prison record. Full marks for owning up like a man, of course, but still . . .

Nonetheless this *is* a book about flagellation; and in one way at least I believe it to be unlike most of its predecessors. For although over the last two centuries the subject has been regularly discussed and dissertated upon, the consensual conclusions of these works are unambiguously negative. The subject has remorselessly acquired a worse and worse ambiance. Today, it is closely associated in the public mind with such unpleasant social entities as cruelty, fascism (or at least near-fascist authoritarianism), male chauvinism, brutality, child abuse – and, of course, sexual perversion. Its ancient and even proper purposes – mystical, initiatory, medical and, yes, penitential – have been either almost completely forgotten or calumnified beyond recognition. As a result it is more taboo than at any time in its long history.

This book is a heresy: its purpose is to offer another, rather more benign, certainly broader, view of flagellation, an impulse which is very ancient and takes many forms, with many layers of complexity barely illuminated by those who have had the telling of the story so far. It is a personal and not a scholarly view. I am not an authority. I have no formal qualifications whatsoever for attempting such a work. For me at least this has been a blessing, since it has freed me from the necessity of observing academic conventions. I have allowed myself to cut corners, employ a free-form chronology, deal economically with those authorities I consider both erroneous and over-exposed (a century of clinical analysis, the reader may be relieved to hear, whizzes by in a single chapter, while the works of the Marquis de Sade are barely discussed at all), in order to cast new light on those areas that, in my opinion, have themselves been dealt with until now in no less ruthless a manner. If some readers find parts of the book superficial, I can only apologise in advance, and offer, in mitigation, the observation that superficiality is absolutely nothing new where the subject of flagellation is concerned. I can at least hope to have been superficial in different ways, thereby to some extent redressing the balance.

In any case not all activities yield the secrets of their purpose to methodological analysis. Even when the integers are all accurately listed and described, and the sequence in which they fit together and act upon one another is perfectly well understood, the essential point of the event may still elude the analyst. Similarly, the scenarios, personae, modes, settings, implements, furniture, costumes and other periphera referred to at various times in this book are merely components of a larger mechanism, and do not, in themselves, or even in combination, necessarily explain *why* flagellationists do what they do – which some might feel is the crux.

For rather a lot of people, there is no mystery, only a grotesque and disturbing reality. The arguments and examples I have advanced will not convince them to change their gut feelings about flagellation. Such readers will perceive the depth and intricacy of the subject and its associated fantasies only as testimony to human beings' capacity to take pains for both good or ill – in this case the latter. And it is true that refinement, attention to detail and a passionate wholeheartedness are in themselves no indices whatever of moral rectitude, while artistic merit has to be abnormally high before it will even begin to mitigate a deliberately wicked artistic intention. For many, it can never do so.

*

So where does flagellationism come from? Are people justified in denigrating it as a perversion, or is it a natural impulse, part of our genetic inheritance in some mysterious way? Is it learned behaviour? How long have people been doing it? Above all, why?

Said, originally by the French, to be an English vice, flagellationism is of much greater antiquity than any modern nation or culture. In its ecstatic (rather than punitive) form, it has been linked with Dionysism and the Rites of Attis; with the Eleusinian Mysteries, and with the Great Goddess. The same goddess, in her aspect as Artemis, was worshipped in Sparta by ceremonies in which teenage youths were voluntarily whipped for valour's sake at her altar. Frescoes from Pompeii, such as those in the Villa of the Mysteries, show that the Romans of the late Republican period were no strangers to the concept of voluptuous correction, while their festival of Lupercalia was distinguished by many acts of tolerated licentiousness, in which flagellation featured strongly. The onset of official imperial Christianity in both halves of the Roman empire brought a downturn in the fortunes of all rival religions and sects, especially the ecstatic ones; it also heralded, in much of Europe, a Dark Age from which records are scarce. We know, however, that judicial flagellation never ceased. As for the scholastic rod, this had been a Roman and even a Greek tradition, used with zeal and often with more than zeal, as many contemporary chroniclers record. Whatever else may have perished in the downfall of the Western empire, the tradition of chastising delinquents with rods (whose manufacture and employment was often specified with the utmost care by the dissertating monks) survived. This is hardly surprising considering the close attention paid in those days to Scripture, in which dozens of Solomonic spare-the-rod injunctions left those *in loco parentis* in no doubt as to where their duty lay. On this moral basis the monk-teacher Abélard chastised his girl-pupil Héloise. Intended to be punitive, the stripes had instead a voluptuous effect – not the first such confusion to occur, but certainly one of the most famous.

It was in the fourteenth century – the era of the Black Death, the Hundred Years' War and the most disastrous of all Crusades – that flagellationism became a mass movement. Long suppressed by the stern fathers of the mediæval Church, Christianity's Dionysian side suddenly re-emerged in the form of an ecstatic sect whose declared aim was atonement through pain for mankind. The pain they took upon themselves. For years their strange processions wound through the spectral, war-ruined countrysides of northern Italy, Bohemia and Germany as they thrashed themselves and each other with rods, switches and chains, engendering hysteria and affray wherever they passed, thousands of people sharing the same whip-induced ecstatic trance.

The Church, alarmed, fought back by calumnifying the flagellants as voluptuaries – a standard charge used *ab initio* against most heretics – and undoubtedly, in the truest sense of the term Bacchanalian, there were times when religious frenzy gave way to distinctly more orgiastic behaviour. But beyond all doubt the phenomenon was at root a devotional one. By and large historians make no attempt to explain it in terms that modern people can understand. This may not be their fault – the mediæval mind is hard to reach from this distance, and in any case modern people have not recently experienced a plague that slew one person in three across the known world inside a period of twenty years. Moreover, outbreaks of strange behaviour are not always susceptible to easy explanation, even at the time of occurrence.

Meanwhile, the ancient link between devotion, ecstasy, atonement and physical suffering had been re-established in a spectacular fashion, and although the flagellants were eventually, though not entirely, suppressed, from that time on the practice of whipping as a nominal aid to religious devotion, already institutionalised within some religious orders, became positively promoted. The Church laid down rules for the construction and use of 'disciplines', as the scourges and rods used in monasteries and convents were known. Many divines of both sexes – including saints Brigid, Geneviève and Teresa of Avila – became famous for their zeal in its use, and on their own persons. The flagellation of Christ became a popular theme for religious paintings.

By the onset of the Renaissance religious and scholastic flagellations were long, drawn-out affairs, often involving ceremonies prescribed down to the smallest detail – no schoolroom-scene woodcut of the period is complete without a birch rod resembling a small tree somewhere in the picture, often in use. From the point of view of harsh discipline, it was probably the worst time ever to be a child. During the seventeenth century, openly voluptuous, bawdy flagellation made its first reappearance since the Pompeiian wall frescoes. This is probably the moment of its birth as a 'vice' in the modern sense of the word. Certainly there is a nudge-nudge quality to Restoration literature, and especially its drama, which would not be out of place in *Blackadder* or *Monty Python's Flying Circus*. This persists through the eighteenth century – Cleland's *Fanny Hill* and Hogarth's *Harlot's Progress* etchings show clearly that the administering of whippings was an understood part of a prostitute's stock-in-trade. The first flagellation-specific erotic literature arrived: mock theological and medical treatises, chiefly, and of course the much-discussed works of de Sade. We also receive our first intimations of that necessary concomitant to all sexual pleasure: guilt. In the *Confessions* of the philosopher and educationalist Jean-Jacques Rousseau we have one of the most melancholy of all flagellatory memoirs. Chastised as a boy by his young, female guardian, he found that in some strange, bewitching way he liked the experience. He did his utmost to receive more of it, had little further success – and spent the rest of his life feeling ashamed and ridiculous about his longings.

With the introduction of the guilt motif, the confusion was almost complete. From early Victorian times through to our own day, physical chastisement has been perceived variously and often simultaneously (though in widely differing quarters) as (1) a legitimate and desirable form of punishment for children, criminals, soldiers, sailors and other animals; (2) an act of religious or mystical devotion; (3) a sexual perversion; (4) a type of physiotherapy; (5) a form of insanity; (6) a commercial activity; with mutual exclusivity by no means taken for granted. It is hardly any wonder that misunderstanding continues.

The organisation of the book follows my own system of priorities. Part I, 'This Filthy Vice', takes its title from a famously charitable declaration by George Bernard Shaw. Since Shaw was in many ways the emotional patron of the school of thought which today affirms the thoroughgoing unwholesomeness of everything to do with flagellation, it is a fitting heading for a section which deals with the rise to influence of this viewpoint and, as I see it, the distressing results of its mass acceptance in Western society. Everything that is negative, or said to be negative, about the impulse will be found here.

The reason is simple: to get it out of the way. Thereafter, I attempt to show that this predilection, though it can indeed, like all human activities, appear in an excessive and sinister light, has its joyous, therapeutic and romantic sides, too – not to mention its funny side. Since *Thy Rod and Staff* is intended ultimately to serve as a panegyric rather than a counter-polemic, it was important to reserve the greater part of the book to describe not what flagellation is *not*, but what I believe it *is* – a less gloomy view altogether, provided one approaches it with an open mind.

Part I also contains what was by far the most difficult part of the book to write because it is contentious. It would be preposterous to deny that much of the imagery and incidence of flagellation concerns, or is derived from, childhood. It was always, in my view, going to be impossible to complete the book without confronting this aspect of the subject, since so much of what some people find objectionable about flagellation concerns – or, more properly, appears to concern – children. To press ahead as if this problem did not exist would have been evasive and self-defeating.

The reader may be surprised to learn that among SM communities and schools of thought there is an almost universal consensus that children are better kept out of it. A predilection for spanking (or being spanked by) one's partner does not by any means imply approval of physical punishment for children. Yet there is perhaps more than a whiff of political correctness (or perhaps simple prudence) in the often fervent, and certainly frequent expressions of such views by SM celebrities, and by conceding without argument the thesis that spanking ineluctably harms children, even that harm *might* be done, the flagellationist is also admitting that what he is doing is rooted in this 'harmfulness' and is therefore tainted, even depraved. So he is, after all, a 'deviant', just as Richard Krafft-Ebing told him he was a hundred years ago, and any attempts to pretend otherwise are a waste of time.

Mine is a different view and leads in the opposite direction. While I concede that it often appears to commence in childhood, though the reasons it does so are not as obvious as many appear to think, I do not regard the flagellant impulse *per se* as self-evidently aberrant or disgusting. On the contrary, it has nearly always seemed to me to be as 'normal' as many other human impulses, representing a fundamental ingredient of the human personality which, like so many others, we now choose to deny. I further believe that our modern reluctance to acknowledge this impulse within ourselves, free from the usual accompanying package of pre-programmed condemnation, prevents understanding of what it actually is, and represents, and will continue to generate neurosis in both individuals and society at large.

It therefore seemed to me reasonable that if the harm theory is to be sustained, the adult penchant for flagellation must be shown to be a Bad Thing. This – again, in my personal view – has never conclusively been done, though it has been attempted with fair regularity. Nor does it appear to me in any way proven that physical discipline inevitably or even usually damages children, though I would never deny that it can harm some children, as may many different things done to them in childhood. Nevertheless, important conclusions remain to be drawn about the nature of the involvement of children, such as it is, in the subject of flagellation, since it is the apparent inclusion of this particular group which above all causes feelings of uneasiness among many otherwise sexually tolerant people.

Part II, 'The Flagellant Experience,' examines, I believe in unprecedented detail, each of the disparate components which together make up an individual's personal experience of this impulse. It also shows how they act upon each other so that, as is the case with all types of human interaction, no two experiences are identical. It examines the many different motivations for the practice; the archetypes who appear again and again in flagellant imagery; the scenarios in which they perform, the equipment and liturgies they use; the clothes or costumes they may wear; the rituals that are deemed necessary and how all these factors work together.

By contrast, Part III, 'Flagellation and Society,' attempts to analyse why flagellants do what they do, and what they get out of it. It examines the hidden causes of the behaviour, and identifies many unacknowledged anomalies in modern life which, consciously or unconsciously, the practising flagellant is endeavouring to rectify.

Throughout I have quoted from other works where these are apposite to my case. To do so is more or less traditional for this type of book, but I guess the majority of the quotations will be unfamiliar to most of those who read them here. The literature of this subject, such as it is, is littered with the same old extracts repeated again and again. I felt the least I could do, hoping as I am for a change of heart, was to offer a change of diet.

The passages themselves are fairly evenly sourced between erotic and non-erotic literature; that is to say, many were created specifically to arouse the flagellationist impulse, while others have this effect although they were never consciously intended to do so. This latter group is surprisingly large and varied.

I have also made use of interviews and depositions privately obtained by me in the course of researching the book. Here at least

I have followed convention and changed names to protect identities. In an ideal world it would not be necessary, but the world of the 'deviant' is far from ideal. I am grateful to those who confided in me and the best way to show it is to protect their anonymity.

Since one of the main purposes of *Thy Rod and Staff* is to define flagellation in new and more accurate ways, it might be thought odd that there is no single chapter dedicated to this specific task. The reason is that I could see no benefit in replacing one set of labels with another. The clinical or forensic approach to classification of behaviour – identifying one or two readily obvious components, looking up their Greek or Latin roots, and then combining these into an ugly new portmanteau term – is not helpful. The inevitable restrictions of the 'label-driven' method of classification preclude more than two or three such roots, otherwise the resulting conglomerate word would be far too long and unwieldy. Therefore only the most immediately obvious of the contributory components may be borrowed. All other components – and there may be dozens – will be left off the label. In time the label itself inevitably becomes the definition, shorn of all but its most obvious attributes, which may not even be the most important. So misunderstanding and ignorance arise.

However, all of the more interesting human behaviours suffer from (at best) imprecise descriptive terminology. The best example is, of course, romantic physical love. To the behaviourist this activity is 'pair-bonding'; to the legal mind 'carnal knowledge'; to the biologist 'mating'; to the ardent feminist Andrea Dworkin 'symbolic rape', to the libertine 'screwing', and so on. Not one of these labels – and there are many more – comes remotely close to describing what is indeed indescribable.

For example, although I might personally conclude that 'domination and submission' is a more generally useful term than 'sadomasochism' to describe the most important single component of flagellation, it too is ultimately unsatisfactory because, like 'sadomasochism' and 'algolagnia', it only tells part of the story. 'Disciplinism' (my coining) might have served, but discipline may be exercised without flagellation, and vice versa. 'Pœnophilia' ('punishment-love') has an equivalent disadvantage, since by no means all instances of flagellation are punitive or penitential in intent, nor are all punishments flagellatory. If we abandon the classical in favour of a more colloquial approach, the word 'spanking' suggests itself as a short, sharp, all-round 'thought-bite' – except that a flagellatory transaction may be disciplinist, pœnophiliac, algolagnic and sadomasochistic all at once, with lashings and lashings of domination and submission, yet still not involve actual 'spanking', which is a specific style or mode of corporal punishment. Many aficionados of the subject use a range of acronyms – 'SM', 'B&D' (bondage and discipline), 'CP' (corporal punishment), and so on. These are just as unsatisfactory, and even more unlovely.

So we come back to 'flagellation', which, even if it too is brutally imprecise, at least has the merit of being the traditional term. I have described above what it has been held to mean. I have used most of this book to describe what I believe it *does* mean, using every device at my disposal.

Some people who read *Thy Rod and Staff* will find it shocking or horrifying, and of these many will take stern issue with its hypotheses and conclusions. Others will be aroused erotically, and will admit it to themselves. Many will find it simultaneously exciting and deplorable – they too are part of the problem. And many, I hope, will find it funny, at least in places. No human activity is altogether free from moments of innate, near-palpable ludicrousness, and by its nature flagellation is no less vulnerable than any to third-party guffawing from the wings. That is surely as it should be, for while hypocrisy, prejudice and ignorance are potent, if entirely negative, forces, laughter, even with a touch of *Schadenfreude*, is an excellent antidote to them all, and may even be the begetter of their opposite qualities: honesty, tolerance and understanding.

E. A.
10 November, 1994

PART I

'This Filthy Vice'

1

FAIR GAME?

We are tainted with flagellomania from our childhood.
George Bernard Shaw[1]

It does not even have the advantage of being a euphonious word: *flagellation* is awkwardly balanced and strangely difficult to say out loud – not least, perhaps, because the impulses for which it stands are generally held to be embarrassing, incomprehensible, ludicrous, distasteful, bizarre, lunatic, criminal or irredeemably wicked.

This is a wide enough range of responses to raise the possibility that not all of us have the same activity in mind. Although the verb 'to flagellate' has a specific meaning – to strike with a whip – most would accept that it stands for much more than the physical action in its simplest sense. It is the introduction of context which causes confusion.

It is its sexually perverse connotations which have done most to prevent the subject from being discussed on a lay level with anything other than extreme diffidence. These resonances are not new – connections between flagellation and sexuality have been widely recognised for well over a century – but they have latterly come to dominate public perceptions of the subject as never before.

---

1. Preface to *Misalliance* (1914). Shaw was a vociferous campaigner against the use and culture of the rod, and his powerfully expressed views are often cited by present-day campaigners in the same cause ('Flagellomania' is a Shavian coining). His equally passionate support for eugenics (improvement of the human species by compulsory selective breeding) is less frequently recalled.

This is not the place to examine the long relationship between sex and shame in Western culture; it is enough to note that any negative feelings affecting an individual's willingness or otherwise to discuss or reveal his or her sexual preferences are greatly intensified when the taste in question is deemed a 'perversion'. At this point self-censorship is usually total – the perversion is 'kept dark' for fear of shame, ridicule, odium or prosecution. So while a man who enjoys making love to women in the orthodox fashion can usually be persuaded to admit as much, and may even habitually volunteer the information without being invited to do so, another man preferring coitus with ladies' high-heeled shoes is considerably less likely to make his tastes known. Whatever other considerations may obtain, the degree of reticence is therefore directly related to the 'normality' of the sexual activity in question.

Yet even among perversions there are hierarchical forces at work, and scales of odium. Those that involve, or appear to involve, coercion, if not cruelty, are viewed in a sharply different light to the activities of the foot fetishist or the transvestite. The most notorious form of sexual coercion is rape, and its most extreme form sexual murder. This crime, especially when a child is the victim, excites more horror and revulsion than any other. It is 'sadism' in its worst form; abhorrent, evil, unpardonable.

With such a frightful exemplar at the end of a circumstantial causal chain, it is at least understandable that any act of coercive physical violence, deliberately administered to an unwilling recipient, should come to be seen by some as the first step down this dangerous road.

Even greater wickedness may be inferred from other acknowledged components of this strange impulse. It can hardly be denied that the physical disciplining of children is an act both coercive and violent. Nor can it be disputed that the image of the disciplined child is central to many, if not all, flagellant fantasies[2]. The

2. See Part II. Flagellant scenarios often require one of the participants to take the role of a child while the other assumes the part of a coercive authoritarian adult.

two are therefore self-evidently and unwholesomely linked, most likely in a vicious cycle: concomitantly, those who administer or advocate corporal punishment for children probably do so, consciously or not, for reasons of sexual gratification. If they were themselves spanked as children the existence of the cycle is 'proven' – unequivocal evidence of the harm such punishments in early life bestow, and reason enough both to prohibit the practice and to regard with the deepest suspicion all those who advocate it.

Even when what is taking place is an interaction between two consenting adults – no children, no coercion – the practice is still perceived, if not necessarily as a wicked vice, then as a grotesque one. Its practitioners are seen as greater menaces to themselves than to society, but that does not prevent them being denounced and hounded by the popular press, nor does it shield them from other forms of public contempt or even legislation.

In the vanguard, we have the wholly condemnatory, neo-Shavian viewpoint, personified most recently by Miss Patsy Chapman, who, while editor of the *News of the World* Sunday newspaper, commented that 'This country [Britain] will never get itself straight until we get rid of this spanking thing.' Those who believe that tabloid newspapers are sure custodians of all that is best and noblest in the human conscience will doubtless agree with her; the remaining 99 per cent may judge it unhelpful to her cause that such publications have always done as much as possible to keep this particular activity firmly before the eyes of their readers. Instances of discipline enthusiasts getting together to enjoy themselves (and there can be no denying that enjoyment, if not fulfilment of some sort, is the prime purpose of all such encounters) are assiduously reported. The protagonists are followed, wire-tapped, secretly photographed and gleefully exposed. Often they are well-known personalities; but no less often they are ordinary citizens. In all cases lives can be damaged, if not ruined, by the exposure.

In 1974, the *News of the World* revealed that a retired Army officer, Lieutenant-Colonel John Brooks, who owned a cruiser moored on the Thames, enjoyed smacking the bare bottoms of young ladies who crewed for him. There was no suggestion that the girls thus treated had been coerced into such games, but one of them had talked to a friend about the experience, and the friend in turn spoke to the newspaper, who promptly inserted a stool-pigeon into the Colonel's riverborne disciplinary environment. The resulting exposure was entirely according to form, but, untypically, Lieutenant-Colonel Brooks decided that what he had done was no crime but an honest expression of sexual passion between consenting adults, and he sued the newspaper. He won – only to be awarded a token halfpenny damages, which of course meant that as he had still to pay his costs, he was nearly bankrupted by the affair. Lieutenant-Colonel Brooks handled his case with honesty and moral courage, but needless to say emerged very much the loser – he was portrayed from start to finish not as a wicked or debauched man, but as a slightly 'funny' one. Even the 'respectable' broadsheet newspapers were unable to resist repeated sly references to the affair, with, of course, the totemic word 'spanking' prominent in their headlines.

The affair of Harvey Proctor, former MP for Billericay in Essex, was more complex.[3] Again, it was a newspaper which played the exposer's role. It seemed – and was not denied by Proctor – that he had been holding (consensual) spanking games in his flat with sixteen-year-old boys. The complexities arose from the homosexual connotations, and, following from these, the precise status of British law, which stated that while teenagers over sixteen were perfectly entitled to have carnal relationships so long as these were heterosexual, the same licence was not granted to homosexual encounters.[4] Proctor was therefore breaking the law and, after a bitter battle, was forced to resign his seat in Parliament.

The additional complications in Proctor's case were that he

---

3. March 1987.
4. Since amended to an age of consent of eighteen. At no time was it alleged that Proctor's activities had involved coercion – indeed, he had actually paid the youths concerned.

was, firstly, a Conservative MP, and therefore an automatic target for the political left, who might otherwise have been expected to sympathise with the victim of a law which discriminated against male homosexuals. Secondly, he was on the extreme right of his party, with strong and frequently aired views concerning the immigration of ethnic minorities (he opposed it), which had long made him a particular target. It was obvious that the savagery of the attacks made against him was not motivated so much by his spanking activities as by these other considerations. But it was the former motif which dictated the usual headlines.

The Proctor case demonstrates to perfection a further ingredient in this stew of negative perceptions. A penchant for flagellation is a Disgusting Vice, an English Vice and a Male Vice, but above all perhaps it is a Right Wing Vice, a Tory Vice – even a Fascist Vice. This tinge of blue, as it were, long ago placed it, in terms of the British socio-political lexicon, squarely amid the landed gentry, the red-faced ex-colonels, the city brokers and the aristocracy.

Whether or not these common perceptions represent objective truths – I hope to show in due course that each falls somewhat short of those – the four-square identification of flagellationism (the vice) with Conservatism (the political colour) was established long ago. Inevitably, its principal opponents, then as now, were the left. This enmeshing of the subject firmly within the iron matrix of party attitudes has long impoverished the quality of debate. A still unhappier result is that the contemporary tolerance extended by liberals towards sexual minorities has never been extended to flagellationists, the supposed Toryness of the tendency being enough to disqualify them from all such consideration.

Then there is the case of Frank Bough.

Mr Bough is – or was – one of the most familiar faces on British television, an avuncular, middle-aged former sportscaster who for many years was the anchorman on *Nationwide*, then BBC TV's early-evening news magazine. Later on, he was chosen to lead the corporation's new breakfast television programme at a time when this service had just been launched in the UK by an independent channel and was already running into difficulties. With uncharacteristic opportunism, the BBC decided to create a last-minute 'spoiler' programme, choosing Bough as the front-man. By common consent he did an excellent job, the casual, besweatered BBC approach immediately proving a far more popular formula than that of the independent. If perhaps a little bland, Bough was clearly the supreme TV professional, possessed of a 'nice-guy' image that few could emulate.

The first scandal which broke about the head of this unfortunate man was an exposé (again, by a newspaper) of private sessions involving call-girls and cocaine. A pop star might well have survived such an affair; even prospered as a result under the markedly more tolerant rules extended to members of the artistic avant-garde. The definitively un-hip Bough did not: he was immediately jettisoned by his employers and for several years did not work in TV at all, except for private contracting companies. This is perhaps only to be expected: public corporations like the BBC must, in theory, be beyond reproach, and that condition nominally extends to those they employ in prominent positions. But unlike the broadly similar cases of the American TV fundamentalist Jim Bakker (caught with his hand in the till), or the disgraced British Director of Public Prosecutions, Sir Alan Greene (arrested for kerb-crawling), Bough had never openly preached pious values or enforced the law and was not therefore an immediately obvious hypocrite.

Worse was to come. In 1990, several years after the cocaine and call-girls affair, Bough was followed and secretly photographed by an investigative team from a Sunday newspaper. The film, several frames of which were reproduced on the front page, appeared to show him descending to a London basement apartment and being admitted. The apartment belonged to a professional dominatrix: a woman specialising in catering for sexual submissives of a sadomasochistic kind. Bough was therefore exposed as one of her clients.

The lady was interviewed, money changed hands and as a result the newspaper was able to print for its readers' benefit a menu of tortures the dominatrix offered her clients. It was not directly claimed that Bough had availed himself of any in particular of these activities, but the guilt-by-association ploy seldom fails and did not do so here.

Since then this man has been an open target for the nastier kinds of newspaper.[5] As far as I can see, he has broken no law (the cocaine aside), and has at no time done harm to anyone, except himself and certainly his wife, through his extramarital activities.

Many may feel – or think they feel – that such is the fate the victims of such exposés deserve: after all, they are self-evidently 'perverts'[6]. And to organisations so expert at causing pain by means of the printed word, to prefer some other medium for its infliction – let alone choosing to receive, rather than administer it – may well seem so extraordinary as to be perverse. Yet if the activity these 'perverts' pursue is so distasteful and repulsive to the sensibilities of decent citizens, why parade it so often and with such evident delight? If Joe Soap, or Miss Soap for that matter, is caught playing parlour games of a disciplinary nature, the resulting story will, at the very least, be a page lead in whichever tabloid newspaper has been playing KGB games that week. If the protagonist is even remotely famous, the story will be on the front page.

The true reason is that flagellation is a media *frisson* – it sells newspapers. In the justified belief that the nation as a whole is

---

5. The most recent example I can find is 'A HAT OR A HORSEWHIP – BOUGH'S BALD CHOICE' (Bough is thin on top), in the *Mail on Sunday*, 6 September 1992, by Victor Lewis-Smith. It seems likely that the newspaper had mounted yet another covert anti-Bough operation, and failed, producing this unpleasant article as a last-minute substitute. Without such a reason, the degree of spite was inexplicable. Bough was a 'sleazebag' who, if he really desired humiliation, need only watch himself on TV, and so forth.

6. *Chambers Revised English Dictionary* (1935 edition) defines 'pervert' as 'one who has abandoned the doctrine assumed to be true'.

guiltily fascinated by the subject, the British popular press deploys the argot of physical discipline as frequently as opportunity allows. TEACHERS CANED (i.e. their pay award is rejected). SIX OF THE BEST (recipes for fruit cake in a women's magazine). CLINTON CAN WHIP BUSH (he can defeat him in the United States presidential elections). RETURN OF THE STRAP (as a fashionable element of ladies' shoe design). A THRASHING FOR ENGLAND (they lost a cricket match against Australia). THE SMACK OF FIRM GOVERNMENT (elucidation unnecessary). Some years ago, when there was apparently a threat that a British woman might be caned by the Saudi Arabians for an illegal bottle party, the daily papers almost exploded with excitement, speculation and interviews with the males who had already experienced the Saudi judicial cane. In 1980, when the birch rod was finally abolished in the Isle of Man as a method of judicial punishment for juvenile males, it was what the media call a top story for weeks, with a plethora of photographs, reminiscences, video footage of the weapon in question being examined rather wistfully by a rotund Manx police constable (possibly the very man whose job was on the line), and a furious public correspondence, with passions clearly roused on all sides. This was no mere debate on an issue of law and order. Plainly the ancient *frisson* was in full cry.

As I write this, the British interest in corporal punishment is being both fuelled and exploited by the press to an unprecedented degree, due to two events, widely separated in both space and time. The first of these is the sentence of caning imposed by the Singapore courts on a sixteen-year-old American for the crime of vandalism. The second is the near-simultaneous publication in Britain of an official history of Eton College – the 'top people's' boys' school – in which a late headmaster is recalled as a flagellant of the first order.

The Singaporeans' interpretation of judicial caning is dealt with later on. So far as press coverage ranged, there were two 'angles': firstly, the revelation that it was so severe as to amount to a form of judicial mutilation; secondly, that a great number of people (see Chapter 2) – particularly Americans, to everyone's

22

surprise – nevertheless appeared to feel that the sentence was justified, and might profitably be emulated in those Western countries which have abolished such penalties. There was of course much lurid press speculation about the event, virtually all of it nominally disapproving in tone, yet oddly unsparing of detail for all that. On 21 April 1994, for example, the London *Evening Standard*, a newspaper with a long and oft-proclaimed history of opposition to corporal punishment, saw fit to publish, large size, a Press Association photograph, originating from the Singapore penal department[7], of a singleted warder applying a four-foot cane with terrific force to a dummy strapped into the punishment A-frame. The accompanying article gravely supplied the fullest account of the procedure; it described the gruesome physical effects; it speculated on the terror the guilty youth must be feeling, and it included a horrifying account from an unnamed Singaporean boy who had received the same treatment, whose wounds had taken four months to dry properly and who was now scarred for life. The nominal purpose of the article was condemnatory; the effect was two-faced in the extreme; prurience, hypocrisy and gloating cruelty masquerading as 'the public's right to know', but in fact feeding the public's desire to know, which is not at all the same thing.

Equally telling was the massive coverage of *Eton Renewed*. Here it must be made plain that at least some of the attraction of the story was that Eton is unquestionably the most prestigious boys' school in England, and the class motif is therefore involved. The last school in England to abolish the use of the birch rod, Eton has always had a tradition of stern and frequent corporal punishment. *Eton Renewed* revealed that the last head but two, the late Anthony Chevenix-Trench, had been well up in the tradition of Doctors Keate and Hawtrey, like them a flagellator of passionate energy and questionable motives.

---

7. The release of this photograph, not to mention a videotaped reconstruction, which was shown on TV, would itself seem to provide evidence that the Western *frisson* is fully understood, and shared, in Singapore.

This unprecedented *nostra culpa* stimulated a vast correspondence across the press spectrum, much of it from Old Etonians. No one appeared to dispute that Chevenix-Trench had indeed been a mighty and fearsome whacker throughout his career as a schoolmaster – indeed, the evidence entirely supports this contention – but many claimed not to have resented it, and indeed rejected the idea that they had been harmed by it. One exception was Richard Hornsby. In an article published in (again) the *Evening Standard*[8], he recalled being beaten at Eton by the late accused, and now reckoned himself scarred for life by the memory. His was a valid and no doubt genuinely held point of view, but once more it was curious that the *Standard* chose to cover this long-ago tale of corporal punishment with a virtually unprecedented full-page layout complete with specially commissioned artwork. To draw attention to this 'special', they trailed the article and the drawing on page 1.

There are other areas in which evidence of the longstanding national predilection for flagellatory references occurs with considerable frequency.[9] Television comedy, which has to touch the pulse of its target culture with consistency and acuity if it is to be successful, is an excellent example. Throughout the fifties the hit BBC TV comedy series *Whack–o!,* starring Jimmy Edwards as a moustachioed, cane-wielding blimp prep-school headmaster, deployed spanking jokes and scenes almost non-stop (as the title of the series indicates). The late Benny Hill, one of the very few British comedians to be successful in America, also played on the naughty-schoolboy smack-bottom theme with remarkable frequency, as did his contemporary the late Dick Emery. In a more sophisticated mould, the BBC *Blackadder* series, starring

---

8. 27 April 1994.
9. For an excellent example of the theme being linked with sex in visual form and openly used to sell a product, readers should examine the jacket of both hardback and paperback editions of Jilly Cooper's novel *Riders* (Arlington Books, 1985/Corgi Books).

Rowan Atkinson, an enormous success throughout the 1980s, was joyously unrestrained:

> NURSE (*reprovingly, to* QUEEN ELIZABETH I): Now, now, dearie, it'll soon be time for Mr and Mrs Spank to pay a visit to Botty-land![10]

> WORLD WAR I ARMY OFFICER: We'll give the Hun a damned good thrashing, British-style – six of the best, trousers down![11]

In both cases the reaction of the studio audience was uproarious. Clearly the references touched a well-defined button in the public consciousness. An earlier example of the same sly jibe at this offbeat sub-department of British sexuality was found in an episode of *Monty Python's Flying Circus* – a sketch called 'Blackmail', a parody of a standard game show in which a nondescript man (face obscured by the usual raincoat) is clandestinely filmed entering a suburban house. Moments later, he appears in silhouette at an upstairs window, accompanied by another silhouette of a whip-brandishing female. The 'presenter' (Michael Palin) then allows the man ten seconds to call the studio and promise to pay up before his face and identity are revealed. It was hugely funny, but although the butt of the satire was twofold – the pervert who made himself vulnerable by his activities, and the unscrupulous nature of some TV programme-makers – hindsight and reflection reveal that 'Blackmail', though a parody, is actually exceedingly close to the real-life activities of some British newsgathering organisations; in the final analysis, not funny at all.

*

10. *Blackadder Two.* On the face of it, this is an hilarious exaggeration of what may be termed 'nanny-speak', though the present writer has discovered the scarcely less baroque threat 'Do you want to pay a visit to Lapland?' (i.e., do you want me to put you over my knee?) in a Victorian women's publication, while French mothers of the same era warned naughty children of 'a visit to the Pays-Bas [Low Countries]'.
11. *Blackadder Goes Forth.*

So on the one hand flagellation is a 'disgusting' activity, a 'vice' or self-contained branch of wickedness, without which this country and culture will never get itself straight, and whose practice justifies the most revolting deceits on the part of the mass media and the cruel pursuit of individuals. On the other it is also clearly accepted, by many, with a degree of understanding that almost amounts to affection, even if this is only of the type normally felt towards reliable and consistent sources of bawdy humour. Such mutual exclusivity, in an individual, would unhesitatingly be diagnosed as neurotic; for surely both views cannot both simultaneously be 'true'.

2

THE SLOW DEATH
OF CORPORAL
PUNISHMENT

Smacking has to be wrong because we all agree that hitting people is wrong and children are people – aren't they?

EPOCH manifesto[1]

Since recorded history began, for most human beings life outside the womb has commenced with a sharp smack on the bottom.

It is the very first thing that happens to us, the earliest manifestation of 'them', an act of unmistakable violence which is nevertheless generally held to be necessary, if not vital: for the spank just after the moment of delivery – traditionally administered to an upside-down patient, so adding insult to injury – is applied, not for motives of discipline, cruelty or sexual perversion, but for an overwhelmingly humane reason. Its summary shock generates indignation and rage. Infants instinctively manifest rage by bawling, an urgent operation which requires sharp,

---

1. EPOCH was founded in 1989 by the child psychologist Penelope Leach and Peter Newell. The latter has had a long, dedicated and successful career in abolitionism, being the editor of *A Last Resort? Corporal Punishment in Schools* (Penguin, 1972), produced by The Society of Teachers Opposed to Physical Punishment (STOPP), itself founded in 1968, and EPOCH's direct ancestor.

lusty, repeated intakes of life-giving oxygen. So, assuming all motors function as they should, our reaction to the natal spank is a prompt inflation of tiny lungs to maximum capacity, and we let our injured feelings show. Like a car with a flat battery, the breathing clockwork has been jump-started.

If our umbilical cords have been severed and we do not start breathing, before long we will die, or suffer irremediable brain damage; and, since death at the moment of birth – let alone catastrophic brain damage – is usually the very last thing those in charge would want, they accept the risk of hurt feelings or even trauma without hesitation. Indeed, this is rather the point of the exercise, and issues like injustice, assault et al simply do not enter into the calculations. There are larger imperatives.

For many of us, particularly those born in the civilised West[2], that may well be the last time we ever feel the impact of a deliberately violent hand. We will glide through childhood without so much as a punch or kick from schoolmate or sibling, let alone a cuff or spank from a grown-up. Wars, civil disturbances, crime and domestic violence (in its criminal sense) aside, with the passing of childhood the likelihood of receiving a blow in form of penalty diminishes sharply, almost to vanishing point. In the West, the possibility today of adults or children being judicially punished in this way for a criminal offence is nil.

For others, the spank at the dawn of life is merely a harbinger of more – sometimes many more – smacks, wallops, strokes or lashes they will receive during their progress through childhood: because they are part of a family where traditional modes of child-rearing are still observed, because they attend one of the few remaining schools where the traditional sanction may still lawfully be applied to the naughtier pupils, or because they have been born into a culture which is simply more traditional in every sense of the word. If theirs is an Islamic society, they may well continue to be liable to physical sanctions well into

---

2. I use this term to mean North America, (most of) Europe and Australasia. At ` the time of writing, Russia is attempting to join the club.

adulthood, for Islam unhesitatingly prescribes corporal punishment of several types for certain offences against God or state – the most notorious of these being the canings administered to believers (and visiting infidels) who violate Islam's strict taboos against alcohol. In other places, chiefly African and some Asian countries, criminals are also sometimes judicially beaten.

It is difficult even for the reluctant Westerner to escape the feeling that the incidence of officially sanctioned corporal punishment remains higher where the peoples are poorest, most ignorant and non-white, and lower where Western values prevail. Nevertheless, corporal punishment lingers embarrassingly on, usually on individual or familial bases, in most countries of the Western club – excepting those, like Sweden, where it has become altogether illegal to smack a child. But many people are deeply ashamed of these lingering blemishes, as they see them, on their societies, citing each and every one as evidence that the Nirvana of civilised values is still a long way off. For them, violence of almost any sort is an incontestable outrage. It can never be a justified proceeding. Wars can be avoided, delinquents reasoned out of their anti-social behaviour, dogs and horses trained, all our daily affairs carried on in peace and harmony without so much as an upraised hand. And for many this hope may turn out to be perfectly realisable. They will pass through life without once fighting in a war (or lending one their moral support), smacking an errant child or cuffing an unruly dog – without even raising the possibility of retributive violence. They have identified it as a demon and cast it out of their lives.

This is to identify an extreme position which is nevertheless a longstanding and, latterly, a successful one. So widespread is the viewpoint that corporal discipline is wicked or at best of dubious value among those who shape public opinion that their terms of reference have become an unchallenged part of modern speech.

Yet explaining away the corporal punishment (distribution of) world map remains difficult. Without descending into something very like cultural imperialism, how can one possibly point out to a citizen of a Third World country that his culture habitually acts in a barbarous manner towards its children, its womenfolk, its criminals and whomsoever it maltreats with the rod in this degrading fashion? Is it possible, without incurring racialist guilt, even to *notice* such associations?

An even bigger embarrassment is represented by the world's most successful economy, certainly a civilised one by its own and many other standards, maybe even a super-civilised one if the capacity for near-infinite refinement of almost any activity is a valid yardstick. Like South Africa and Israel, but for entirely different reasons, Japan is a joker in the civilisation pack. Despite superficial changes in recent years, it remains at root a highly traditional, authoritarian culture, and one which notoriously beats its children, not so much for their own good as for the good of Japan.

It would be provocative at this stage to logic-chop. (1) The Japanese physically chastise their children. (2) Japan owes much of its success (and certainly its low inflation rate) to the legendary discipline of its population, therefore (3) the secret of economic success is to beat young people whenever it seems appropriate. Or: (1) over the last twenty years, all Western countries have ceased, in whole or in part, to discipline their young by physical means. (2) The same countries have mainly experienced absolute declines of economic power, not to mention moral authority and loss of control over their own populations, within the same period, therefore, etc., etc.

These arguments are specious, not to say mischievous. I introduce them here only because it is debate of this precise nature that has all but won the day for the opposite point of view, whose purest form runs as follows: (1) most evil manifests in the form of violence, therefore (2) violence is evil. (3) Smacking is violence, therefore evil. (4) A smacked child is likely to grow up to smack his or her own children, thus perpetuating the evil. (5) So by criminalising the smacking of children we break the cycle and strike a mighty blow against evil.

The conviction that violence equates with evil lies at the root of most forms of pacifism, an honourable system or pattern of belief as old as recorded history. It is always a difficult under-taking to dispute another's article of faith, but is *all* violence evil? The universe, after all, is a demonstrably violent place. When a star goes supernova and a nuclear fireball 200 million miles in diameter swallows half a dozen planets, one or two of which may harbour intelligent life, one may call to mind several potent adjectives, but 'evil' is surely not among them. When a cheetah runs down and slaughters a gazelle, has actual 'wicked-ness' taken place? And in the reverse sense, is it really true that *no* forms of human violence may be said to produce a 'good' (i.e., non-evil) result? What about the war of self-defence, or the cru-sade to rescue a weaker neighbour cruelly invaded and subjected? The frantic mother who drags her baby back from the arms of the child-snatcher and is not too careful where or how hard she kicks him in the process? The straight left that knocks the school bully flat? The swift stroke of the police truncheon that puts paid to the career of a notorious rapist, or – an extreme version of the same – the officially dispatched police bullet that cuts short the demented life of an individual who has already killed fourteen people with a high-powered rifle and apparently intends to kill more? Are these evil motives, evil undertakings? Deplorable, certainly; to be avoided if humanly possible; last resorts – but evil?

Of course, it is not necessary to show an overall equation between evil and violence for strong arguments against corporal punishment to be sustained. These take the form: some violence may, after all, be inevitable, but most of it is not; and physical punishment is not, and has never been, an unavoidable pro-ceeding – it is the lazy or brutal disciplinarian's way of achieving results. A blow delivered is an opportunity for reason lost; worse, it is more likely than not to harm or debase both donor and recipient in ways that are wholly to be regretted. It is degrad-ing. It is an uncivilised demonstration of superior physical force. It is that totemic word of the last decade: abuse.

This is no modernist viewpoint. Mankind has dissertated

upon the subject of corporal punishment since earliest times. Scriptural references, the earliest we have, are wholeheartedly in its favour[3]; Plato approved of it, perhaps unsurprisingly, and his greatest pupil Aristotle is generally supposed to have employed it to shape the character of his own greatest pupil, Alexander the Great of Macedon. But by the Roman era we begin to encounter disapproving sentiments, such as these from the poet Martial:

> What have you to do with us, accursed pedagogue, a fellow odious to boys and girls? Not yet have crested cocks broken the hush of night, already with menacing voice and with thwacks you raise an uproar.[4]

Other Roman poets – Ovid, Juvenal, Horace – likewise condemned or satirised the use of the rod, albeit obliquely, in their works. The prose-writer Cicero of Quintilian offered a comprehensive humanistic condemnation which Bernard Shaw himself could hardly have bettered:

> I cannot approve of children being beaten, though the practice is so common . . . Firstly, beating is odious, slavish and dishonourable at any age; secondly, anyone who is so base that he could not be improved by suggestion will also be as insensible to blows as the lowest of slaves; finally, because such measures are not necessary if the child is under continual supervision. It cannot be stated without shameful blushes what still more shameful orgies are performed by unworthy persons who abuse the right to chastise, and to

---

3. The Book of Proverbs is particularly reactionary. The existence of these texts is held by fundamentalist Christians, perhaps not unnaturally, to be a positive instruction from God not to spare the rod when raising their children. Similar injunctions may be found in the Qoran. In secular Western countries which claim to guarantee freedom of worship but nevertheless wish to outlaw corporal punishment, a conflict therefore arises between constitution and law.
4. Ep. IX, 68.

what, at times, the treatment of these unfortunate children leads others.[5]

Plutarch supported much of this view[6]; and, from another standpoint, a near-contemporary, St Augustine of Hippo Regius[7], set down all the classic anguish of the schoolboy in whose life the scholastic rod is an ever-present threat:

If idle in learning, I was flogged . . . I used to ask Thee [God], though small, yet with no small earnestness, that I might not be flogged at school . . .

Though with small effect, it seems, since:

My elders, yea my very parents, who yet wished me no ill, laughed at my stripes, then my great and grievous ill . . .

In view of the unequivocal scriptural injunctions concerning corporal discipline, it might be thought odd that notable religious figures of the Renaissance – when 'religious correctness' was as never before a dominant element in daily life – might inveigh against it. Martin Luther, perhaps remembering an occasion in his boyhood when he is said to have received fifteen thrashings in a single morning from a schoolmaster, believed that 'the apple ought always to lie beside the rod', which, while not precisely abolitionist, bespeaks an awareness that coercion ought not to be the pedagogue's first response – let us call this an amendment to the classical (Solomonic) position. Another famously, and fatally, devout man, Sir (later Saint) Thomas More, fudged the issue of child-beating in an original way by using

---

5. *Institutio Oratoria*, Harvard University Press, 1936, trans. H.E. Butler.
6. Children should always be kept to their studies by kindly persuasion and loving admonitions, never by means of blows or maltreatment. Beating trains only slavish natures, embitters the nature of the child, and destroys all joy in his tasks.' (*De Educ. Liberis*, xii.)
7. *Confessions*, ch. 9.

only a peacock feather to chastise his offspring; while the great Dutch philosopher Erasmus was wholly against it, like Luther for reasons not unconnected with personal experiences of ferocious school floggings.

Hitherto arguments against corporal punishment had been based on two secular premises, often in combination: the humanitarian (beating is unkind, not to say cruel), and the practical (it is counter-productive and therefore inefficient). The Quakers, who suffered grievously in the seventeenth century from the tyranny of the judicial rod employed as a manifestation of religious intolerance, introduced a new concept: beating as a violation of the temple of the body and therefore of the laws of God. And with the growing humanism of the eighteenth and nineteenth centuries, manifested most obviously in the success of the Emancipation Movement, what may be termed the Quintilianic view was once again put forward, this time with far greater public acceptance: that whippings were wholly and unacceptably degrading, the portion of the slave. But all arguments against physical discipline took on an entirely new momentum with the growing public realisation, which sharpened throughout the nineteenth century and is today common currency, that there was, or at least might be, a pronounced sexual component in the act of physical chastisement.

The eighteenth century produced two remarkable men, each of whom placed his own stamp upon the subject. The first was the rationalist philosopher and educational theorist Jean-Jacques Rousseau (1712–78). The second, and by far the more notorious, was Donatien Alphonse François, Marquis de Sade (1740-1814).

Both men were flagellants. It might be said that they were of different and perhaps opposed classes, since while de Sade's name has since become indissolubly associated with the active principal in any human combination of sexual stimulation and cruelty, the opposite type, the sadist's natural partner, as it were, is supposed to derive equivalent passive gratification from being so treated, and is today popularly called a 'masochist', after

Baron Leopold von Sacher-Masoch (1836-95). But in the early nineteenth century, *Venus in Furs*, Sacher-Masoch's definitive fictional portrayal of the obsessive pain-fancier, had not yet been written, and those who discoursed on the condition had no handy label to deploy. If the word 'masochist' had been available, however, it would most certainly have been applied to Rousseau, since (accepting the standard definition for a moment) that is what he was – to his great discontent. Nor, like his notorious contemporary, did he use fiction as a vehicle for his musings on the subject. In his *Confessions* we have one of the most honest – and dolorous – personal accounts of how a perfectly conventional childhood spanking can cause unwelcome sexual notes to resonate into adulthood, with unhappy results; a classic instance, it is said, of unthinking, if kindly motivated, abuse.

> Since Mlle Lambercier [Rousseau's guardian] treated us with a mother's love, she had also a mother's authority, which she exercised sometimes by inflicting on us such childish chastisements as we had earned. For a long while she confined herself to threats, and the threat of a punishment entirely unknown to me frightened me sufficiently. But when in the end I was beaten I found the experience less dreadful in fact than anticipation; and the very strange thing was that this punishment increased my affection for the inflicter. It required all the strength of my devotion and all my natural gentleness to prevent my deliberately earning another beating; I had discovered in the shame and pain of the punishment an admixture of sensuality which had left me rather eager than otherwise for a repetition by the same hand . . .

A nineteenth-century liberal educationalist might well read this famous passage as a matter of course and derive much food for thought thereby. He would be less likely to encounter the works of de Sade in his normal reading (they were already classed as pornography which is, indeed, by any yardstick, what they are), but once he had done so, he would be led, doubtless horrified and unwillingly, into a sub-world of literary eroticism in which the use of the rod played a central part. This genre, already thriving before Victoria's reign, is more fully discussed elsewhere; the point here is that its very existence offered further, conclusive proof that for many people there was sexual stimulation to be had in the contemplation of the act of physical discipline. Even were the humanitarian and practical arguments against it not also to be judged compelling in a society already beginning to declare holy war upon the sexual impulse, this one fact alone served to call the practice into serious question for the first time. Whipping a delinquent – criminal, soldier, sailor, child – might be a deterrent, maybe even a deserved penalty, certainly a quick and economical one, and there was no doubt that scripture and tradition both condoned it, but the ancient writers of scripture and the generations in between were naive and untutored folk who had never appreciated the unwholesome connection between physical discipline and sexual excitement. Now that such a connection was proven, the practice must be stopped, and if it could not be stopped altogether (early abolitionists were realistic) it should be modified as far as possible to remove the likelihood of obtainable sexual gratification – a good thing in itself which might also help to lower the incidence and so make eventual abolition all the more likely.[8]

As far as the everyday lives of nineteenth-century children were concerned, certainly in Europe, the most noticeable modification to disciplinary practice as a result of these ideas was the progressive eclipse of the antique birch rod as the primary instrument of scholastic and domestic correction. Since this instrument, despite its fearsome reputation, may only be applied

---

8. The motives of some early abolitionists are mixed indeed. Many appear to be unconcerned by whipping per se, yet deeply disturbed by the possibility of a whipper obtaining gratification – hence the mid-nineteenth century proliferation of strange machines designed to inflict judicial corporal punishment with mechanical dispassion.

with any effect at all to the bare skin, its use was clearly in breach of the new rules of propriety and it was in sharp decline by the middle of the century. The birch was replaced, particularly in Germany, Holland and England, by the imported rattan cane, an implement less fundamentally indecent in use since it did not necessitate the baring of bottoms in order to be effective; but also much more penetrating and capable of causing considerable pain – even, in extreme cases, real injury. Since many disciplinarians continued, for a variety of reasons including the lamentable, to decree that bottoms should nonetheless be bared for punishment, the end result of this 'advance' was, in many cases, a profound increase in severity – not, presumably, what the reformers had in mind.

Before the middle of the century humanitarian concerns with whipping had been brought to the notice of a wider audience by means of popular fiction. Charles Dickens' Mr Creakle (*David Copperfield*) and Mr Squeers (*Nicholas Nickleby*) are the same figure repeated: ultimate literary exemplars of the early Victorian provincial English brutish schoolmaster, gloating over his prey and rejoicing unwholesomely in the use of the rod.

'Now, boys, this is a new half. Take care what you're about, in this new half. Come fresh up to the lessons, I advise you, for I come fresh up to the punishment. I won't flinch. It will be of no use your rubbing yourselves; you won't rub the marks out that I shall give you. Now get to work, every boy!'

When this dreadful exordium was over . . . Mr Creakle came to where I sat, and told me that if I were famous for biting, he was famous for biting, too. He then showed me the cane, and asked me what I thought of *that,* for a tooth? Was it a sharp tooth, hey? Was it a double tooth, hey? Had it a deep prong, hey? Did it bite, hey? Did it bite? At every question he gave me a fleshy cut with it that made me writhe; so I was very soon made free of Salem House (as Steerforth said), and was very soon in tears also.

Not that I mean to say these were special marks of distinction, which only I received. On the contrary, a large majority of the boys (especially the smaller ones) were visited with similar instances of notice, as Mr Creakle made the round of the schoolroom. Half the establishment was writhing and crying, before the day's work began; and how much of it had writhed and cried before the day's work was over I am really afraid to recollect, lest I should seem to exaggerate.

I should think there never can have been a man who enjoyed his profession more than Mr Creakle did. He had a delight in cutting at the boys, which was like the satisfaction of a craving appetite. I am confident that he couldn't resist a chubby boy, especially; that there was a fascination in such a subject, which made him restless in his mind, until he had scored and marked him for the day. I was chubby myself, and ought to know.[9]

By now the sexual innuendo attached to corporal punishment was part of the common sensibility, even if still largely unmentionable. The personal attacks levelled at Dr Thomas Arnold, the nationally famous headmaster of Rugby School, during a campaign for a parliamentary seat, and with the purely political purpose of discrediting him locally and thereby promoting the candidate he opposed, took the form of allegations[10] that he birched Rugby schoolboys, not so much because they needed it, but because *he* did. This is the earliest direct example I can find of alleged sexual flagellationism being used as a political smear against an individual. Arnold coolly ignored the rumours – he would hardly have admitted them had they been true – yet whatever his other faults and misconceptions, he is not recalled as an ogre of the birch, as was Keate of Eton. But on its own the use of

9. *David Copperfield*, ch. VII.
10. *Northampton Herald*, 21 March 1835. The candidate Arnold opposed – and presumably the agency behind the smear campaign – was the future Lord Cardigan, who led the Charge of the Light Brigade.

the smear clearly demonstrates a contemporary public understanding of the link between whipping and sexuality. If the
allegations had not been widely comprehensible they would
have been useless, and therefore not worth the making.

The development of these perceptions into their finished form
therefore took place a century and a half ago, long enough, one
might think, for public opinion to catch up with reformist
thought and for corporal punishment to be abolished as a
method of governing the immature and the unruly. Society was
far quicker to register, in terms of legislation, public disapproval
of little boys working as human chimney sweeps. In Britain,
public executions had ceased by the later part of the century.
Slavery was abolished, by degrees, over no more than four
decades, its most famously disputed extinction taking place, it
has been said, as the result of the popular impact of a single
novel. Across the Western world, the franchise was remorselessly extended; the poor of one continent were cordially invited
to 'breathe free' on another, and did so, in their grateful millions. But throughout this century-long tidal wave of humanistic
success the old attachment to corporal punishment resisted more
staunchly than might have been expected.

Britain ceased to flog female criminals in 1828; her soldiers
and sailors had to wait a further forty years for the same privilege
(both Army and Navy retained rights of corporal discipline over
boy entrants until the 1950s). Male criminals were liable to be
flogged on the shoulders with a judicial 'cat' until 1948, male
prisoners until 1967. Delinquent boys, in mainland Britain historically subject to the birch rod, remained so also until 1948. In
the UK-dependent Isle of Man and Channel Islands they were
still liable to this penalty as late as 1980, when a judgement by
the European Court of Human Rights pronounced judicial
birching beyond the pale of Euro-tolerability.

So much for judicial and military penalties. In England,
schools have put up an even stouter resistance. At the time of
writing it is still not quite illegal for private schools to use the

cane or slipper, though since 1987 it has been wholly illegal in England and Wales for state schools to do so. Even so, the numbers of private schools that use corporal punishment are few indeed, and dwindling.

As for domestic discipline – physical punishments administered by parent or guardian – here the most dogged fight of all has been put up, and although ground has been lost, and the Solomonic method of child-raising criminalised in, to date, Sweden (1979), Finland (1983), Austria (1989), Norway (1987) and Denmark (1985), with more states, including Germany, wavering in the balance, a few Western governments[11] have largely hesitated to take this final step. There are several reasons: public worries over child crime; a reluctance to interfere in private matters; the urge to defend the institution of the family and, not least, the near-impossibility of enforcing such a law. It must also be said that in many countries, even Western ones, there is almost certainly a majority[12] of responsible parents who believe that the biblical remedy can, on occasion, be exactly the right one to apply. Journalist Katherine Whitehorn is unrepentantly one of these:

Should you smack? People who approve say 'smack' and people who disapprove say 'hit', so that shows you where I stand. *Where?* [magazine] did a survey of a fortnight's punishments in a variety of families and came to the conclusion

---

11. Notably the ones with the strongest libertarian traditions, particularly England and the United States. In 1993 over 1 million American children were 'paddled' in school, one quarter of them in a single state, Texas.

12. Surveys on this subject regularly show that between 70 and 80 per cent of English mothers are unwilling to rule it out. A 1990 survey carried out in *Woman's Own* magazine returned a figure of 90 per cent for those who admitted having smacked their children on at least one occasion. A TV programme, *The Time, The Place*, which devoted a half-hour show to the issue of corporal punishment the morning after the flogging of American teenager Michael Fay in Singapore in May 1994, invited viewers to phone in with their votes (for/against). By the end of the programme, an unprecedented 65,000 people had phoned. The result of the straw poll was 95 per cent in favour, 5 per cent against.

that everybody smacks; all that varies is the amount of guilt you feel about it. It's unlikely that anything so nearly universal will warp your child forever.

On the other hand, speaking as one who has laid about her pretty freely on occasion, I can't say it's done as much good as I hoped, for the same reason it doesn't do harm: they get used to it . . . What I now wish I'd done was to make smacking much more rare and awesome; and I bet what stopped me, as it stops plenty of parents, is that idiotic remark of Shaw's about it being better to hit a child in anger, even at the risk of maiming it for life, than to strike a child in cold blood. Everyone was riveted when he said it because the current view was you should *never* strike a child in anger, but he's quite wrong. It puts the motives of the parents above the likely effects: it *is not* better to be maimed for life than to have a nasty half-hour with Father. And if you can only forgive yourself for smacking if you've lost control of your temper, you probably won't hand it out to best effect . . . The message that should come across is that this time he's done something really bad, like running in front of the car or making the helper cry; not just that Mummy's in a bad mood again.

And it is no good saying smugly 'I never spank my children' if everyone's inwardly groaning 'More's the pity.'[13]

Marshalled against the unreconstructed public is a formidable array of expert opinion: child psychologists, behaviourists, activists and lobbyists of many kinds. Where such voices and opinions sway policy, corporal punishment has been outlawed.

The abolitionist view has always been accounted progressive, and those who adhere to it, for whichever of the many possible reasons I have ascribed, are mainly to be found in the centre and on the left of politics and national debate, and among the intelligentsia and the pædiatric professions. It is also true that

---

13. *How to Survive Children*, p. 22.

those who are most robust and 'old-school' in their stated views are more noticeably to be found among non-intellectual, conservative circles. This division of opinion is, however, not reflected in the country as a whole. A majority of working-class people of all political persuasions, particularly those over thirty-five, is still against blanket abolition.

The abolitionist is himself far from liberal in his attitude to those who take an opposing position. He finds it genuinely difficult to extend understanding to a person whom he is compelled to see as an apologist for cruelty, whose views are, at best, the gross naivety of a miserable deviant who refuses to confront the fact of his own perversion – at worst inhumanity, if not actual incitement to child abuse. Pity for the flogged compels hatred for the flogger; that the flogger was almost certainly in his day one of the flogged is an acknowledged key component in the overall abolitionist case but it evokes curiously little sympathy in a social climate where the search for exciting new classes of victim is one of the few genuine growth industries.

The fair-minded abolitionist will occasionally concede that the pro-smackers may also be victims. But there is an unspoken hierarchy of victimhood, with children automatically heading most ad hoc personal lists. The Solomonites – most of whom are white, middle-class and middle-aged – do badly in this chart. The only crumbs of sympathy which come their way do so when they themselves are adduced as evidence of the truth of the abolitionists' assertions; hopelessly damned out of their own mouths, unthinking dupes of their own crippled sexuality, vampires tragically driven to promulgate the evil that destroyed them.

In England, once famous for its legendary attachment to the Solomonic penalty, there remain only two fortresses to be stormed before the practice is abolished *in toto*. Firstly, the ban on corporal punishment in state schools must be extended to private establishments. Secondly, it must be extended to the home. The former seems relatively easy to achieve and is almost certainly inevitable; the latter is another matter entirely, with enormous residual resistance from the public.[14] Therefore, in order to bring into being Swedish-style legislation forbidding all forms of corporal discipline on pain of criminal penalty, UK abolitionist groups such as EPOCH have played their strongest card and invoked the spectre of child abuse as the new foundation pillar of their case.

14. In March 1994 Mrs Anne Davis, a childminder from Sutton, Surrey (England), won a longstanding legal battle with Sutton Council, who had refused her official registration (thereby depriving her of her livelihood) because she would not promise not to smack naughty children in her care if she deemed fit; even though no British law was being broken, and despite her having received full permission from the parents involved. As an example of creeping abolitionism, unsupported by any wider legislation or the consent of the electorate, this policy, implemented by 95 per cent of British local authorities, is noteworthy – and, according to the High Court judgement, illegal. Its nominal justification was a recent set of Ministry of Health guidelines which advocated such a policy. These no-smack guidelines were quietly drawn up in 1990 with no reference to any public body of opinion save, apparently, the EPOCH pressure group. Outside the High Court, Mrs Davis told reporters: 'It's only the experts who can't tell the difference between loving discipline and child abuse.'

3

SUFFER THE CHILDREN

*Corporal punishment is tremendous fun for adults, but
out of the question for children. Everybody should spank
their partner and cuddle up afterwards. But hitting children? No thank you.*

Tim Woodward[1]

We now find ourselves in dangerous terrain, since the subjects of
children and sexuality have been drawn together within the
same arena. In few other areas of public debate is there such a
dense minefield of lethal preconceptions to be navigated.

Every age has its characteristic no-go areas for respectable discourse. To dispute the king's will (Thomas More), the Church's
teaching (Galileo, Bruno), fundamentalist cosmology (Darwin),
or the morality of the class system (Marx *inter alia)* have each, in
their various eras, been awkward, dangerous, and sometimes
fatal undertakings. Those who openly questioned the legitimacy
of either world war were ignored, scorned, ostracised, hounded,
interned and sometimes made away with – in virtually all the
countries that participated, on either side. Relatively few voices
were raised in their defence, not, at least in the West, because of
fear of consequences, but because so few people agreed with
them. Lone voices they may have been, even gallant ones, and of
high moral courage there can be small doubt; but they suffered as

---

1. Quoted in the *Independent on Sunday*, 24 April 1994. Mr Woodward is the
editor of *Skin Two* magazine, probably the world's most intelligent 'fetish' publication, and this viewpoint is standard throughout the so-called SM
community.

they did chiefly because their views were bitterly incompatible with those of the vast majority of their fellows; because theirs were considered to be perverse (see chapter 1), and not merely mistaken, views.

Today, one may quite safely be unchristian, anti-royalist under a monarchy, outspokenly pacifist, or all three at once, and no great popular odium will accrue.[2] One may be a diehard communist, even a full-time street-fighting anti-establishmentarian with a pocketful of ball-bearings to break the legs of police horses, and no harm will befall one simply for stating one's opinions – street demonstrations may be a different story, but there different conditions obtain. Wholly respectable national journals of opinion regularly publish articles in which radical views of different types are freely aired without untoward consequence to their authors. The views themselves may be contentious, even to some offensive, but their regular voicing is seen as the proper exercise of free speech, their unfettered publication the hallmark of a free press.

There are exceptions to this admirable liberality of principle. For example, *Time Out* magazine, the respected weekly London journal of metropolitan life, arts and leisure, refuses to accept personal ads it deems sadomasochist (though it apparently places no such bar on any other kind of sexuality). Politicians who oppose further non-white immigration into the UK will find very few respectable journals willing to give them column-space. They will not be invited on TV to promote 'repatriation'. Supporters of the view that many former colonial possessions of European powers have suffered catastrophic reverses of fortune since (and, by implication, because) they have been decolonised will not exactly be inundated with offers to promulgate their opinions, which fly in the face of

---

2. Voluble opponents of the Second World War were quietly persuaded to silence, shunted away to less harmful arenas, or – *faute de mieux* – incarcerated. Opponents of the Vietnam, Falklands and Gulf wars were invited on television to air their views in comfortable studios.

fashionable thought. Since fashion is not the least influential of the mass of disparate components which at any time make up what is called public opinion, this is often enough to bring about what amounts to an ad hoc self-suppression of ideas. So strong is the impulse to conform that many who hold (unfashionably) awkward views learn to conceal them as a matter of course.

Self-imposed constraints of this type currently affect Western public opinion on the various forms of unpleasantness that have historically been visited upon some children by those in authority over them.

There is no doubt that the sexual and physical maltreatment of children triggers a particular horror in modern society. I concede without argument that this should be so. Nebulous and clichéd though the term may be, there is such a thing as abuse, it can have long-lasting effects on its victims, which can utterly ruin their enjoyment of life; it may indeed be perpetuated, in some cases, as a form of subconsciously deferred revenge – and it is and should be a crime.

The problem with 'abuse' is that it is an indistinct term which can mean whatever the user wishes. There can hardly be anybody who would dispute that the rape of a four-year-old girl is the very worst type of abuse; or that to break the ribs of an eight-year-old boy is not and can never be 'discipline', but is common assault of a particularly cowardly and odious kind. Both are rightly deemed criminal acts. But for many people, the difference between the grievous bodily and mental harm described above and a bottom briskly smacked in the traditional nursery manner is only nominal: merely a matter of degree. Granted, the physical injury in the former cases is more serious, but the spanking, even though it may have left no physical trace whatsoever, is deemed no less of an outrage. All are 'abuses' – equally, in the last analysis, to be abhorred and condemned.

Openly to dispute the unchallenged extension of the 'abuse' definition into regions which are, to say the least, contestable, is to run a considerable risk of being vilified – to no less an extreme degree than the sixteenth-century doubter of papal infallibility might be unsurprised to find himself regarded with horror and loathing as a heretic, while the mild questioner of a Tudor king's absolute right to do as he pleased at all times might inevitably be dubbed 'traitor', the convinced Second World War pacifist a 'Nazi sympathiser' or the 1980s CND activist a 'commie stooge'.

Such is the righteous contemporary hatred for child abusers that those who appear even to press for a closer definition can find themselves somehow on the defensive, as potential abusers themselves. This is particularly true of those who honestly believe, and boldly state, that judicious and reasonable corporal punishment is by no means the worst thing one can do to a child, and may indeed be to his long-term advantage. But the odium of the 'abuser-friendly' label being more than most are willing to court, increasingly, no matter what they feel, they keep quiet. It is a form of censorship by received opinion. As Mrs Lynette Burrowes, one of the few who does not keep quiet, recently wrote:

> Why are we so squeamish about saying it? We delude ourselves with being uniquely free-thinking and outspoken on almost every subject but when it comes to saying what our fathers and grandfathers would have taken as the merest common sense, that punishment has to be painful in order to be effective, the words stick in our throats.
>
> The truth is that we are brainwashed by child-care professionals into denying our own experience of children and deferring, instead, to theirs. Since most of them are men or career women, this experience is hopelessly inadequate for the authority they claim. But they are the only people who are sufficiently organised to mount a propaganda offensive in favour of their latest theories. This inevitably attracts the attention of the media and then becomes an influence on the professions.

The particular theory they favour at the moment is a mirror image of the one they had fifty years ago. Then it was that physical affection between parents and children was indistinguishable from sexual activity so kissing and cuddling should be avoided. Now they maintain that physical correction is indistinguishable from violence and so must be avoided. Like any theories, its logic is plausible; the only problem is that it is not true.[3]

There are many who may well have agreed with some if not all of the arguments deployed thus far, but who nevertheless will withhold final approval of corporal punishment on either or both of the following grounds:

(1) Even allowing a great deal of elasticity over definitions, real, indisputable physical abuse does undoubtedly occur from time to time. *For this reason alone* corporal punishment should be universally discouraged and eventually banned. Whatever their actual numbers and rates of incidence, individual abuses are a far greater evil than any supposed pandemic of indiscipline resulting from the permanent exclusion of physical sanctions from school and home. The risk of other, possibly damaging replacement penalties should be accepted, since however bad they may be they cannot be worse than physical abuse.

(2) The potential, if not inevitable, sexual connotations in any traditional act of physical discipline are *by themselves sufficient grounds* for its complete rejection as a suitable punishment. When the obtaining of sexual gratification is an element, unconscious or not, in a supposedly disciplinary

---

3. The *Sunday Telegraph*, 13 February 1993. Mrs Burrowes, the author of *Good Children* and other works on childcare, is robustly of the old school and occasionally invited to state the case for reasonable corporal punishment in home and school.

proceeding, what is actually taking place is a sexual assault. Even the possibility of such an interaction is too disturbing to be permitted.

The first argument may be met by citing the motor car and the jet aeroplane, veritable whipping-boys of the late industrial world. Because a low percentage of drivers commits motoring offences of an irresponsible and dangerous kind, is that a serious reason for grounding the vast majority who do not? Because airliners sometimes crash, should air travel be abandoned? There are indeed opponents of both forms of transport who would like nothing better than to see them done away with overnight, but this is almost always on other grounds such as environmental damage. To propose a universal ban on either mode of locomotion merely for the reasons stated above would be considered an impossible over-reaction, though there are few of us who are not shocked and distressed by the spectacle of a car crash or the contemplation of an airline disaster. The personal mobility represented by the car and the aeroplane are considered vital to modern life, so the risk is accepted. Everything is done to minimise it, not least the continuous devising of new regulations, but the idea of eliminating risk altogether by eliminating the only theatres of activity in which it can occur is not seriously considered for one moment.

As for the notion that other, non-corporal, punishments are less open to abuse, offenders who, as a result of truancy, brawling and other classic bad-boy activities, have been punished in the new ways and have as a result found themselves in 'special schools', 'behaviour units' or 'secure accommodation' – where they have been locked in, deprived of clothing, semi-starved, assaulted on a routine basis, humiliated at every possible opportunity, and occasionally buggered – may be forgiven for doubting the accuracy of this assumption. Several outrages a year of this type gain public exposure, the most notorious recent example in Britain being the 'Pindown' régime operated by a behaviour unit in Staffordshire throughout the 1980s, where everything listed above (except buggery) actually took place. No prosecutions followed, though some staffers were dismissed.[4]

The second objection – the sexual connection – is more profound and cannot be so easily countered. It rests on the very old idea that sex is original sin, fundamentally wicked, a genie in a bottle, the contents of Pandora's Box, something innately base that may nonetheless be put to occasional virtuous use – but only when securely chained and harnessed: for this is a demon that yearns to be free, and will escape if it can.

The equation of the sexual impulse with all that is most bestial in human nature, and the consequent desire to quarantine it behind a curtain of regulation and convention, even to exclude it entirely from all areas of life other than simple and lawful procreation – in other words, sexual repression – is said by many who deplore it to have begun, for Christian culture at least, with the Pauline 'heresy' (by which they mean St Paul's revisions of the Gospels) nearly 2,000 years ago. Others have associated its genesis with the rise of non-conformism, or the Counter-Reformation, or the Puritans, or the Jesuits, or the British public school system. Almost every historical entity noted in its day for authoritarianism has at some time been accused of setting the wheel of sexual repression in motion – or, at the very least, giving it another firm spin.

Yet the development of this negative and wary view of the sexual impulse is readily explainable. Around 5,000 years ago people began to live in cities. Though it is surely safe to say that the late-neolithic villages of the Tigris, Euphrates and Indus river valleys (from which the first city populations were drawn) would already have had rules and laws concerning many

---

4. The British Home Office refuses to release the numbers of children held in secure units. Since it is also illegal to publish their names in the press (nominally for their protection), these children have effectively disappeared into a gulag. The numbers, names and locations of such units, the identities of those who work in them, and the criteria on which they are selected, are also 'official secrets'.

matters, not least sexual behaviour, metropolitan environments, being more crowded, necessarily and prudently exercised still stricter disciplines upon their inhabitants than the smaller and more diffused rural communities. Sex is a potent impulse which frequently exceeds the bounds of sense and consideration, and if not regulated to some extent it may have undesirable side-effects (quarrelling, feuding, the dilution or over-concentration of blood-lines, the complication of property rights), as well as good ones (the increase of the population and therefore – since numbers usually mean military power – increased chances of survival in a hostile and cruel world). But there have always been at least as many, if not more, 'bad' consequences of sex as 'good' ones, and some of the laws made by Hammurabi of Babylon (c. 1800 BC), as well as their near-contemporary equivalents codified as the Ten Commandments, represent the culmination of many generations' practical experience in how best to deal with, among other things, each other's sexuality. They are overwhelmingly practical in intent and scope.

The usually tragic or unwelcome consequences of the 'wrong' kind of sex form a theme which runs steadily and powerfully throughout human tradition and history from its legendary beginnings: temptation (Adam and Eve); adultery (Helen of Troy, Jezebel); bestiality (Leda and the swan, Pasiphæ and the bull); incest (Oedipus and Jocasta, King Arthur with Morgana); rape (the Sabine Women, Lucretia), and lust (David and Bathsheba, Messalina, Henry VIII of England and at least two of his wives). As long as man has been aware of sex, he has been wary of it; and laws and taboos of such antiquity do not come about, let alone survive, by accident.

In the light of this ancient and deep-rooted worry the sexually based objections to corporal punishment are logical and obvious: the instant old Adam reveals himself, the nature of the event has inevitably and fatally changed for the worse. It has become impure, a 'bad' thing – not because of the coercive or punitive aspect, or even necessarily because of the violence, but because the element of sexual gratification has corrupted everything connected with it. Discipline and lawful authority have been defiled by lust. And if sexual motives are so powerful that their gratification becomes the real, even the only reason why stripes are administered, then injustice is the very least of the offences committed. The worst? Something not quite rape, and not quite torture, but an ugly self-gratifying blend of both to some lesser degree; in all cases, an abhorrent abuse of power, wholly to be condemned.

A moment's reflection will reveal that in fact sexual motives do habitually 'stray' into fields of human life other than the marital/procreational, with little or no apparent guilt or condemnation. It is now conceded that the sexual impulse is more ubiquitous within our commonplace actions than had been appreciated until recent times. Sex is acknowledged to be a constant and powerful, if usually subconscious, factor in our choice of clothing (mating display); in our physical behaviour towards various selected individuals (postures and dances); in our food, drink and styles of consumption; in our language and especially arts, and even in our behaviour towards our children. Many mothers will testify, some guiltily, others with surprise and no little pleasure, that the act of feeding an infant from the breast may often be accompanied by intense sexual pleasure in that region of the female body. This phenomenon, now freely acknowledged, violates – almost exactly, so far as I can see – the gut prohibition of sexuality outside its 'proper' sphere, especially where children are involved: yet I have never read any admonitions against breastfeeding *solely for this reason*. The sexual reaction is perceived as a minor side-effect which may be accepted and even enjoyed with a clear conscience in the light of the greater good represented by the maternal act of nourishing the child.

More contentiously, it is a widespread practice, especially in Third World countries, for mothers and those in charge of very young children to masturbate them in order to induce sleepiness. A worldwide pandemic of child sexual abuse, or simple practicality?

It may also be noted that there are other classes of supposed sexual perversion – all of which are as socially *de trop* as flagellation – which appear to commence in infancy, as a direct result of caring treatment by the mother or whoever has charge of the infant. Many people are erotically excited by the tactile sensations occasioned by certain materials – notably, and significantly, rubber and plastic. Both of these materials are in everyday use around the world for an overwhelmingly practical reason: as incontinence safeguards. Plastic and rubber baby pants have been in use for over a century, which is, interestingly, about as long as the associated fetishes have been in existence (or at least documented, which is the only evidence one may rely upon). Before that, infants were swaddled in linen (or not swaddled at all). Therefore, by applying the same implacable 'abuse test', it may be claimed that all mothers who clothe their babies in these materials – in order, let it be said, to save their infants from discomfort and themselves from regular, unpleasant, cleaning-up of the family furniture or the car seats – and all companies who manufacture and sell such garments are actively creating and maintaining a widespread sexual neurosis and are therefore 'abusers'. If this were true, then the only answer would be to ban nappies and all baby garments made from such materials forthwith. Except that very few mothers would tolerate such a reversion to an earlier system. Many might be struck by the above argument, but, faced with the unpleasant consequences of a reversion to linen or towelling (or nothing at all), would decide that life is already quite complicated enough, and would continue as before. In other words, the risk of sexual perversion later in life would be accepted in the light of a greater and more immediate good.

Man obtains stimulation – at varying levels, many of them below the level of everyday consciousness – from a variety of sources which have nothing very obviously to do with procreation. It will be said that many of these activities involve some form of sensuality, and therefore that the follow-through into straight sexuality is an inevitable concomitant. Even if one accepts both the dichotomy and the transition, this approach still raises more problems than it solves, since if sensuality is an ineluctable path to sexuality, then, in order to maintain the strictest social controls on the latter, one must therefore include as many manifestations of the former in any list of specific prohibitions.

To impose bans on sensuality might be thought unwise, even impossible: it has been tried nevertheless, throughout history. In the main, however, ruling authorities have recognised the essential impossibility of regulating their subjects' behaviour to such extraordinary degrees, and have evolved systems of remarkable casuistry which attempt to distinguish between the two, in order to permit the one while continuing to attempt regulation of the other.

But if the argument is accepted that a mild incidence of sexual arousal, for either party, is not in itself an inevitable 'brand of evil' in the execution of an otherwise reasonable duty, then this apparently key objection is substantially undermined.

Finally there is the associated belief that the receipt of corporal punishment, whatever the motives of the donor, can excite sensual urges in an immature mind and body, and thus generate a specific neurosis: the wish to be whipped.

The occurrence of this phenomenon of course is not denied, even though its mechanics remain mysterious. Yet although experiences of this type may indeed cause unhappiness in individual cases and are therefore ultimately 'harmful'[5], they are not, I suggest, intrinsically so, any more than other, no less traditional traumas of childhood, which are not, and cannot be, guarded against.

In fact it is not the means that is being condemned – though this is what is claimed – but the end.

---

5. A great deal of unhappiness is not caused by the 'perversion' itself, whose practice or contemplation may afford the keenest pleasure, but the longstanding fear of being exposed.

Let us suppose that on a single occasion in his life a child behaves badly and is spanked. As an apparently direct and self-contained result, like Rousseau, he becomes, in later life, a flagellant, to the extent that the mere contemplation of the idea of spanking or being spanked causes erotic arousal. Whatever else may befall him, and no matter how he copes with his 'imprinting', his life's course has been deviated to some degree: we may fairly say without his consent. Even those not automatically predisposed to disapprove of physical discipline may find grounds for objecting to 'inheritances' of this apparent magnitude: children are neither property nor surrogates, and to influence or colour another human being's life pattern to such a degree is, at best, irresponsible; at worst, self-evidently abusive.

Now consider the case of the child who has the good fortune to be born to wealthy, non-spanking parents with highly developed musical sensibilities. Himself displaying modest evidence of infant musical talent, he is encouraged, pressured, even forced, to learn a musical instrument. He may desire ardently to grow up to be a footballer, or a soldier, or a racing driver, or even a chartered accountant, but if he shows promise on the violin all such childish desires will be dismissed by his parents, who 'know better'. In due course, after a hothouse childhood devoted to the intensive study of the violin, he becomes a professional musician, perhaps a world-class one. His life will have been shaped against his originally expressed wishes, and indeed he may dutifully proclaim himself grateful for it once he attains adulthood. Nevertheless exactly the same class of coercion has taken place; in fact, being continuous, it has been even more intensive and in this instance deliberate.

How much condemnation will accrue to the parents as a result? I suggest little enough. The relentless long-term pressure, the brushing aside or smothering of the child's own immature hopes, the desperate stress experienced by many gifted children with over-expectant parents, all are virtually discounted because musical virtuosity is universally held to be a desirable goal. The end has justified the means, and the proud parents have done nothing more than their duty; to their child, and to the world. As a recent correspondent to *The Times* put it:

> Causing a slight physical pain with somewhat symbolic smacking or spanking may be more effective and less harmful than a frosty or acid reprimand, a parent's or minder's sulk. Everyone is subject to the law in extreme cases.
>
> Unfortunately, far deeper and more lasting injury is widely inflicted on children and yet ignored, if not encouraged, by society. What right, for example, have parents to impose their religious 'faith' on their children? What right have they to impose their 'ethnic' origins/prejudices? What right to have their children circumcised?
>
> Parental love is, possibly, our most beautiful and fulfilling gift from nature. Parenting, however, is a most difficult and morally demanding art. Special and additional legislation has no place in either.[6]

Since it is high time the present writer placed his own view on record, let it be as follows: that there is at best a middling case for a wholesale return to corporal punishment for delinquency in home, school or society at large; that some individuals may indeed be harmed by it beyond all intention of the punishing authority; and that there have indeed been a shameful number of cases in the past where theoretically legitimate corporal punishment has been applied in an over-severe, inappropriate or indecent manner – cruel punishments indeed.

In this connection, there is a widespread point of view which holds that juvenile males (or adults, for that matter) who commit certain crimes deserve to be judicially beaten. By and large, I agree: a beating is very often exactly what some of them deserve. Should it therefore be restored as a judicial penalty? In my view, only if methods very different to the way it was done in the past can be developed. The historical British penalty of judicial flogging with

---

6. 26 March 1994.

a heavy birch rod when the culprit might be a boy as young as eight years old has always appeared to require the active participation of at least two and probably more grown adult males as well as the use of restraints, not to mention the presence of a doctor. Such spectacles, even in the mind's eye, strike an appalling note. The punishments themselves were likely to be savage enough, with little account taken of age, size or malnourishment, while the statutory requirement for a doctor is itself distinctly disturbing. No matter what a bad boy may have done, to be punished in such a way that there is any danger whatsoever to his physical health (for if there is not, why is a doctor's presence necessary?) exceeds the limits of acceptability, even to many of those otherwise keen to see this penalty restored to the statute books. Yet this is how it was done in the past, and would, if the law were indeed changed, as is most unlikely, probably be done again (one may, I think, trust the British Home Office to make a dog's breakfast of it from the very beginning). Public sympathy would inevitably accrue to the early victims, whose wealed bodies would instantly be on page 1 of all the tabloid newspapers[7] (though on TV news only after 9pm), and whose crimes – which might well have been appalling – would thus be largely overlooked in the apparent disproportion of the judicial response. There would be artistic reconstructions of the vital scene on the middle pages, and the editions containing such artwork would sell out faster than any edition in any tabloid's history. All this would follow were the birch to be brought back, as many devoutly wish (or think they wish); which is a compelling reason for doing no such thing. But there will still be many who deserve it.

As for domestic or pedagogic discipline, a practice which is still in being, though its incidence has been vastly reduced in the last twenty years, a course of action or established practice is not

---

7. The newly appointed literary agent for Michael Fay, the American boy caned in Singapore in 1994, publicly predicted that his client would make a lot of money. 'His buttocks are worth a fortune,' he said. 'Everybody wants to see Michael's buttocks.'

necessarily fully invalidated by occasional manifestations of an unexpected, excessive or extreme form, or by exceptions to the rule. There is no class of human activity which is not badly or wrongly done by some people some of the time, or which does not provoke occasional unlooked-for reactions; and because some individuals have been cruelly or excessively punished, *of itself* that is no evidence that all or even most corporal punishments have been objectively reprehensible and wicked – least of all that the practice itself is wholly evil and should be stopped. Similarly, just as some recipients of corporal punishment have certainly developed an affinity for it, like Rousseau, Gladstone, C.S. Lewis and T.E. Lawrence – while others, like the late Lord Olivier, have manifested an unusual horror – that is proof only that some children are different to others and react differently to certain treatment. Other children may be in their turn especially vulnerable to other, as yet largely uncondemned forms of daily discipline: relentless over-criticism, for example, may produce a catastrophic absence of self-confidence later in life. As 'non-violent' behaviour such parental approaches are not legally classifiable as child abuse (though there are many, including me, who would see them as such), not least because they cannot be prevented or policed.

There are, I suggest, strong residual arguments in favour of physical discipline *in certain cases*, many of them still largely unaddressed by its opponents.

Firstly, it is (or can be, or should be) the quickest of all punishments, succeeding the crime which triggers it as swiftly as possible to underscore the fatal connection between the two in the mind of an immature culprit.

Secondly, the trauma associated with its infliction can nevertheless satisfy all parties' requirement for a dramatic clearing of the air, in the same way that many happily married couples resolutely testify that occasional ultimately reconciled rows are actually good for long-term domestic harmony.

Above all, perhaps, it is held by many to be a 'natural' (i.e., untutored) impulse. As if in physiological confirmation of this notion, the traditional target is indeed the best-padded area of the human body, where nerve endings are few and far between and recovery of the muscles and epidermis from the effects of a spanking will be rapid.

Although there have been many instances when corporal punishment has been misapplied, or has produced unsought results – and entire epochs like the Tudor, when it was habitually invoked both over-zealously and to degrees of severity which now seem almost insane – nevertheless most adult Britons and Americans alive today were subjected in their childhoods to this sanction, at least in theory, as were their parents and grandparents and all the generations before them, not necessarily encountering the rod in person but being fully aware at all times of its potential for intervention in their lives in certain circumstances; yet they might well scoff at the idea that they have suffered damage as a result.

To be fair, there are also many who went through the same experiences and today harbour manifold doubts – and there are certainly irreconcilables, still deeply incensed by outrages perpetrated upon their young and defenceless bodies and minds by those whose duty, as they see it, it was to be kind.

Finally there is the very important proposition, entirely ignored by those who take an abolitionist view, that in many cases corporal punishment may actually be a more merciful and less psychologically damaging form of correction than those they offer as replacements.

A parent whose child is behaving atrociously, who feels in her heart (or remembers from her own experience) that a good smack is now required for a fast, satisfactory result and an end to indiscipline, but who is absolutely barred, by law, convention or acquired conviction from taking any such step, may, in her frustration, express her anger in much more psychologically damaging ways. Harsh or contemptuous words, in particular, may adversely colour the relationship for a very long time, if not in perpetuity. A spanking will cause pain and probably humiliation.

The words 'I don't love you!' or 'I wish you'd never been born!' –
even 'Why can't you be like your brother?' – can do much greater
and more long-lasting psychological damage.

Since objections to corporal punishment are so longstanding –
a fact to which abolitionists are fond of drawing attention – it is
only fair to recall some of the punishments their predecessors
have substituted for the hated rod. Joseph Lancaster
(1778–1838), author of *Improvements in Education* (1805), was,
as a Quaker, naturally opposed to beating as a form of discipline. Instead, he came up with the following:

> When a boy is disobedient to his parents, profane in his
> language, or has committed any offence against morality, or
> is remarkable for slovenliness, it is usual for him to be
> dressed up with labels, describing his offence, and a tin or
> paper crown on his head. In that manner he walks round the
> school, two boys preceding him, and proclaiming his fault;
> varying the proclamation according to the different offences.
> When a boy comes to school with dirty face or hands, and it
> seems to be more the effect of habit than of accident, a girl is
> appointed to wash his face in the sight of the whole school.
> This usually creates much diversion, especially when (as
> previously directed) she gives his cheeks a few gentle
> strokes of correction with her hand. The same event takes
> place as to girls, when in habits of slothfulness.
> Occasionally, such offenders against cleanliness walk round
> the school, preceded by a boy proclaiming her fault – and
> the same as to boys. A proceeding that usually turns the
> public spirit of the whole school against the culprit . . .

This man, so careful not to use the rod, yet so attentive to the
finest detail of as many other cruelties as he could devise, also
recommended shackling pupils to logs, to their desks (to save the
employment of masters) and to each other. Offenders of some
kinds, he considered, might be suspended in a cage from the ceiling. Nor was his an isolated case of anti-rod zealotry producing a

regime incalculably more inhuman. Other Quaker schools did likewise. The punishment book of the senior of these, near Pontefract, Yorkshire, relates how naughty children had to confess publicly before the assembled school, beg forgiveness, and ask for 'sponsors' for future good behaviour.

Disturbing echoes of this approach, specialising in the profounder kinds of humiliation, may be detected in the way misbehaviour is now routinely dealt with in British state schools. Until quite recently, say, fifteen years ago, the offenders would have been recognised for what they almost always are – attention-seekers, restless spirits, bullies, clowns – and physically checked with palm, slipper or cane in the age-old manner. When the last whack had been delivered, the boy was accounted newly purged of sin, and was indeed free to make the same mistake all over again – if he wished to. The theory was that the pain and disgrace of the chastisement would be automatically recalled to memory whenever recidivism was contemplated and would so deter it. If he returned to his classroom in tears or visible discomfort, the deterrent effect was distributed even more widely by the most dramatic possible means. Others would learn from the same experience, thereby reducing the incidence of its application – a classic example of a force multiplier.

But in modern educational and pædiatric theory one of the key components of the old disciplinary approach – physical pain – has been entirely removed, leaving no alternative when sanctions are required but to increase the other: disgrace. There is no longer any such thing as 'naughtiness', only 'hyperactivity', 'behavioural difficulties', 'anti-social conduct', and the like. Instead of the stinging and cathartic rite of passage in the head's study, which clears the slate and washes away all sin – and, if courageously borne, can sometimes be the wellspring of self-respect – offences result in exclusions, solemn case conferences[8], massively humiliating parental involvement, psychiatric studies

---

8. It would be interesting to discover how many jobs in the educational bureaucracy have been created specifically as a result of the abolition of the cane.

and, ultimately, the inevitable banishment to 'special' classes, 'special schools' or 'behaviour units'[9], where the stigma of failure and/or madness is hung around the delinquent's neck like a shame placard from Joseph Lancaster's 'humane' school – never, so long as his or her school career lasts and almost certainly longer than that, to be shaken off. Other children, the most pitiless of all ad hoc natural disciplinarians, will see to that.

---

9. It is a hallmark of many totalitarian regimes officially and deliberately to deem all unwelcome manifestations of individualism, especially when these take a disrespectful or disruptive form, to be prima facie evidence of insanity, to be 'treated', or their perpetrators 're-educated' rather than punished (since only an insane person could possibly oppose the benevolent regime). Needless to say, 'treatments' are indistinguishable, at the sharp end, from punishments, but a branded lunatic is less likely than an imprisoned freedom fighter to gain martyrdom and so attract emulators, which is the real point.

4

THE LEXICON
OF DEVIANCE

*My particular horror of others knowing I had been pun-
ished led me to imagine the whipping, with which the
daydream always began, as taking place before the whole
school. I was either leaning on a desk or bent forward in
the middle of the room. Sometimes the whipping took
place in tight drawers which pressed on the bladder or
sex parts. Sometimes the drawers were unbuttoned and I
was exposed to view with great chagrin and shame. I
read in a book that at some girls' boarding schools in the
olden time, it was the custom to undress the victim and
put on her a chemise reaching only to the waist; thus
attired and mounted on a servant's back she was
whipped before the whole school. This was a new idea for
my daydream and included much extra shame.*

'Florrie'

'Florrie' was the patient of Henry Havelock Ellis (1859–1939); or
rather, his correspondent, since over a three-year period the
future author of *Studies in the Psychology of Sex* received no less
than sixty written communications from this lady, whom he
later described as 'robust and rather stout . . . her matronly
appearance being to some extent belied by a somewhat girlish,
timid expression which, however, still remained compatible
with a complete and quiet self-possession'. So prolific was she
('while not unwilling to make oral communications the subject
was much more accomplished and instructive with a pen') that

in due course he gave her a chapter to herself in his *opus magnus*, and as a result hers has become perhaps the most widely celebrated case in the entire clinical history of the flagellant passion.[1]

She was a passive heterosexual flagellant of classic dimensions. A child of the Victorian age – a child-whipping milieu *par excellence* – Florrie had never been to school at all, least of all one of the type which formed the backdrop for her thirteen-year-old imaginings, but nevertheless she had been physically chastised, as a small child, by her father[2], and there seemed small doubt that the two were connected. For various reasons, most notably the conviction that her feelings were sinful, her predilection had not made her happy. Her matrimonial essays had also not been fortunate: she had never, for example, had an orgasm.

She was fortunate to discover Ellis, who paid her the compliment of treating her as an intelligent woman, and uncovered what he really wished to learn in the gentlest, least challenging manner.[3] Being thus encouraged to talk or write through her feelings had a wonderfully fulfilling effect upon Florrie. Ellis did not 'cure' her, but he gave her the wherewithal to 'cure' herself, to the extent that, by the time he

---

1. 'The History of Florrie and the Mechanism of Sexual Deviation' (*Psychology of Sex*, pt 2, ch. III, first published in the *Psychoanalytic Review*, vol. VI, 1919).
2. Though always at the direct instigation of the family governess, who disliked her. At an earlier stage, she had also been spanked by another governess for failure to urinate on demand, and this separate punishment had apparently added a urolagnic dimension to her fantasies.
3. 'In the present case I was careful to play as passive a part as possible, and to avoid the risks of suggestion; but it was sometimes necessary to throw out a question, which was always put in a casual way as regarding some quite innocent and harmless subject. It might then happen that the subject, without the slightest embarrassment or violence, quietly put the question aside, as though it were of no concern to her, that I refrained from any comment, and that subsequently she spontaneously showed that the subject thus put aside was of vital bearing on the case. Such a method of investigation naturally takes time.'

finally lost touch with her, he was able to conclude that:

> Florrie is not, and never will be, completely what we are
> pleased to term 'normal'. She is reconciled to 'normal' sex
> relationships, but they do not afford her any intense gratifi-
> cation. Her disposition . . . remain[s] essentially what [it]
> always has been. *But now she understands.* She is no longer
> obsessed and tortured. She is content and at peace.[4] The
> therapeutic result – here as always in this field – does not lie
> in the personality being forced into a rigid alien mould . . .
> it lies in enabling the subject to see himself or herself under-
> standingly, not in being artificially changed but in being
> rightly harmonised.

Harmonisation of the deviant with society was not the approach
favoured by all. In 1923–24 Dr Wilhelm Stekel of Vienna
obtained permission from Havelock Ellis to republish the history
of Florrie, albeit with a commentary of his own. In general Stekel
approved of Ellis's conclusions, and in his *Sadismus und
Masochismus*[5] he lauded the careful methods used, but he went
much further. Ellis felt sufficiently disturbed about Stekel's
desire 'to find points which the history as it stands does not
contain, and which, from my own standpoint, there is no occasion to seek' to take the unusual step of publishing a riposte.[6]

Besides interpreting Florrie's dreams in a way the lady herself
thought 'fantastic', Stekel postulated homosexual inclinations,
abnormally early sexual experience (not least, with her brothers)
and rectal enemas – all indignantly denied by Florrie (with
whom Ellis was still at that time in touch). He also had no hesitation in referring to the father's 'sadism', the first item Ellis
sought to address in the long list of instances where, in his opinion, his colleague had gone too far. While granting without

---

4. She had also experienced her first-ever orgasm.
5. Published 1925.
6. As a chapter postscript (1933 edition onwards).

argument some connection between Florrie's predilection and the punishments she had received at her father's hand, he noted mildly that 'it seems unnecessary to call the father a sadist', since a rigid and perhaps rather stupid adherence to scriptural injunctions (Ellis was no believer in corporal punishment) would explain all without recourse to this, for some, rather extreme label. 'It is likely that he regarded himself as merely carrying out a proper and necessary tradition . . . Florrie bore him no ill-will . . .'

Invoking Occam's Razor[7] as an analytical principle was hardly sufficient to stop a Freudian in full cry. In addition Ellis was up against the urge, entirely (some may say menacingly) typical of its era, to classify human species according to millimetrically precise degrees of accuracy in every way, including the psychological – and, in the Freudians' specific instance, to promote psychoanalysis as an exact tool for making assessments of the latter type. This classification fever had properly got underway two generations earlier, in 1886, when Dr Richard Krafft-Ebing (1840-1903), the foremost neurologist of his day, published *Psychopathia Sexualis* (first translated into English six years later).[8] Krafft-Ebing's work received guarded endorsement, with refinements and departures of his own, from Sigmund Freud; and since then a host of Freudians and near-Freudians like Stekel had pushed the parameters of sub-definition ever outward, each contributing his own particular refinement or variation on the theme.

In sharp contrast to the fevered didacticism of contemporary European opinion, Havelock Ellis's approach was gentler, less pedantic, almost pastoral, though he too employed the terminology of the developing classification system for sexual deviation. His reluctance to use the term 'sadist' without clear justification was out of step with the general rush to apply this

---

7. 'Hypotheses should not be multiplied without necessity.'
8. He was not the first to use this title. A Ukrainian physician, Heinrich Kaan, had published an identically named work in 1844, in Leipzig.

label wherever possible.[9] But it is rare to find anything like a condemnatory note in *Psychology of Sex* or Ellis's other work. He stands apart from the mainstream, on a lonely, kindly pinnacle of his own: less eager to condemn than to learn, with every desire to assist, and never forgetting for one moment that his patient is a human being like himself.[10]

The opposite assumption, that unusual sexual behaviours are *ipso facto* malign in nature and effect – psychopathologies indeed – was built in from the very beginning, so far as the 'father' of this particular science had been concerned. Earlier dissertators – notably Meibomius[11] – had dealt with the subject almost exclusively from a physiological viewpoint: the activity and its effects were seen as a phenomenon, not necessarily a malady. The stonier concept of sexual deviance, and the negative responses such a term engenders, remain Krafft-Ebing's single most lasting influence on the subject – together with the word 'masochism'. He did not invent the term 'sadist'[12], but its

---

9. Ellis's own preference was for 'algolagnia' (pleasure from pain), a rather more precise term for at least one component of the overall flagellationist impulse.

10. Fairness obliges us to record the existence of a theory which, if true, might discredit Ellis's unusual sympathy for Florrie and other flagellants. It is that he was himself of this predilection, being supposedly the secret author of *Gynecocracy*, one of the most remarkable and literate fictional works on discipline ever written (see Bibliography). The present writer is suspicious of this suggestion, however. It was first advanced a generation ago by the New York-born bibliophile and erotic expert Gershon Legman, whose own fiercely condemnatory views on sadomasochism have long been evident in a great deal of his commentary. Since the humane approach favoured by Ellis is a serious inconvenience to those seeking to calumnify flagellationism root and branch, it must either be ignored or, for more lasting results, undermined. To suggest that Ellis had a hidden agenda and was therefore not being properly objective might well achieve this aim. No hard evidence for the Ellis theory has been advanced, and the original candidate for authorship of *Gynecocracy* – a successful London lawyer called Stanislas de Rhodes, who died in 1932 in Eastbourne, aged over ninety – remains the most likely candidate.

11. Dr Johann Heinrich Meibom (1590-1655): *De Flagrorum Usu in Re Veneria & Lumborum Renumque Officio*, published 1629.

12. The *Oxford English Dictionary* adduces the year 1888 for its first appearance. Gibson (*TEV*, I, p.35) prefers 1836–39 in the French form *sadisme*.

co-equal opposite is one of his most celebrated coinings.

In an era when the legal differences between the criminal and the insane were very much more blurred even than they are today, Krafft-Ebing held a series of important consultative and supervisory posts within the mental hospital systems of the German and the Austro-Hungarian empires, which allowed him access to unlimited, if wretched, human study material. His subjects, condemned to incarceration as a result of their activities, were already officially odd. There is no clear record of his treating patients, or arranging for their release, or involving himself in their welfare. He simply examined them. His concern was not the higher cause of whether or not they had been justly or appropriately dealt with, or what might be done to cure them, but to question, record, analyse and arrange the resulting case studies according to his own developing system of deviance classification. He published the latter, and published it again when he had added more material and refined some earlier conclusions, and once again when still more case-study material had come his way.[13] *Psychopathia Sexualis* grew into a veritable monster, and it had an enormous and lasting impact. It is the *Malleus Maleficarum* of perverts.

At least one of his conclusions, that some forms of sexual deviation, particularly masochism, might be congenital – that is, inherited – did not survive Freud, and although the idea won tentative support from Havelock Ellis, it has never found ready acceptance since, largely because Fabio-Freudian considerations require environment to take precedence over any other factors that might shape a human personality.

Freud himself took only a spasmodic interest in sexual flagellationism. Broadly speaking, he endorsed Krafft-Ebing's general classifications, added some of his own, dismissed the theory of inheritance and attributed everything to the parents. This general view then became the definitive approach, and the combined Ebing-Freud lexicon of deviance became common

---

13. He borrowed extensively from other scholars' works.

currency wherever these matters were discussed. So matters stand.

The final establishment of the belief that corporal punishment is definitively inflicted in order to gratify a sexual impulse (acknowledged or otherwise) dates from this time. This, as a key extension of the earlier, more relaxed notion that it *might* be for such motives, lent very considerable force to the abolitionist argument at a time – between the wars – when flagellation, both disciplinary and recreational, had reached an apogee of devotion that puts the Victorian era, so often thought of as the epitome of a whipping culture, firmly into the shade.

The society which had given birth to the desire to classify *homo sapiens* down to the last buttonhole was the first to take the final, logical step and act upon the conclusions thus obtained. Having analysed and graded most types of human being according to all available criteria, it found some severely wanting and therefore, under the new rules, to be with no automatic entitlement to existence, let alone the pursuit of happiness. Flagellatory and other 'perverted' books were burned in Nazi *autos-da-fé* up and down the Reich, together with other 'immoral' material – art and literature, as well as jazz records by black American artists and (irony!) the works of Freud and other Jewish pioneers of psychoanalysis. Spankers, corset devotees and rubber-wearers joined homosexuals, gypsies, freemasons, epileptics, the mentally handicapped, fortune-tellers and Jews as bacteria in the pure bloodstream of culture.[14] Much of what Krafft-Ebing had condemned as sexual degeneracy was proscribed – the Nazis were inclined to accept his hereditary theories without question – with fearful penalties which the world now knows all too well.

So the residual legacies of a century's clinical study are the assumption that 'different' forms of sexual activity are fundamentally

---

14. The Nazis abolished corporal punishment in schools but retained it as a judicial penalty.

pathological (therefore undesirable), and their associated lexicon of deviance, of which sadism is the most well-known example.

It is a word with horrible connotations: Gilles de Raiz, concentration camp guards, Mr Creakle, Jack the Ripper, the Moors Murderers, de Sade himself . . . the sadist has replaced the vampire as the contemporary incarnation of the fiend, a glowing-eyed haunter of the dark, gloating as his tortured victim slowly writhes in an agony induced wholly for the purpose of feeding his ghastly lusts.

Such dreadful creatures have certainly existed, and still exist, but this particular cap fits only about one in ten of those to whom it has been applied. Even the wholly dreadful Gilles de Raiz may not have been a pure sadist (his deeds, fairly meriting the description 'satanic abuse', were at least partly motivated by a desire for political power); and some famous theories hold that Jack the Ripper was pursuing quite another end in his series of awful murders, but disguised these as sadistic acts to throw the police off the scent. But Mr Creakle and Mr Squeers were certainly intended by their creator to be seen enjoying a strange gratification from administering whippings, and there can be small argument that Ian Brady, the Moors Murderer, conforms almost exactly to the classic definition in its most dangerous form. There is some doubt whether de Sade himself qualifies unequivocally (since he was as much masochist as sadist); and although a great many concentration-camp atrocities and Japanese PoW abuses may genuinely have been sadistically motivated, it is also likely – since true sadism requires a degree of planning ahead – that much of what went on was simply soulless, expedient brutality, with little or no sex-gratification motive, which is not in any way to diminish the horror of what was done, and continues to be done, in such places around the world. Sadism should be an explicit term, but it continues to be used without thought and as a result has seldom been helpful to any debate.

Modern usage is remarkably imprecise. The man who is erotically aroused by ritually smacking his wife's bottom (let us suppose she enjoys it no less than he) is actually excited by what?

The love of giving pain to another? Only that? In that case, why not pull her hair, or punch her face, or slash her skin, or humiliate her in public with a few cruel words? The answer is that these activities would almost certainly have the opposite effect to that sought: they would subdue desire. The spanking excites the man and his wife for a mixture of reasons, many of them affectionate, most of them entirely unrelated to cruelty or the giving of pain: for many men of this type, even a hint that too much[15] pain had been inflicted would instantly extinguish all traces of sexual desire. So he is not, after all, 'sadistic' – except that he is, because this is the only adjective in the public domain. The presence in his psycho-sexual make-up, in no matter how small a proportion or in what contexts, of a wish to give pain, makes him so – Krafft-Ebing decreed it, and no single behaviourist has yet disagreed. Factors like consent, control and complete absence of any desire to harm or frighten make no difference. There is no escape from the term.

'Masochist' is no less unsatisfactory. For example, it is conceded that 'masochistic' pleasure may be obtained without any specific infliction of physical pain – the masochist may attain a state of being so exalted and intense that more dynamic procedures become wholly unnecessary. Simply being under orders will do; a keen consciousness of being at another's beck and call, within his power, at her disposal. Such refined fancies can invoke the keenest arousal, though sometimes a yearning for deeper waters will compel him to ask (the masochist can only ask) for reinforcement of a more immediate and tangible kind:

'Severin, I warn you for the last time,' began Wanda.

'If you love me, be cruel towards me,' I pleaded with upraised eyes.

'If I love you,' repeated Wanda. 'Very well!' She stepped

---

15. How much is 'too much'? I suggest that it is a variable, dependent on personal taste and circumstance, which nevertheless falls self-evidently beyond the limits of any 'contract', whether or not this is a precise agreement or an empirically evolved common base of understanding between the two parties.

back and looked at me with a sombre smile. '*Be then my slave, and know what it means to be delivered into the hand of a woman!*' At the same moment she gave me a kick.

'How do you like that, slave?'

Then she flourished the whip.

'Get up!'

I was about to rise.

'Not that way,' she commanded. 'On your knees.'

I obeyed, and she began to apply the lash.

The blows fell rapidly and powerfully on my back and arms. Each one cut into my flesh and burned there, but the pains enraptured me. They came from her whom I adored, and for whom I was ready at any hour to lay down my life.

She stopped. 'I am beginning to enjoy it,' she said, 'but enough for today. I am beginning to feel a demonic curiosity to see how far your strength goes. I take a cruel joy in seeing you tremble and writhe beneath my whip, and in hearing your groans and wails; I want to go on whipping without pity until you beg for mercy, until you lose your senses. You have awakened dangerous elements in my being . . .'[16]

The above passage, from the most famous of all 'masochistic' fictional works, with its kowtowing and whips and fur-clad dominatrix, epitomises the masochistic passion in its contemporary form – as it ought: after all, the entire inclination was named after its author.[17] It is certainly true that, for some whose inclinations run along such lines, contempt as well as blows is what they seek. Furs and bullwhips may indeed be essential components of their scenario, though nowadays it is more likely to be leather and canes. And it is also true that the popular image of the masochist invariably involves hideous self-abasement.

The first person I saw was Anni. She was standing in the

---

16. *Venus in Furs.*
17. It is probably true to say that while de Sade may not have been exclusively a sadist, Sacher-Masoch was a definitive masochist.

middle of the room. Arthur cringed on the floor at her feet. He had removed several more of his garments, and was now dressed, lightly but with perfect decency, in a suit of mauve silk underwear, a rubber abdominal belt and a pair of socks. In one hand he held a brush and in the other a yellow shoe-rag. Olga towered behind him, brandishing a heavy leather whip.

'You call that clean, you swine!' she cried in a terrible voice. 'Do them again this minute! And if I find a speck of dirt on them I'll thrash you till you can't sit down for a week.'.

As she spoke she gave Arthur a smart cut across the buttocks. He uttered a squeal of pain and pleasure, and began to brush and polish Anni's boots with feverish haste.

'Mercy! Mercy!' Arthur's voice was shrill and gleeful, like a child's when it is shamming. 'Stop! You're killing me.'

'Killing's too good for you,' retorted Olga, administering another cut. 'I'll skin you alive!'[18]

This is masochism in its most satisfyingly grotesque form. There is no danger of unexpected sympathy being afforded the victim. He is not physically attractive, being plump, white, male and middle-aged. He is well-off and so 'deserves all he gets'. Worst of all, he is being horribly, inexplicably, disgustingly abject. In a pit-bull culture like ours, this is disgrace indeed.

Unfortunately, one must also use the same word, 'masochistic' to describe, in clinical terms anyway, the type of pleasure experienced by the hypothetical wife of the earlier example, who, once in a while, thoroughly enjoys being taken across her husband's knee, lingeringly undressed, scolded, lightly (or not so lightly) smacked, and then, having been 'forgiven', made love to in a more orthodox fashion. She may joyfully subscribe to this passion and yet conform in no single way to the caricature presented above.[19] But she is still 'masochistic'.

---

18. *Mr Norris Changes Trains*, p.33.
19. One of the main sub-points of disagreement between Krafft-Ebing and Freud was on the very question of whether men or women are more 'naturally' masochistic. Krafft-Ebing thought women, Freud men.

'Sadomasochist' is a little more flexible. Attributed to Freud, it carries at least three distinct meanings: a person whose moods and desires alternate between the two modes (what Americans call a 'switch'); or one who properly belongs to one or the other of the root categories but is called sadomasochistic for reasons of verbal economy; or one able to experience both modes at the same time. The notion that sadism and masochism are but two faces of the same coin is pure Freud. When, in his fully developed form, the sadomasochist commits a 'sadistic' act, he draws pleasure, not only from the sadism, but also, by osmosis or intense identification, from the masochism of the victim, who, ideally, is doing the same thing in reverse: a true communion.[20] From this hypothetical pinnacle of perfect harmony, types and classifications trend off in the two mutually exclusive directions, with the extremes at either end of the 'mutual sympathy' scale possessing the most advanced forms.

Partly because it is indeed a less specific and therefore more flexible word than either of its contributor roots, and partly because of the widespread contemporary usage of the associated acronym SM[21], the once-obscure neuropathological term 'sadomasochism' has become part of the 'thought-bite' language of the late twentieth century. It is frequently used in books, newspapers, magazines and films and on television. In recent years it has become confused to some extent with the activities of an exhibitionist tendency with roots in at least four distinct 'perversions' (sadism, masochism, fetishism and bondage[22], not to mention fashion). The 'public' SM participant or 'fetishist'[23] wears tight-fitting rubber or leather clothing of

---

20. Though for the definition to hold good, there must be corresponding pleasure on the part of the victim. Theoretically, the only way a genuine sadist may act in a genuinely sadistic way towards a genuine masochist is to behave in a kindly and understanding manner.

21. Also S/M, S–M and S&M.

22. Connoisseurs of deviance are able to detect several more, including infantilism, urolagnia and coprophagia, though not usually in nightclubs.

23. This particular term has become the umbrella name for a portmanteau of related and overlapping activities, including SM.

bizarre and sexually explicit design, and regularly attends *outré* nightclubs where much goes on of a silly and occasionally alarming nature – including, it must be said, some fairly heavy-duty public 'discipline' (the equivalent of go-go dancing). Yet these clubs advertise publicly and continue to do excellent, unharassed, business.[24] Their more publicity-conscious habitués have become mildly celebrated, and are occasionally invited on late-night TV to talk about their hobby in a serious manner.

Though it would be tempting to regard these phenomena as signs of increasing public understanding, it might more realistically be seen as a small and thus far tolerated (the Spanner case[25] strikes a warning note) advance into the public eye on the

---

24. A classic recent example of the use of the word 'sadomasochism' for its reflex shock-horror value, comes, rather disappointingly, from the conservative British political journal the *Spectator* (9 October 1993). In an article entitled 'The Smack of Firm Governesses', journalist Tabitha Troughton wrote: 'The Torture Garden [nightclub] is there for fetishists (people who get a kick out of dressing up in rubber and leather), bondage fans (people who get a kick out of tying each other up), and sadomasochists, *which should need no explanation.*' (My italics.) Nor did she attempt one – wisely enough, perhaps, since to do so in any spirit of serious enquiry might have compromised the panoply of prejudice with which Miss Troughton approached her subject.

25. The clearest description of this case and its particular anomalies I have read comes from an American professor, Anne McLintock: 'In 1990, the notorious Spanner investigation became a £2.5 million showcase for the policing of gay SM in Britain . . . fifteen men were sentenced by Judge James Rant at the Old Bailey for willingly and privately engaging in SM acts with each other for sexual pleasure. Eight of the men were given custodial sentences ranging up to four and a half years. In February 1992, five of the men failed to have their conviction overturned by the Court of Appeals. The presiding Lord Chief Justice, Lord Lane, ruled that the men's consent and the privacy of their acts were no defence, and that SM libido did not constitute causing bodily harm "for good reason".

'By contrast, activities such as boxing, football, rugby or cosmetic surgery apparently constitute, in the eyes of the law, well-recognised cases of licit, consensual bodily harm, for they are conducted for "good reason", that is, for the profitable, public consumption of "natural" female vanity, "natural" male aggression and the law of male, market competition – for the proper maintenance, that is, of heterosexual difference. In violent contact sports, men touch each other in furious and often wounding intimacy, but the homoerotic implications are scrupulously disavowed.

part of a special-interest group. But in the longer term, the blanket identification of a specific and highly complex type of human relationship with the antics of a contemporary group of urban exhibitionists, or even a certain fashion look – a process which is already well underway and may soon become irreversible – is not, in my estimation, likely to advance genuine understanding.

Sadism, masochism, sadomasochism, fetishism, infantilism . . . Has human knowledge, let alone the ability or wish to love our neighbours, been very greatly advanced by this century-old reductionist approach, with its slide-rule gradations of perversity and its drearily impoverished terminology? Many forms of sexual 'deviation' have a pronounced, sometimes overwhelming, affectionate, spiritual or mystical flavour; yet, since these are not classifiable entities, their existence, and how their presence might alter the quality of the event so far as everyday perceptions are concerned, has been ignored. Many 'isms' are to be found in the works of the great behaviourists, but – with Havelock Ellis once more the exception – the word 'love' is at a sharp discount. There is no place for the unmeasurable in the clinical universe.

Superficiality and prejudice – and, concomitantly, injustice – are inevitable in the media and in mass public opinion, if only because when something has to be said about everything very little can be said about anything. But will it do for more serious debate, where the object is, or ought to be, the acquisition of real understanding, and the possible improvement of the human condition, rather than the enhancement of a professional reputation, the knee-jerk recitation of a distasteful labelling

---

Footnote 25 – *contd.*

'[These sentences] exceed, in many cases, those for the violent, non-consensual rape or battery of women or for cases of lesbian and gay bashing.' *(Dirty Looks.)*

system derived from a discredited clinical approach, the promotion of a politically correct point of view, the editorial constraints of a TV programme or the profitability of a newspaper chain? A century after Krafft-Ebing, we are not much further on.

5

THE PERVERT
HUNTERS

*Sexual perversion is not funny, not rare, and not to be
taken lightly, as anyone who has ever been married to a
homosexual or sadist or other pervert knows. It is hard for
normals even to bear to look at the pitiful lineaments of
sexual perversion. . . . The Marquis de Sade is the classic
case, and his worshipping imitators are seldom far
behind. For example, Baudelaire and Swinburne and the
other 'poets of evil,' also the entire Futurist-Dadaist-
Surrealist movement promulgating anti-human literature,
'music' and art since the early years of this century . . .*

Gershon Legman: Introduction to *The Private Case*[1]

In addition to the clinical writers on the subject of flagellation
and associated deviations, there have been a number of secular
authors who have also discoursed upon the condition, superficially at least in a serious spirit of enquiry. In many ways this
body of work is a better paradigm for public attitudes over the
same period than that produced by the scientists, for, not being
obliged to adhere to the conventions of academic publishing,
the authors have been able to strike a more populist note, and in

---

1. Although the writer of this passage is rightly adjudged one of the foremost
living authorities on erotic literature, many will feel that the credentials accru-
ing to Mr Legman nevertheless do not begin to justify the hysterical
immoderation – a kind term – displayed in this and his other polemics on the
subject of sadomasochism. His use of the term 'normals' is particularly to be
noted by connoisseurs of dehumanising terminology.

so doing have revealed, far more clearly than the clinicians, the curious blend of condemnation, excitement, hypocrisy and prurience which has characterised public attitudes for so long. They are, in fact, a case study in themselves.

Until comparatively recent times, non-fictional works about sexual matters by lay authors were seldom produced by mainstream publishers. In keeping with Victorian conventions, they were relegated to medical imprints, or published in some other, even less respectable mode – as under the counter books or private editions. In other words, as pornography.[2] Whatever the motives – real or apparent – of the authors, market forces (in other words, the publishers) made the primary decision concerning the likely readership of these books. Nor, from their own point of view, were they mistaken in doing so.

Many, if not all, such books, have an almost transparently dual purpose: primarily that of exciting and arousing, while maintaining, at least superficially, and whenever the author remembers to reinvoke it, a veneer of condemnation – the classic facing-both-ways posture, implemented to differing levels of success depending on the author's self-control (or self-delusion).

It is not a new form. A famous treatise on flogging (from the 'medicinal' angle), published in 1732 by the 'Abbé Boileau', is revealed in its true colours without the necessity for reading it when one realises that *boileau* is French for birch-tree. *An Illustrated History of the Rod*, from the pen of the Reverend W.M. Cooper, first published around 1870, is perhaps the definitive example. In its 'preliminary' (i.e., preface), the author resolutely states that it was:

neither compiled for the prurient nor the prudish, the

---

2. There has at times been a very thin line between medical publishing and pornography. For example, the famous Paris-based publisher of erotica Charles Carrington, whose many offerings between 1900 and 1920 are the foundation for the legendary link between erotic publishing in English and the city of Paris, originally published much of his catalogue in the form of supposedly medical books. It was excellent camouflage.

writer's sole aim being to give (to the best of his ability) a true History of the Rod as an instrument for correctional purposes in the Church, the State and the Family.

Even if the reader was unaware, as he might well be, that the Rev. W. M. Cooper was actually one James G. Bertram – author of one of the most famous Victorian works of flagellatory fiction, *Personal Recollections of the Use of the Rod*, otherwise known as *The Merry Order of St Bridget* – this massively ingenuous claim would rapidly have been dispelled, if indeed it had ever been accepted, once reading had begun. Certainly a number of chapters – there are forty-nine altogether – dutifully concern themselves with relatively obscure aspects of the topic ('Discipline among the Carthusians', 'Flagellation in Africa'); but even more are aimed at a target much closer to the epicentre of the passion ('Father Gerard and Miss Cadière', 'The Flogging of Slaves', 'Anecdotes of Domestic Birch at Home' etc.). There is also a considerable miscellany, including poems, doggerel, unsubstantiated anecdotes – one or two of which bear hallmarks of Bertram's own style – and of course the illustrations, which must have been a major selling point.[3]

Although *History of the Rod* is flawed as a work of scholarship – few direct references are supplied, for example, though in a list of sources the author demonstrates his own very wide reading – it is massive (550 pages) and every edition, including the most recent reprint[4], has been well produced. Is it pornography? In original intent, yes. In form, not quite – it is 'scholarly'. It was

---

3. One delighted customer was the Australian composer Percy Grainger, who bought the volume in 1909. To his favourite correspondent on flagellatory matters, Karen Holten, he wrote: 'Yesterday I bought a book entitled "The History of the rod" [*sic*] dealing with the use of the whip in all countries and times. Seldom in my life have I gone through such a lecherous day as yesterday. My head ached, eyes burnt, body shook, of the excitement of reading what people have invented in my greatest speciality . . .' Letter dated 18 July 1909 to Karen Holten (*The Farthest North of Humanness*, p. 301).
4. I am informed that the edition, priced at £25.00, sold out with gratifying speed.

intended, perhaps naively, to bridge both worlds, like the 1950s UK nudist magazine *Health and Efficiency*, which ostensibly, and sincerely, promoted the cause of naturism while actually providing an entire generation of adolescent British boys with their first glimpses of the unadorned female form; or the modern videotape which purports to instruct in lovemaking techniques – romantic DIY – while in reality providing acceptable soft-porn images for quite another purpose. (One wonders, indeed, how many copies of *Psychopathia Sexualis* were read by medical practitioners and how many by those who wished to use them for the classic pornographic purpose in an era when overtly erotic writing was much harder to obtain than it is today.)

Successive books displaying a similar blend of condemnation and excitement have appeared at frequent intervals, none of them, despite their nominally serious purpose, with titles one would readily display in a domestic bookcase[5]: examples are *Kiss of the Whip* by Professor E. J. Henri; *Flagellation: The Story of Corporal Punishment* (George Ryley Scott); *Chastisement Across the Ages* (Gervas D'Olbert). Whatever their supposed purpose, most of these titles seem to have been published in one or the other of the notorious imprints (Olympia, Luxor, Diamond Star), whose slightly larger-than-usual formats and yellow card jackets proclaim their genre without ambivalence. Of the three mentioned above, while Henri and Ryley Scott largely plunder 'Cooper' and Krafft-Ebing, D'Olbert, a genuine enthusiast, has done his own copious research, and his collection of literary references is without parallel. He at least strikes an honest note: he makes no secret of his approval of some forms of corporal punishment, while deploring others (I think sincerely). For all the dreadfulness of its title, *Chastisement Across the Ages* had pretensions to scholarship, but it was still not one for the family bookcase.

There are other ways to skin a cat, and other ways in which

---

5. A good way to appreciate the *frisson* which attaches to this subject is to imagine oneself walking into a public library and asking for any of these titles in a clear, loud, confident voice.

pornography may be disguised as something else. In south Germany, thirty years before 'Cooper', *Lenchen im Züchthause,* otherwise known as *Nell in Bridewell*, had been published, telling the cruel, and allegedly true, tale of a young German maiden wrongfully imprisoned in a house of correction and there subjected to . . . you can guess. While not absolutely documentary in form, its strictly maintained first-person narrative style carries a certain authority and apparent verisimilitude. As an example of unusual self-control it is impressive, and no less than the 'studies' it serves the two opposed principles of erotic excitement and social condemnation almost faultlessly, for at no time does the narrator lose her grasp on the prevailing message – that such goings-on are cruel, and wrong, and should be stopped – even while she is recounting them in luscious detail. *Nell in Bridewell* is perhaps more harrowing even than *Jane Eyre*, but like its better-known contemporary (which it resembles in one or two curious ways) it has a happy ending.

Yet none of these books (excepting, possibly, D'Olbert's) was ever truly likely – or intended – to make an abolitionist or reformist case. Therein lies the hypocrisy (or the self-delusion), and the damage: for by using the terminology of condemnation to frame and present the literature of sexual excitement they do nothing to promote understanding, let alone Havelock Ellis's objective of harmony, and indeed strongly reinforce any associations of wrongdoing, guilt and fear with this form of sexuality.

It is of course more than likely that the writing of such a book may have represented an author's deliberate personal catharsis. The presence within himself of obsessions he believed to be unhealthy, and the assumption that these were the direct result of actions perpetrated against him during childhood, and therefore 'not his fault', can take the form of a righteous (and, in the circumstances, by no means incomprehensible) reaction against the perpetrators, with the degree of anger related, however, not to the quality of the original event so much as the depth, and staying power, of the obsession. In these instances authorship may therefore have been a form of exorcism. However, one may realistically doubt whether the writing of the book ever did much to remove the obsession, any more than its reading ever served any real purpose other than to gratify an already present sexual taste, while purporting to do the opposite. To be deliberately excited while being scolded at the same time for the sinfulness of one's excitement might itself be seen as a classically sadomasochistic transaction.

By far the most respectable, indeed in many ways most objectively admirable, of all serious lay works to date on the specific subject of flagellation is *The English Vice* by Ian Gibson. To my certain knowledge, no other book approaches it for forcefulness of argument as well as its quality of scholarship, which can only be described as immaculate. It is the best-researched, best-written, most powerfully presented polemic on the subject in existence – and nearly all of its conclusions are diametrically opposed to those advanced in this book; indeed, the whole purpose of *The English Vice* is to damn flagellation and flagellants once and for all.

Gibson's thesis, as the title proclaims without ambiguity, is that flagellationism is a specific product of Anglo-Saxon culture:

> I became gradually convinced that the 'English Vice' was not simply sadism but flagellomania, and my belief was confirmed when I read the three great bibliographies of erotica published in the late Victorian period by Pisanus Fraxi (Henry Spencer Ashbee). There seemed to be no question about it: flagellomania, while almost totally absent in France, Spain and Italy, was widespread in Britain, especially in England.[6]

It is also almost exclusively a male predilection, at least in the 'active' mode:

> As regards the beater, all analytic writers seem to agree . . .

---

6. *TEV*, p. x.

that behind the manifest beater – the stern, masterful
female – there lurks a father figure . . . if the adult passive
flagellant prefers to imagine himself being fustigated by a
female, it is because he is unable to admit to himself that,
when he was a child, the idea of being beaten by an authoritative male was sexually exciting to him . . .

There seems to be no doubt that, in the original fantasy,
the beater was undisguisedly male . . .[7]

And, of course, upper-class:

We shall never know how many people have been crushed
and rendered impotent by the flogging system of which the
British preparatory and public school Establishment has
been so proud, for the victims have not gone around proclaiming themselves in public.[8]

To which one might respond: is it any wonder, if this is the
degree of understanding they might reasonably expect? Male
homosexuality, too, in its day, called, by some the 'English
vice' – and also widely associated with the English public-school
system – produced a very great crop of victims; not so much of
their sexuality, it is now admitted, as of prejudice. Until very
recently, homosexuals did not readily go around proclaiming
themselves in public, for to do so meant (as it still does in certain
quarters) running an unacceptable risk of contempt, disgust, vil-
ification, assault and prosecution. To keep a low profile is not
necessarily an admission of moral guilt.

Gibson's target, the upper- or middle-class 'public school'
English male – not to mention the wickedly depraved practices he
has spread around the world by means of colonial aggression –
will be familiar to many. Indeed, he is distinguished from many
other national, ethnic, cultural and gender-based groups by the

7. Ibid., p. 295.
8. Ibid., p. 314.

unusual number of shell-craters around the positions he still man-
ages – not without success – to defend. He has been a target for
over a century: for Marxists, socialists, anti-colonialists, feminists,
Mr Rupert Murdoch and the French.

But *The English Vice* is no half-educated diatribe: it is a well-
argued, precisely (if selectively) researched, chillingly angry
statement of the abolitionist position, from an angle not usually
mentioned by STOPP or EPOCH or other abolitionist groups:
that the practice of flagellation as a means of discipline leads to
flagellomania the vice, and is a cultural neurosis of massive
proportions. The only way to stop the cycle is by legislation. 'An
Act of Parliament making beating illegal in all British schools
without exception is long overdue[9],' according to its author.

Writing in 1977, Gibson was not sanguine about this prospect,
but in fact much of what he recommended had been implemented within a decade. As we saw in chapter 2, beating of any
sort is now illegal in all British state schools. But of course that
still leaves at least two (or three) generations of 'live white males'
who have been adversely affected by the practice – new victims
of the English vice, as Gibson gloomily concludes, at whose
expense 'the purveyors of flagellant pornography will continue
to make a good living . . .'

In the light of the latter statement one wonders if the author
really took a moment to consider who might buy his book. While
doubtless many copies (it was reprinted after one year) went to
researchers, paediatricians, behaviourists, political theorists and
the like, I have never yet seen it in a public library (which is not
to say no libraries bought it), while I have certainly encountered it, many times, in places of which its author would surely
not approve: pornographic bookshops and erotic mail-order catalogues. This of course is not the author's fault, for although
The English Vice is a less embarrassing title than *Kiss of the
Whip* or *Chastisement Across The Ages*, it is still a little ripe for
most bookcases and it may simply be that the publishers, having

---

9. *TEV*, p. 315.

over-estimated the 'respectable' market, were more than happy to sell it to those who wanted it for another purpose: for despite Gibson's loathing of flagellant pornographers, he nonetheless found himself obliged, in support of his case, to deploy a great deal of material of outstanding interest to connoisseurs of this particular *oeuvre* – the double-bind working in an old way, for how is it possible to document atrocities sufficiently to bring down upon them the odium they deserve without simultaneously providing some juicy reading for those whose unhappy appetites are precisely for such stuff?

It will be obvious that I take issue with Gibson, no less than with the clinicians. The author of *The English Vice* assembles his own lexicon of deviance by picking and choosing, with great care and fastidiousness, among the latter (though he makes barely a mention of Havelock Ellis). That the subject is irredeemably deviant, pathological and malign he does not question for one moment. In sour pursuit of the thesis embodied in his title, he ignores or overlooks the enormous bodies of flagellant tradition and erotica produced by other cultures and national groups – many of these, like the French, Russians and Germans, not hitherto noted for having fallen in the past under the wicked spell of Anglo-Saxonism. To prove the feminist case that flagellationism is something women don't do, he unhesitatingly deploys the most tortuous sub-Freudian rationalisations. Those whom he quotes in approval of physical discipline rarely survive the context into which they are summoned: those who disapprove are far more numerous and invariably benefit from context to precisely the opposite degree. And nowhere at all in the book is there more than the most fleeting mention of any emotion other than the most bestial, cruel, creepy and guilty. In the world of the flagellant, as seen by Gibson and those for whom he speaks, there are no finer feelings, no affection, honour, trust, love, respect, gratitude, spiritual aspiration, solace, humour or charm. The words are not mentioned; the possibility of their existence is not even raised.

Flagellation as a divinely inspired activity: the 'Arcadian' fancy of the goddess Venus as the inspiratrix of all things flagellatory is shown in the 18th-century allegorical oil-painting *[below]* in which she bestows the Rod upon an eager world, as well as in the etching from the same period *[upper left)*, where she does the job on her son Cupid (Amor) with a weapon that looks like a cudgel.

Despite a blurring of Venus with the Virgin in this form of allegory *[see next pages]* the original model remained popular with those of more pagan stamp and still pops up now and again in a disciplinary context. The late 19th-century drawing *(upper right)* where the Goddess breaks her brother Mars' spear and displays disapproval of his behaviour in still more forthright ways, might serve as proto-CND propaganda!

As a semi-satanic impulse: the darker notes of the passion were recognised early on, especially after the advent of the Flagellant movement *(top left),* a disturbing feature of the early Renaissance landscape. The etching *(centre left)* is a satire on the temptations that afflicted the *flagellanti,* as, in its own way, is the 1920s drawing *(lower left).*

FACING PAGE
As a system of canonical discipline: the Christian Church played a key rôle in maintaining flagellant tradition and expertise. *Lower left:* Saxon engraving of a priest armed with a 'discipline', *c.* 800 AD. *Top:* King Henry II receives his penance at the altar of Canterbury Cathedral after the murder of Thomas à Becket. This was a true penance, properly

administered, but afterwards standards slipped badly. In the 16th-century wood-painting *(centre),* a friar chastises an errant nun with a pig's bladder. The image of canonical discipline reached its erotic apogee (and spiritual nadir) in the 'whipping nun' archetype *(lower right).* This persona is not without substance, as the childhood saying 'There is no mercy in the Sisters of Mercy, and no charity in the Sisters of Charity' sadly confirms.

As a Maternal act: nearly all 'début' spankings have been administered by mothers, a fact acknowledged in the very large body of artistic tradition depicting such events. The Surrealist Max Ernst's 'The Virgin Chastises the Infant Jesus in the Presence of Three Witnesses' *[above left]* first exhibited in Vienna in 1923,

caused an outcry, though in depicting Virgin-as-spanker Ernst was merely following an already old tradition. The French woodcut *[lower left]* details disciplinary goings-on in 'The School of Mary', with a similar outcome for a Jacobean Boy Jesus. *Above:* The famous engraving by Hans Holbein (16th-century) encapsulates the essence of maternal chastisement—the deadly combination of calmness and controlled violence, as, in a different way, does the breathtaking American advertisement *[facing page, upper]* for a stove ('base burner'—get it?). This ad (*c.* 1880) might not readily be accepted in today's climate! The Victorian 'Stereoptikon' (fairground viewing slot-machine) plate *[facing page, lower]* is entitled 'Mama settles the pillow fight'.

BASE BURNER

CO-OPERATIVE
FOUNDRY CO.
Rochester,
N.Y.

A BASE BURNER

The Schoolmistress: this Archetype has barely changed down the centuries. Grim, virginal, often bespectacled—and always a fearsome wielder of the rod—she is caricatured in the 18th century 'Dame' *[lower right]*, as 'Mrs Trimmer' from a sombre poem in an 1808 children's book *[left]*, and in the drawing *[lower left]* from a 1920s French edition of the erotic (flagellant) classic *Verbena House*.

Her more attractive form is still more potent—as painted by Fragonard *[opposite page, top]*, by the illustration for an early 20th-century magazine cover *[lower right]*, and above all by the 1880s American children's book illustration *[above]*, which encapsulates both the essence of that pre-flagellatory moment (note the pleased and interested spectators) and the classroom atmosphere. The stern expression of the handsome young schoolmistress, and the curve of the switch clasped in her determined hand, are devastating to the male flagellatory sensibility.

The Schoolmaster:
never in his long career
has he been a stranger to
the use of the rod. *Top:*
interestingly, it is a
birch-rod (and not the
traditional *ferula)*, in
this tracing from a
Pompeiian wall-painting
(*c.* 100 BC) which is
being wielded by an
usher. But it was in
mediæval and Tudor
times that the archetype
took on his definitive
form *[left]*—an image of
power and terror that
was to last for centuries
and is by no means
extinct.

FACING PAGE:
**The Schoolmaster as
cartoon character:** two
satires of the 18th and
early 19th centuries
make fun of the
archetype. In the upper
example, Westminster
College's Nicholas Udall
disciplines the entire
House of Commons
(cartoon by Gillray).
Below: a village
'dominie' (schoolmaster)
in frenzied action.

6

THE HIDDEN
HAND

*'Well, I suppose you've been back in the woods laying in
a supply of switches for tomorrow?' was his greeting as
Anne came up the veranda steps.*

*'No, indeed,' said Anne indignantly. She was an excel-
lent target for teasing because she always took things so
seriously. 'I shall never have a switch in my school, Mr
Harrison. Of course I shall have to have a pointer, but I
shall use it for pointing only.'*

*'So you mean to strap them instead? Well, I don't
know but you're right. A switch stings more at the time
but the strap lasts longer, that's a fact.'*

*'I shall not use anything of the sort. I'm not going to
whip my pupils.'*

*'Bless my soul,' exclaimed Mr Harrison in genuine
astonishment, 'how do you lay out to keep order, then?'*

'I shall govern by affection, Mr Harrison.'

L.M. Montgomery: *Anne of Avonlea*[1]

The sternly abolitionist stance to which Miss Montgomery's
ineffable heroine Anne Shirley is committed at the outset of
her teaching career is not, of course, fated to last more than a
few chapters. As her many followers will know, the local
naughty boy, Anthony Pye, deliberately falls foul of the vivacious

---

1. pp. 30–33.

sixteen-year-old pupil-teacher, and despite her own best intentions, Anne finds herself obliged to administer the supreme penalty.

'Who put that mouse in my desk?' said Anne. Her voice was quite low but it made a shiver go up and down Paul Irving's spine. Joe Sloane caught her eye, felt responsible from the crown of his head to the soles of his feet, stuttered out wildly,

'N . . . n . . . not m . . . m . . . me t . . . t . . . teacher, n . . . n . . . not m . . . m . . . me.'

Anne paid no attention to the wretched Joseph. She looked at Anthony Pye and Anthony Pye looked back, unabashed and unashamed.

'Anthony, was it you?'

'Yes, it was,' said Anthony insolently.

Anne took her pointer from her desk. It was a long heavy hardwood pointer.

'Come here, Anthony.'

It was far from being the most severe punishment Anthony Pye had ever undergone. Anne, even the stormy-souled Anne she was at that moment, could not have punished any child cruelly. But the pointer nipped keenly and finally Anthony's bravado failed him and the tears came to his eyes.[2]

L.M. Montgomery was, of course, writing at a time (the early 1920s) when the lascivious cruelty of such forms of classroom discipline had not been made apparent to most pedagogues. She was a former teacher herself, and certainly approved of such methods, since throughout her books there are constant, and by no means disapproving, references to corporal punishment for unruly juveniles. The naivety of a Canadian backwoodswoman? Or the unselfconsciousness of someone who

2. Ibid., p. 88.

had resolutely administered many such punishments, and did not for a moment believe that children were harmed by them, or that they were resented? The most likely answer is a bit of both. But like the successful English authors of a later generation, Elinor M. Brent-Dyer and Enid Blyton, L.M. Montgomery combined a belief in the efficacy of corporal punishment for children with a talent for writing fiction for them which captured their allegiance as few other authors have, before or since. A certain sympathy with, and liking for, children is therefore inarguable.

There is a little more to observe about the downfall of Anthony Pye. He is shown consciously to have provoked the situation – presumably knowing what would, or might, happen. And afterwards, Anne is unexpectedly gratified by his amended attitude towards her, his late *fesseuse*. First of all, he offers to carry her books home, and:

> Anne suddenly felt that if she had not yet won Anthony's liking she had, somehow or other, won his respect.
>
> Mrs Rachel Lynde came up the next Saturday and confirmed this.
>
> 'Well, Anne, I guess you've won over Anthony Pye, that's what. He says he believes you are some good after all, even if you are a girl. Says that whipping you gave him was "just as good as a man's".'[3]

All three of the passages quoted above contain many of the elements most valued in flagellatory erotica. The first has the discerning talk of rods, and the expert knowledge of their effects displayed by Mr Harrison (which is, of course, Miss Montgomery's own expertise). The second contains an even stronger *frisson*, for it offers the spectacle of an attractive sixteen-year-old girl administering corporal punishment to a twelve-year-old boy in front of a mixed class, to a point where

---

3. Ibid., p. 90.

he weeps, if only a little.[4] Finally, the curious way the culprit both provokes the chastisement and is subsequently shown to be wholly transformed by its infliction into an adoring acolyte might, with only a little effort, be seen in a darker light than that usually associated with one of the great children's writers of the century.

To calumnify the immortal heroine of the *Green Gables* saga as a teenage sadist might be thought a hazardous undertaking. In any case, Miss Montgomery provides her heroine with a partial alibi in the clear recitation of abolitionist principles quoted in the first passage. The punishment (with a heavy hardwood pointer) was forced upon her: Anne would therefore have been more humane to have taken a switch from the woods, as Mr Harrison advised, and the overall moral is therefore an old and home-spun one: traditional ways are usually best. The real comeuppance is not Anthony Pye's, but Anne's, for thinking she knows better.

That the key scene has caused embarrassment to the liberally inclined makers of TV programmes cannot be doubted, since in various versions of *Green Gables* that have been produced it is either severely watered down or altered beyond recognition. I have seen two of these: the 1975 BBC TV production, starring Kim Braden, has her applying the stick to Anthony Pye's palm (the context makes it quite clear that she whipped another part of him). A later Canadian production shifts the incident entirely – and weirdly – to a later point in her career, and requires her to administer the discipline to a girl of very nearly her own age, again, on the hand. This might be thought to contain an even greater *frisson* than the original, but no doubt sexual perversion is in the eye of the beholder.

Were Miss Montgomery not a veritable icon of children's writers,

---

4. This short episode alone contains so many flagellant-emotive grace notes and icons that to deconstruct them all would be a formidable undertaking. Some idea of what these are may be obtained by imagining the above scene reversed – that is, with a teenage male pupil-teacher beating a twelve-year-old girl with a 'heavy, hardwood pointer', presumably across the buttocks. For some, including its author, the original scene has a poignant charm. For all, its reversed image evokes instinctive – if sexist – outrage.

and a Canadian national heroine besides, it is hard to resist the feeling that despite the quality of her work she would have been written off long ago as a spokeswoman for the peculiar tendency[5] and scrubbed from most publishing and TV schedules – as happened to the British children's author Frank Richards, author of the Billy Bunter series among others, and would indeed happen to the late Enid Blyton were it not for the uncomfortable fact that she is the best-selling British children's author of all time, and still, despite the 'incorrectness' of her views, the most popular.[6] All that the censors – that is to say, her present publishers – have been able to do, bearing in mind the contiguous desire to extract continuing income from the late Miss Blyton, is to remove any supposedly racist terms and images from her books, and of course to cut the occasional references to spanking. So far as I know, this has not yet been done to the *Chalet School* books of the late Miss Brent-Dyer – another huge canon of children's writing by an author who clearly approved of corporal punishment every bit as much as Miss Blyton, and not only for boys.

To make changes and excisions in the work of Frank Richards[7], probably also in his day the best-selling British children's writer, has presumably been seen as an impossible undertaking:

'Well?' hooted Mr Quelch.
　'I— I think I've got it right, sir!' gasped Bunter.
　'You utterly obtuse boy.'
　'Oh, really, sir.'

---

5. One of her many works is a book of short stories entitled *The Woman Who Spanked the King*. The title story tells of an aged Scottish crofter lady who puts the future King Edward VII across her knee – he is a small, and, moreover, kilted boy at the time – for reckless misbehaviour. For some reason mention of this book is omitted from most bibliographies of Miss Montgomery, but I can assure readers it exists nonetheless. The Anne stories also make reference to an incident in which a boy is 'petticoated' – obliged to wear girl's clothing – as a punishment.
6. Based on the 1993 Public Lending Right (fees payable to authors whose books have been borrowed from public libraries) returns.
7. Real name Charles Hamilton (1875–1961).

'If you had prepared this lesson, Bunter, you could not possibly have made such absurd mistakes. You have done no preparation. You are making wild guesses at the meaning of that passage. Your translation, Bunter, would disgrace a small boy in the Second Form. I will not permit such idleness, such slackness— in my form! I have warned you, Bunter, of the consequences of idleness and slackness. I shall now cane you.'

'Oh, lor'!'

'Stand out before the class, Bunter.'

Billy Bunter rolled out reluctantly. Mr Quelch picked up the cane from his desk. Billy Bunter eyed it with apprehension.

'Bend over that chair, Bunter.'

Whack!

'Ow!'

Whack!

'Wow!'[8]

It is no exaggeration, as any unrepentant Bunterphile will attest, to say that Richards' *Greyfriars* and other school stories contain literally hundreds of scenes resembling the above, with over-used onomatopoeia, a plethora of exclamation marks and more paragraphs per page than any prose outside the tabloid newspapers. One might cut dozens of them from the Richards *oeuvre*, and still leave dozens more to harm the sensibilities of the innocents who still, despite relentless indoctrination to the contrary, unaccountably seem to enjoy wallowing in middle-class never-never-lands of long ago, canes and all. Greyfriars never existed, and one hopes that Bunter himself – a remarkably early example of the all-round anti-hero – had few equivalents in real life. But all the same, is this not a eulogy of the hated public-school system, and, moreover, self-evidently perverted? Even though as late as the end of the 1950s, the BBC was regularly screening Children's TV dramatisations of the Bunter books (with Gerald Campion as the Fat Owl),

---

8. *Billy Bunter of Greyfriars School.*

and with most of the whackings left unrepentantly in place, in the last twenty years those who now control much of the British public library system have decided that while the public school motif is in any case an *ipso facto* objection, and the *oeuvre* itself hopelessly dated (and therefore irrelevant to the generation of baseball-capped Nintendoids they are currently servicing on our behalf), it is above all the whacking that dooms the Fat Owl of the Remove to be removed from the kiddies' shelves.

Nonetheless it is difficult, even with the necessary will, to identify actual sadism in the Greyfriars books. Bunter-whackings are always pure burlesque (or Benny Hill). The victim, no masochist he!, makes a fuss ('Yaroooh!!!' with all three exclamation marks being the best-known Bunterism of all), not because the canings he receives are cruel – other boys are whacked in stoical silence – or because the whacker, the form-master Samuel Quelch, is a sadist – for though he is most certainly a martinet, he is also usually a just one – but because William George Bunter is a laughable, lily-livered coward. Nor are his frequent punishments ever shown as undeserved. He cheats, and steals, and lies, and blames others for his own misdemeanours: the cane-based comeuppances that so frequently come his way do not do so without due cause, and are clearly intended to depict the workings of a remorseless, demiurgic justice. Schoolboy justice, to be sure – it is markedly less hedged about with complexities and socio-political imperatives than the adult kind – and therefore banal; but still not a wholly immoral literary objective.

Nevertheless three of the four distinguished and prolific children's authors mentioned above – three women and one man, all incidentally deceased – who display approval, in varying degrees, of school discipline based on physical punishment, have been subjected to varying degrees of censorship. One has nearly disappeared, another has her film or TV dramatisations bowdlerised while, for the present at least, her books are left intact, and the third has had her books 'edited' in order to remove 'forbidden' concepts.

Who are the censors, and on what system do they operate?

*

If there is a conspiracy, it is largely an unconscious one. Those who object to the deracination of modern society by means of retroactive thought-control techniques are often tempted to see secret cabals getting together to wreak their mischief, but I do not share this perception. Librarians may legitimately belong to professional associations and unions, and since many of these bodies are strongly influenced by progressive thought and policy there is also likely to be some considerable diffusion of ideas of this type. Nor may one reasonably object: not for the world does one wish to censor the free exchange and promulgation of ideas. It is with the uninhibited passing on of these ideological constraints to the general public that issue is taken. Frequently, indeed, library customers do so themselves, and the expurgation or removal of this or that particular title for reasons similar to those discussed earlier does not by any means pass without comment. But the libraries have the last word on the books they will purchase, stock or display, and those who make such decisions represent 'weak spots' in any national system of resistance to this kind of bossiness. What is the true value of wholly unfettered national newspapers when our library system is subjected to continued, anonymous and virtually unaccountable censorship? TV, films, advertisements and videos are also censored – on a national level by national bodies – but even if we have no part in their appointments, at least we know who the censors are.

It is awkward indicting an entire profession, and one does not happily do so; but who else is really to blame for the inexorable creep of censorship into the largest single source of low-cost reading available to the British public? In the United Kingdom, book prices are currently subject to the Net Book Agreement, in effect a cartel which fixes the retail price of books at profitably high levels. Public libraries are therefore very much in demand, especially where incomes are lower. Some book publishers themselves operate their own in-house censorship schemes; but even were this not the case – and not all publishers are equally guilty by any means – some libraries are apparently more than willing to do it for them. Time is on their side. When well-known books are struck from an existing list someone may notice, and trouble may ensue. But after a while, when the generation that remembers it best has died out, no one will be left among the general public to recall, and possibly demand, such examples of the old, unreconstructed thinking, and so a wicked concept will die out from our culture. All the censors have to do is hold on, ride out the storms, and in the end 'natural wastage' will do the business. By what right does this process continue?[9]

Book publishing is another area where direct censorship – there is no other word for it – takes place. Of course, it is not by any means axiomatic that if a new book is refused publication it has been 'censored' (though especially aggrieved authors have been known to reach such conclusions). It might simply be not good enough, or uncommercial, or a bad risk in other ways; publishers are fully entitled to make the best decisions they can concerning these matters where new works are concerned – it is their money, after all.[10]

Where they take it upon themselves to edit – that is, to alter – existing work, which may have been on their catalogues for years, in the light of new thinking on this or that contentious topic – the

---

9. The following subjects are known to have been subjected in recent years to official or ad hoc (local branch) library censorship: spanking, racism, middle-classism ('bourgeois value systems'), fur couture and blood sports. While each may represent a genuine area of personal concern on the part of an individual librarian, the collective effect is of a massive, self-righteous and miserably illiberal assault on what we are allowed to know and opinions we are eligible to read.

10. Not all such decisions are free from non-commercial motives, or pass without comment. A few years ago, the Virago publishing house was excited to receive an editorial submission of unusual excellence, and moreover, one that conformed wholly to this famously radical house's cocktail of ideologies. The novel took the form of a first-person narrative by a young Asian girl, and dealt in a sensitive manner with the tribulations of growing up in modern Britain. Virago accepted the work and put it into their forthcoming schedule. Only then was it revealed that the author was not, after all, either Asian or female, but a white English male clergyman. The company instantly, angrily and unrepentantly dropped the book; its merits, apparently, were wholly devalued by its being the work of the wrong sex. One wonders if the Brontë sisters (who wrote under the names Currer, Ellis and Acton Bell), or Aurore Dudevant (George Sand) would have approved.

classic 'projection of ideology into the past' – one might say they were on shakier ground. It is inevitably done to deceased authors since objections might very reasonably be anticipated from successful living ones. As yet unsuccessful living authors may also encounter ad hoc versions of the above tinkering: whole passages 'corrected', not in line with the definitive editorial objectives of greater clarity, better grammar, fewer spelling mistakes and no libels, but to conform to a set of rules which has not by any means been agreed in advance, but is the propaganda of a discontented minority – who are disproportionately represented in the editorial departments of a great many newspapers, magazines and book publishing houses. There are not many employment possibilities (other than teaching) open to English graduates, and editorial work of some description is easily the most popular (one reason why it is so miserably remunerated). The amending, excising or writing in of views and opinions is one way in which the world may be changed. A stroke of the pen and a 'racist' or 'perverted' or 'sexist' term has vanished, or been replaced with something more acceptable to the progressive mind, even though the original meaning may have been lost, or a subtlety of phraseology destroyed, or mistakes of grammar or spelling written in. And who will ever notice, after all? Only the author. So unless he is of the temperament to make a fuss – and many are not, especially when new to authorship – no repercussions will result. The work will remain in its amended form.

There are a few checks and balances. A combination of literary fame and continuing good health on the part of the author is the ultimate guarantee against half-baked tinkering of this or any other kind, since if a successful author is not entirely pleased with the way his works are delivered to the public he may be tempted elsewhere. When an author dies much of this protection is withdrawn, as in the cases of Enid Blyton and Agatha Christie[11], both of whom

---

11. The huge embarrassment caused by the title *Ten Little Niggers* (one of her best novels), remains an enjoyable recollection of early (1950s) political correctness. It was changed to *Ten Little Indians* for the film, and the book was reissued as *And Then There Were None*.

have been 'corrected' in ways they would surely not have approved during their lifetimes. If the canon is also of waning commercial value as well as being difficult to 'correct' without wholesale changes – which cannot be said of Miss Blyton or Mrs Christie but is certainly true of Frank Richards – then it stands a good chance of being dropped entirely.

Another reason for a book to escape revision when it contains an episode or phraseology which one might otherwise guess would attract it is when the book, or its author, is already an icon of the progressives, and a bona-fide literary classic besides. Here entirely different rules apply.

A good example comes from *My Brilliant Career*, a remarkable Australian novel written at the end of the last century. The heroine, Sybylla, a teenage governess, is in charge of a collection of rowdy children on a remote and impoverished Australian farm. Her first attempt to impose discipline is frustrated by the mother of the brood. After an evening spent in despair, Sybylla determines to prevail on the morrow.

During the dinner-hour I slipped away unnoticed to where some quince-trees were growing and procured a sharp rod, which I secreted among the flour-bags in the schoolroom. At half-past one I brought my scholars in and ordered them to their work with a confident air. Things went without a ripple until three o'clock, when the writing lesson began. Jimmy struck his pen on the bottom of the bottle every time he replenished it with ink.

'Jimmy,' I gently remonstrated, 'don't jab your pen like that – it will spoil it. There is no necessity to shove it right to the bottom.'

Jab, jab, went Jimmy's pen.

'Jimmy, did you hear me speak to you?'

Jab went the pen.

'James, I am speaking to you!'

Jab went the pen again.

'James,' I said sternly, 'I give you one more chance.'

He deliberately defied me by stabbing into the ink-bottle with increased vigour. Liza giggled triumphantly, and the little ones strove to emulate her. I calmly produced my switch and brought it smartly over the shoulders of my refractory pupil in a way that sent the dust in a cloud from his dirty coat, knocked the pen from his fingers, and upset the ink.

He acted as before — yelled ear-drum-breakingly, letting the saliva from his distended mouth run on his copy-book. His brothers and sisters also started to roar, but bringing the rod down on the table, I threatened to thrash every one of them if they so much as whimpered; and they were so dumbfounded that they sat silent in terrified surprise.

Jimmy continued to bawl. I hit him again.

'Cease instantly, sir.'

Through the cracks [in the wall] Mrs M'Swat could be seen approaching.

Seeing her, Jimmy hollered anew . . . to attract his mother, and I continued to rain blows across his shoulders. Mrs M'Swat approached to within a foot of the door, and then as though changing her mind, retraced her steps . . . I knew I had won, and felt disappointed that the conquest had been so easy.'[12]

---

12. Virago Modern Classics (1988 edition). This extraordinary novel, written by a sixteen-year-old girl (very like the heroine of the story), was first published in 1901 when it attracted much critical attention (interestingly, Havelock Ellis thought the book 'bitter'), though it was later withdrawn from publication (by the author) for over sixty years. It has been successfully filmed and was one of the standard-bearers of the 1970s revolution in Australian cinema. For the crucial scene, director Gill Armstrong and screenwriter Eleanor Witcombe altered the punishment, firstly, to make the boy discharge a catapult at the schoolmistress – thereby 'deserving' punishment rather more than in the original book – and secondly, arranging for the strokes of the switch to fall across the boy's bottom (rather than the shoulders), while the heroine holds him firmly across a desk. The careful camera work – the approaching mother is seen in background while, in foreground, the lashing continues – gives the scene huge flagellant potential. It is one of the most artistic child-whippings in cinema history.

Here again, a teenage heroine's lot is improved and her status elevated by the summary public thrashing of a small boy. If a little unprogressive, the scene is by no means untypical of school-room whippings administered by schoolmistresses a hundred years ago in many countries; which certainly cannot be said for its literary 'twin', written in England fifteen years later, with precisely the same plot objective (overwhelming victory for the teenage schoolma'am) in mind, but with a very different flavour.

'Go in front, Wright,' she said.

She was trembling in every fibre. A big, sullen boy, not bad but very difficult, slouched out to the front. She went on with the lesson, aware that Williams was making faces at Wright, and that Wright was grinning behind her. She was afraid. She turned to the map again. And she was afraid. 'Please Miss, Williams—' came a sharp cry, and a boy on the back row was standing up, with drawn, pained brows, half mocking grin on his face, half real resentment against Williams – 'Please Miss, he's nipped me,' – and he rubbed his leg ruefully.

'Come in front, Williams,' she said.

The rat-like boy sat with his pale smile and did not move.

'Come in front,' she repeated, definite now.

'I shan't,' he cried, snarling, rat-like, grinning. Something went click in Ursula's soul. Her face and eyes set, she went through the class straight. The boy cowered before her glow-ing, fixed eyes. But she advanced on him, seized him by the arm, dragged him from his seat. He clung to the form. It was a battle between him and her. Her instinct had suddenly become calm and quick. She jerked him from his grip and dragged him, struggling and kicking, to the front. He kicked her several times, and clung to the forms as he passed, but she went on. The class was on its feet in excitement. She saw it, but made no move.

She knew if she let go the boy he would dash to the door. Already he had run home once out of her class. So she snatched her cane from the desk, and brought it down on him. He was writhing and kicking. She saw his face beneath her, white, with eyes like the eyes of a fish, stony, yet full of hate and horrible fear. And she loathed him, the hideous writhing thing that was nearly too much for her. In horror lest he should overcome her and yet at the heart quite calm, she brought down the cane again and again, whilst he struggled making inarticulate noises, and lunging vicious kicks at her. With one hand she managed to hold him, and now and then the cane came down on him. He writhed, like a mad thing. But the pain of the strokes cut through his writhing, vicious, coward's courage, bit deeper, till at last, with a long whimper that became a yell, he went limp. She let him go, and he rushed at her, his teeth and eyes glinting. There was a second of agonised terror in her heart: he was a beast thing. Then she caught him, and the cane came down on him. A few times, madly, in a frenzy, he lunged and writhed, to kick her. But again the cane broke him, he sank with a howling yell on the floor, and like a beaten beast lay there yelling.

I have encountered many scenes of corporal punishment in literature both respectable and forbidden, and have no hesitation whatever in describing this episode, from D.H. Lawrence's *The Rainbow*[13], as easily the most distressing I have ever read. Its realism makes it far more genuinely horrible than the demented fantasias of de Sade. It can barely be read – by the present writer at any rate – without strong feelings of almost physical outrage. It is shocking and brutal. But somehow it is entirely 'respectable', and has never been cut from the book. Indeed *The Rainbow* has been a set book many times in British school syllabuses. It has attracted no wrath whatever from any quarter, certainly on this account.

In many ways the plot of the scene in *The Rainbow* bears a close resemblance to that of both *My Brilliant Career* and *Anne of*

---

13. pp. 398–99.

Avonlea[14], though the setting is not a far-flung colonial village school but a British 'board' (state) school in a grim Midlands town at around the same time (Lawrence was writing in 1913–14). The heroine, Ursula Brangwen, a working-class pupil teacher of seventeen, dislikes her job intensely; she also dislikes the headmaster, one Harby, a thunderous bully, patronising at best, odiously concerned for her 'welfare' at his creepiest, who in

---

14. The same plot – of the personable young woman driven to administer corporal punishment to a boy, with satisfactory results – is something of a favourite with lady writers. An early, though obscure, example, is *A Woman's Will* (pp. 233–34), by Frances Hodgson Burnett. A new (French) governess has been plagued by the archetypal bad small boy, but has triumphed, as she relates in a letter to a friend: 'As to the children, I have reached a climax with them, and do not think I shall have any more trouble. Yesterday occurred my battle royal with Master Hugh Dysart, and it is my opinion – yes, I really think – that, upon the whole, I came off victor. He is a young savage, this master Hugh Dysart, and from the first he has continually done all he dared to defy and annoy me. But yesterday the crisis arrived. He brought into the school-room a dog I hate (and secretly stand in fear of), a big fierce-looking creature, belonging to Sir Roderick, and he also brought a whip with which he teased it. I ordered the dog out, and told him to bring the whip to me. He told the dog to remain, and refused to bring me the whip. I am afraid of the dog, as I tell you, but my temper was stronger than my fear; so I went to the animal and took it boldly by its collar and led it out myself. Then I returned to my seat and commanded my young Sir Hugh to come to me, as I had done before. The two girls dropped their books, and sat and stared at me. I really believe there was something in my face which frightened them. For fully two minutes the boy sat in his seat, laughing at me a horridly wicked laugh, and then a sudden passion of fury seemed to seize upon him. He sprang up and ran towards me, all at once, and before I could touch him his whip had struck me across my face.

'You cannot imagine, unless you have once received such a blow, what its effect was upon me. It is already agreed between us that my temper is not a cold one, and between the sting and the humiliation, and my perfect conviction that my time had come, I will confess that it got the better of me. In two seconds I had wrenched the whip from the little animal's hand, and held him with all my strength, and then I beat him – and beat him – and beat him! I beat him until I felt that even the amiable Sir Roderick might have considered I had distinguished myself; after which exploit I flung him upon the floor, broke the whip into half a dozen pieces, and threw it at him where he lay . . .'

It is hard to find reference to this title in biographies of the author of *A Secret Garden*, but once again I can assure readers the book exists.

any case has small opinion of Ursula's ability to keep order among her class of poor, urban children. And it is because she indeed cannot keep order that she has recourse to the cane, though not on an ad hoc basis (like Anne Shirley with her pointer), since despite similar short-lived reservations about caning, Ursula has nonetheless taken the trouble to procure one in advance, albeit with no particular culprit in mind. It might have been Wright. It nearly is – in fact his execution is only deferred. In the event it is the slightly uncanny Williams who is flogged – for that is the best description for what takes place – into a state of hysterical dementia, not to mention serious bodily harm, by the stick-at-nothing teenager. Her aim? To prove to the other teaching staff, especially Harby, that she's every bit as capable as they are. In other words, it is a career move.

Luckily for Ursula's conscience, it hurts her more than it hurts him.

Mr Harby had rushed up towards the end of this performance. 'What's the matter?' he roared.

Ursula felt as if something were going to break in her.

'I've thrashed him,' she said, her breast heaving, forcing out the words on the last breath. The headmaster stood choked with rage, helpless. She looked at the writhing, howling figure on the floor.

'Get up,' she said. The thing writhed away from her. She took a step forward. She had realised the presence of the headmaster for one second, and then she was oblivious of it again.

'Get up,' she said. And with a little dart the boy was on his feet. His yelling dropped to a mad blubber. He had been in a frenzy.

'Go and stand by the radiator,' she said.

As if mechanically, blubbering, he went.

The headmaster stood robbed of speech and movement. His face was yellow, his hands twitched convulsively. But Ursula stood stiff not far from him. Nothing could touch her now: she was beyond Mr Harby. She was as if violated to death . . .

The boy blubbered wildly by the radiator . . .[15]

Who, exactly, has been 'violated to death'? Perhaps the ugliest aspect of the scene is the way the victim is dehumanised so that the thrashing may be presented as something one might administer, *in extremis* no doubt, to a badly behaved animal (though many people observing someone thrashing a dog or horse, let alone a child, in the manner described, might be tempted to intercede – with violence if necessary). It is a *macédoine* of negative anthropomorphism. Williams is several times likened to a rat, with face unnaturally pale; he has fish-like eyes 'stony, yet full of hate and horrible fear. And she loathed him . . .'[16] Driven by these impulses, the heroine of *The Rainbow* and *Women in Love* whips and whips and whips the twelve-year-old *untermensch* to and on the ground – like Anne Shirley in front of a mixed class of near-adolescents – until 'the pain of the strokes cut through'.

Williams does not weep (a real child might do this): he 'blubbers', the most dishonourable and contemptible way in which to shed tears. When he attempts to defend himself (we must remember his original crime was to 'nip' another boy) he is a 'beast thing' – 'thing' and 'beast' being words Lawrence/Ursula felicitously uses more than once to describe a child who, in reality, would have been severely physically damaged, and psychologically scarred for life, by what had just been done to him.

Beforehand, yet again like Anne of Green Gables, Ursula Brangwen had been foolish enough to fancy she might rise above tradition:

So there existed a set of separate wills, each straining itself to the utmost to exert its own authority. Children will never

---

naturally acquiesce to sitting in a class and submitting to knowledge. They must be compelled by a stronger wiser will. Against which will they must always strive to revolt. So that the first great effort of every teacher of a large class must be to bring the will of the children into accordance with his own will. And this he can only do by an abnegation of his personal self, and an application of a system of laws, for the purpose of achieving a certain calculable result, the imparting of certain knowledge. Whereas Ursula thought she was going to become the first wise teacher by making the whole business personal, and using no compulsion. She believed entirely in her own personality.

This is Lawrence himself speaking – the former schoolmaster who regretted the 'punishment book' system[17] since it inhibited the number of times (or how severely) he might cane his pupils; who believed that 'when a parent gives his boy a beating, there is a living passionate interchange'.[18] Here his own voice takes the place of Anne Shirley's Mr Harrison – the voice of experience, whose advice the silly young schoolmistress does not take. Never mind: she will learn. She does indeed, and, unlike Anne Shirley, who undergoes a profound personal crisis of regret immediately after whipping Anthony Pye, at no time does Ursula Brangwen show a moment's pity or remorse, although we are repeatedly reminded she hates what she is doing. The children in her 'care' have become – always were – the enemy; and war is war.

Reconciling the above passage with modern pedagogical theory might be thought a difficult undertaking in its own right, while the flogging alone surely puts *The Rainbow* beyond the pale of any book that might be thought fit for schoolchildren – according to any rules, not just the new, unannounced ones. Nor is that all: there is a fearful snobbery of a kind that sits equally

---

17. For over a century British schools administering corporal punishment have been obliged to record each event in a special ledger kept for the purpose.
18. *Fantasia of the Unconscious.*

poorly with either the heroine of a working-class novel or its author. The boy Williams (it turns out he has a heart condition) has been beaten literally black and blue, and his mother comes to complain, as some mothers indeed might have done, even in that unreconstructed era. She considers (indeed, she is oddly persistent in this assertion) that her son has been assaulted rather than punished, and it proves difficult to dissuade her from consulting another authority on the matter.

Fortunately for Ursula's moral alibi, however, and the sympathetic reader's peace of mind, Mrs Williams is herself a queer, repulsive creature, just like her son, and is finally patronised into withdrawing her complaint.

'I know he is troublesome,' the woman only addressed herself to the male now – 'but if you could have him punished without beating – he is really delicate.'

Ursula was beginning to feel upset. Harby stood in rather superb mastery, the woman cringing to him to tickle him as one tickles trout.

'I had come to complain why he was away this morning, Sir. You will understand.'

She held out her hand. Harby took it and let it go, surprised and angry.

'Good morning,' she said, and she gave her gloved, seedy hand to Ursula. She was not ill-looking, and had a curious insinuating way, very distasteful yet effective.

'Good morning, Mr Harby, and thank you.'

The figure in the grey costume and the purple hat was going across the school yard with a curious lingering walk. Ursula felt a strange pity for her, and revulsion from her. She shuddered. She went into the school again.

So that's all right, and Ursula survives, to cane, and cane again, though of course as usual it hurts her more than it hurts them (and it hurts them considerably):

So the battle went on till her heart was sick. She had several more boys to subjugate before she could establish herself. And Mr Harby hated her almost as if she were a man. She knew now that nothing but a thrashing would settle some of the big louts who wanted to play cat and mouse with her. Mr Harby would not give them the thrashing if he could help it. For he hated the teacher, the stuck-up, insolent highschool miss with her independence.

'Now, Wright, what have you done this time?' he would say genially to the boy who was sent to him from Standard Five for punishment. And he left the lad standing, lounging, wasting his time.

So that Ursula would appeal no more to the headmaster, but, when she was driven wild, she seized her cane, and slashed the boy who was insolent to her, over head and ears and hands. And at length they were afraid of her, she had them in order.

But she had paid a great price out of her own soul, to do this. It seemed as if a great flame had gone through her and burnt her sensitive tissue. She who shrank from the thought of physical suffering in any form, had been forced to fight and beat with a cane and rouse all her instincts to hurt. And afterwards she had been forced to endure the sound of their blubbering and desolation, when she had broken them to order.

Are not these crocodile tears of Miss Brangwen's more odious than any sadism? The overall vision is as 'politically incorrect', surely, as it is possible to be: deliberate, unquestionable, repeated child abuse, by almost anybody's reckoning; uncharitable reactions towards the disadvantaged, if not actually disabled; morally corrupt motives, the abandonment of self-control as a deliberate act of policy and a capacity to dehumanise that Julius Streicher[19] might have envied. And yet the story of Ursula Brangwen and her

19. Editor of *Der Stürmer*, a Nazi propaganda magazine of the early thirties.

battle against the odds is seen as gritty and admirable. The incident described, the experiences that lead up to it and the bout of canings which follow it, are all presented as hurdles *Ursula* must get through, barriers for *her* to cross. Teacher – working-class, young, self-made, intelligent, sensitive, attractive, lesbian-ish – stands up for herself physically, takes no nonsense from males, of whatever age: here is a shining prototype for the modern age with whom it would be unwise to tangle.

Even were this not the case, in Britain the late D.H. Lawrence himself wields an unusual radical cachet: it was the trial for alleged obscenity of one of his books, *Lady Chatterley's Lover*, in 1963, that led to one of the most famous courtroom decisions in British literary history. The book (not one of Lawrence's best) was cleared of the charge and within twenty-four hours Penguin Books had sold out its entire stock. This event did much to usher in, in Britain at any rate, the new age of satire and iconoclasm, not to mention freely available pornography. *Lady Chatterley*, every bit as much as the Beatles, has been held as the true augur of the sixties.

Lawrence, though dead, had won a famous victory against the forces of reaction. Even before *Lady Chatterley*, he had long been regarded, especially by Fabians, as a noteworthy figure of twentieth-century English letters. Many of his books depict working- and lower-middle-class life of the early part of the century. Lawrence is 'sound' on mill-owners and the privations of the workers; while the sex scenes that so often characterise his work have always given him a natural status among the avantgarde. Indeed, the central plot motif of his most celebrated novel is of an upper-class lady being efficiently and repeatedly shagged by her gamekeeper. What could be more symbolic, and radical, than that?

There have been two moving-image versions of *The Rainbow*, one a 1984 film production directed by Ken Russell (who seems to specialise in filming D.H. Lawrence's books), the other a 1989 BBC TV drama. In neither case was the key scene omitted, though each director handled it in a different way – and in both cases it was somewhat altered to give the heroine a justification (both directors seemed to feel she needed a better one than Lawrence had provided). The Russell production kept closest to the original brutality of the caning, though to make the boy 'deserve' it the script was rewritten to show him, firstly, firing a catapult at Ursula (the same device used by the film-makers of *My Brilliant Career*), secondly, resisting violently when she comes to 'arrest' him, and thirdly, actually knocking her over twice, even though he is a mere boy, smaller than her, and bespectacled. He is overcome and dealt with more or less in the mode of the book, with a very heavy cane. Such is Ursula's fury that she actually breaks it in half. Afterwards the boy is not even weeping. In reality, he would have been unconscious and very probably concussed.

The later, and generally superior, BBC TV production addressed the problem by making the caning itself rather less grotesque, though still extremely violent. The boy is hauled out of the class, dragged to the front, bent across a desk, and whipped, very severely indeed, no fewer than sixteen times. Despite all the 'legitimising', the punishment, administered by actress Imogen Stubbs (shown wearing a calm smile throughout the proceedings while apparently thrashing to the limits of her strength) remains excessive.[20] The aftermath is a soft whimpering from the back of the utterly silent class – in real life the boy would have been screaming in pain.

Television is subject to far more severe restraints than film concerning what may or may not be shown, chiefly because it is a far easier business to prevent the young and immature viewing unsuitable films than it is to keep them away from unsuitable television programmes (these days children have learned to wait for the video). There are many viewers who, for one reason or

---

20. The producers, and Miss Stubbs herself, would doubtless be horrified to learn that video clips of this (twice shown) BBC TV play circulate widely among flagellanti, who consider it one of the most breathtaking of all TV or filmed corporal punishments.

another, and on their own accounts, are quite willing to complain about sex and/or violence. Flagellatory scenes certainly evoke this kind of reaction: *The Happy Valley* (a BBC TV play based on the same events as the film *White Mischief)* had caning scenes (with an attractive teenage girl as the victim) which, though dramatically justified, aroused much ire. If *The Rainbow* attracted complaints they cannot have been from very important people, since the TV production was repeated in 1993. Because Lawrence is a touch-me-at-your-peril classic writer with excellent liberal credentials? Because the victim is a boy, and an unattractive one, while the caner is a feminist iconess proving that she's every bit as good as a man? What in any other context would be horrific, eminently censorable, cruelty to children is nothing of the kind, it seems, when it serves a higher purpose.

There is one final point to emphasise about Lawrence's novel. Despite the scene's resonant cast of characters (vengeful young schoolmistress, naughty boy, enthralled audience), its vital prop (a school cane) and the basic outcome of the scene (the application of the cane to the boy by the schoolmistress in front of the audience), all components which regularly find their way into disciplinary erotica, there is little or no flagellatory gratification in this episode – though genuine sadists might identify with Ursula, while far-gone masochists might conceivably long for the kind of psychic death-with-contempt that is dealt out to the boy Williams. At the same time there can hardly be a male passive flagellant who would not joyfully change places with Anthony Pye, and afterwards, like him, offer allegiance to Anne of Green Gables; friendship and adoration having replaced hostility and defiance by means of the sweetest imaginable catharsis.

Such horrible perversions of the human spirit require further exegesis. What do flagellants want? What do they *do*? What *is* flagellation?

PART II

The Flagellant Experience

7

THE ECSTASY
OF THE AGONY

To me, it was a wholly incomprehensible experience. I floated in a state of unimagined bliss and cried heartrendingly for sheer joy . . . every blow became a sweet pain for my own mounting and awakening voluptuary pleasure.

Confessions and Experiences

The capacity to extract pleasure from pain seems to be one of the most baffling paradoxes in human nature. How can it be possible to enjoy, or appreciate — let alone be fulfilled or exalted by — physical hurt? Pain, after all, is nature's warning sign that bodily damage is imminent, if not already an actuality. It is linked to injury and disease; a sign that things are not as they should be. It is negative, one of life's sours; like shame and death, a token of the fall from grace. The instinctive response to pain is to fear it, and avoid it if possible, both for oneself and, to a lesser extent, for others.

Pain has uses nonetheless. Its ability to stimulate — that is, to bring about a reaction, by way of avoidance, flinching or a frantic desire to remove oneself from whatever has caused the pain — constitutes its most common utility. The goad drives the ox, the whip and spur the horse. These are transactions of the most basic kind but there may also be more profound ones, based upon the memory or intelligent anticipation of pain: the burned hand which teaches the child that fire is dangerous; the intensive, rolling pains which warn the mother-to-be that childbirth is imminent; the slightly painful dentist's check-up in order to avoid the certainty of excruciating pain in the unspecified future, and so on. These represent fusions of pain – an animal reaction of the most fundamental level, since nearly all living things appear to feel it – with intellect. Even as dimwitted a creature as a shark knows it must avoid brushing its skin against sharp coral. Whether this knowledge is acquired via experience, that is learned, or is inherited somehow with the shark's DNA is not known: the key point is that the shark is right – some corals can flay even a shark, and a wound will bleed and probably attract predators. Pain is a backstop; the final warning that this is about to happen.

Human beings are not sharks and their ability to mix pain (or its memory, or its anticipation) with the intellect is very much more developed. It is in these amalgams or sensory coalitions that pain begins to lose some of its ancient terror and may be seen in another light, ceasing, albeit temporarily and within carefully defined contexts, to be viewed as a wholly malign entity. Several examples are given above, to which we might add the jogger's famous objective of 'the burn', sharp pains in chest and lungs which are believed by joggers to be a signal that the benefit of the exercise has been duly delivered.[1] At the dining table such pains would cause instant alarm. After five punishing miles in a tracksuit, they are seen as a reward; an experience deliberately sought.

There are other ways in which physical pain, in symbiotic association with other human (or mammalian) impulses, is instinctively, even happily, incorporated into behaviour. For example, courtship rituals among both man and beast often

---

1. 'Going for the burn' is philosophically indistinguishable, so far as I can see, from the austere delights of self-excoriation (usually flagellation) practised by many saints and other religious figures throughout history, and a common penance in the Catholic Church until very recent times. In such cases the benefits are not held to be sexual, but æsthetic: the mortification of the flesh for a higher purpose.

contain an element of ritualised pain and violence: from the Hamar women of East Africa who expect to be sharply thrashed by their suitors as part of the standard courtship ritual (and do not go unsatisfied in this regard), to the mating of domestic cats, which is painful for the female on two counts: the serrated nature of the male's penis, and the sharp, subduing bite he administers to her neck. The purpose of this bite is not known for sure: to restrain the female; to threaten her; because the tom-cat enjoys biting the female at the moment of coitus, or because the female enjoys being bitten? All four at once seems the best bet.

It will be seen that pain is not, after all, an ineluctably grievous or malign matter – as we should expect, since its opposite, plea-sure, also has an obverse side (hedonism, licentiousness, self-gratification). However its transformation from something wholly to be avoided into something to be sought, and even enjoyed, depends on its being experienced in concert with other feelings, where context alone dictates the pain's acceptability or otherwise. The jogger who sprains an ankle will not regard the resulting discomfort as a valid pay-off for his efforts. It will give him no pleasure whatsoever; it is entirely the wrong kind of agony.

Flagellation is obviously an activity where pain and pleasure are mingled, but there is more to it than that. The pain, for exam-ple, must be of a highly specific kind, and, as a general rule, applied to a highly specific part of the human body. Nor is the mere application of pain enough – it must be administered under tightly controlled circumstances, with rules, and only by selected individuals. In short, it must be embedded in procedure. To break any of the rules – by being the wrong person, using the wrong instrument, hitting in the wrong place, hitting without warning, for the wrong reason, too hard or too mildly, saying the wrong things, even wearing the wrong clothes – can reduce the construct to ruins.

It will be seen that in this respect at least the classic flagellant scenario bears a very close resemblance to classic romantic love-making, for it is also true that jarring notes can wreck even the most skilfully planned seductive encounter: inability to pay the restaurant bill, insensitive conversation or a fragment of spinach lodged between the front teeth will all do it. If lovers are on edge, a single word out of place can have disastrous results. And even if the unhappy couple ignore all these grim omens and climb into bed nonetheless, things can still go wrong, as many of us know.

Both activities are forms of sexual theatre. Both have scripts whose details may be varied on an ad hoc basis by skilled actors, but whose plot is known (or hoped for) in advance. Both have traditional props and stage settings (the cane, the chilled champagne, the honeymoon suite, the punishment room), mandatory dialogue ('I love you', 'Bend over!') and both may grow gradually noisier as the night wears on. Even the essentially rhythmic nature of the culminating act is common to both events.

To declare, therefore, that the object of flagellation is to administer or receive pain, is about as comprehensively accurate as saying that the sole purpose of seduction is procreation. Seduction, or another form of courtship ritual, is a prerequisite for mating and not in any way separate from it. If an attempted seduction is bungled, mating (hence possible procreation) may not take place at all. Mating without courtship or consent is rape.

Similarly, those who obtain pleasure or fulfilment from flagellation normally do so as the result of a composite sequential experience, and not just from the culminating physical act.[2] And just as orthodox courtship and seduction may assume many variations, so can their flagellatory mirror images, often with surprisingly close equivalence. Teasing and tantalising, pursuit and capture, deliberate attenuation and sudden decisiveness,

---

2. It might be said that in both cases those for whom the culminating act is the be-all and end-all of the proceedings, to be attained as swiftly as possible, are not well regarded by their partners.

languid calm and controlled physical exertion are sub-themes of behaviour common to both plots.

There are still closer resemblances. Although it is no longer fashionable to say so without wheeling on a dreary host of disapproving caveats, for many orthodox, heterosexual couples, the presence, within their lovemaking scenarios, of a certain amount of ritualised combat, whether physical or verbal – with rules to ensure that the loser loses and the winner wins in the most enjoyable possible ways – may add considerable voluptuous edge to the proceedings: it may be very important indeed, even vital, to one of the parties. Such sexual mock combats are often called domination and submission games, and indeed this is a better term than any we have uncovered so far to describe the core of the flagellant experience. So crucial is the interaction of wills between dominant and submissive that pain itself, supposedly of cardinal importance, usually becomes a secondary affair; a consequence, not a prime mover.

Any careful examination of the erotic literature of this subject will soon produce lists of scenarios, actors, settings, costumes and props which reappear again and again, as they do in all literary genres.[3] The first of these scenarios is also the shortest: the bedroom (or place of conjugal intimacy), the schoolroom (or place of learning and correction), the dungeon (or place of punishment and incarceration). From the fundamental scenario is derived an appropriate cast of characters: the stern spouse or parent, the schoolmistress or governess, the slave-master or tyrant queen. Similarly, the chain of cause and effect, originally dictated by the scenario, extends yet further, into the 'reason' for punishment (unpunctuality, failure to study, *lèse-majesté*), the likely mode of punishment (spanking, caning, whipping), and, in turn, the instrument employed for the purpose (hand, cane,

---

3. Idealised orthodox seduction scenarios are similarly limited to a few well-known favourites: the honeymoon suite, the log cabin with crackling wood fire, the cornfield in summer, the moonlit beach.

cat-o'-nine tails etc.). If the scenario is constructed with dedicated care, the actor-protagonists will even dress the part: every
little helps.

This may seem like a limited number of options, but, just as a
cathode ray tube may produce millions of different colours from
a mere three primary ones, red, green and blue, very considerable variance may be achieved within these parameters alone,
even without introducing elements of individual personality.

What is common to all, however, is the note of domination and
submission. A transaction takes place, whereby one actor
imposes his or her will upon the other, by one means or another,
but always with a fixed end in view.

One beautiful day, my aunt was advised of the return of her
god-daughter who, having finished her studies in
Switzerland, Germany and England, was coming to London
to seek a situation as a lady's companion or family governess. My aunt had invited her to stay until she found
suitable employment.

The young lady of nineteen arrived. Not having seen her
since her fifteenth year, I was agreeably surprised by her
svelte beauty distinguished by regular features, a beautiful
blonde head of hair, wide eyes, a well-formed and energetic
mouth, and fine build with provocative curves.

The sympathetic sentiments with which I greeted the
young lady were reciprocated and she asked me, the first
day, to call her by her first name, Denise. I performed many
small tasks and services for her; and for her part, she assisted
me with my French lessons – she knew that language very
well.

I remember well the occasion when she exclaimed: 'Oh,
what a great number of faults! If I were your aunt, I should
whip you, you lazy creature!' I took this remark – and others
like it – for teasing and took my revenge by means of practical jokes; one time, for example, I dropped a wet sponge on
the back of her neck.

She called after me: 'If I catch you, I'll spank you! Rogue!'
But afterwards she seemed to have forgotten her threat.

Two or three days had passed since the first incident,
when at a certain moment I was leaning out of the window, looking at the business and activity of the street
below. All of a sudden, I felt a sharp smack on my backside.
This burning contact penetrated like a small thunderbolt. I
was startled to see Denise still stooping over me. She
laughed.

'What was that for?' I stammered, though without straight-
ening up. 'Well,' replied Denise, 'that was for your
provocative pose and also for the wet sponge.'

Excited perhaps by my apparent submission, Denise took
hold of the thin material of my trousers, while saying in a
dry tone: 'Wait! I'm going to give you a spanking. Truly you
deserve one!'

'No, no,' I replied. 'People can see us!'

'Not at all,' answered Denise. 'There's only a garden opposite.' And immediately, I felt a series of powerful smacks
falling on my surprised bottom.

'Is that warming you up?' she said. 'I hope you're going to
be more respectful towards me – in fact I'm sure of it. But
next time, I'll take down your trousers and give it to you on
your bare bottom!'

Faint with shame, I murmured: 'But what if I tell my
aunt?'

Immediately Denise released me. 'That's horrible! I don't
love you any more – go away!'

She turned away, visibly offended; but I took her in my
arms. 'Don't be angry, Denise, forgive me, I won't say anything about it to my aunt.'

Denise looked at me with suspicious eyes. 'Promise?'

'I promise you, dear Denise.'

'Even if I take down your trousers?' she asked, after two
seconds of silence.

Blushing, I murmured: 'No.'

> And then, under the influence of a sensation altogether new to me, I added: 'You can do everything!'[4]

This is domination with a very light rein indeed. Far from being an act of violent coercion, the passage above is the story of a seduction – even a conspiracy. The process whereby coercion becomes consent is achieved by old-fashioned coquettishness rather than intimidation or violence. The dominance displayed by the girl depends, in the last analysis, on her emotional rather than physical powers. 'If you do that, I won't love you any more' is pure moral blackmail. Nonetheless it works – and once it has worked, it is a tool which is put away for ever. Hereafter, and the reader may take my word for this, Denise is entirely, conventionally dominant, the narrator completely passive, and what the reader expects to happen happens.

The ability to apply emotional or moral pressure when necessary is therefore a recognised attribute of the dominant, no less than the desire or readiness to administer physical punishment. The willingness to accept pain at another's hands for reasons other than direct physical intimidation – in other words, when it is theoretically an option rather than an inevitability – is also, equally clearly, an attribute of the submissive.

It cannot be denied that these extensions of the dominant and submissive roles into psychology and word-play add complexity to the relationship. There is more to dominance and submission, it seems, than the mere infliction and acceptance of pain. The dominant must 'win' – that at least is an immutable part of the script – but the ways in which this is to be achieved are not restricted to simple domineering. It might even be said that the less a dominant domineers, the more effective the dominance.

---

4. *Monsieur Paulette.* The quoted passage (my translation) is taken from a letter to the author forming, with other letters, an appendix to the novel. The publication of readers' letters (or fantasies) in such a form was common in *fin-de-siècle* (and later) French erotica, since there were so few newspapers or magazines willing to print discussion or fantasy on these topics.

Casilda smiled. 'You know what I'm like, Tony darling,' she murmured, and then, after gazing at me fondly in silence: 'Shall I fetch the stick? . . . I realise I deserve it.'

At my nod she went to the chest of drawers, remarking lightly: 'The bottom drawer, I assume?' and a hint of anxiety crept into her voice as she added, 'This one?' handing me the long, fine, flexible malacca cane.

I pointed to the armchair by the fire. 'Bend over,' I ordered sharply.[5]

The second passage resembles the first most obviously in that once again there is a compact between dominant and submissive; but it is taken one degree further. The submissive actually volunteers for corporal punishment, accepting it as her dreaded due and a necessary preliminary to reconciliation, which she desires. No permanent diminution of status is implied – rather the contrary. She has chosen an honourable and romantic course.

Nor does the process by which dominance and submission merge one into the other end here. As we have seen earlier, and shall again, one may often find, in fiction of various kinds, scenes where the supposed submissive actually pleads with the *soi-disant* dominant to exercise dominance. At this point we run headlong into the most famous of all associated paradoxes.

The first thing I want to make clear is that I am not a 'False Dominant'. Have you heard this theory? I forget where I first read it but it has always seemed to make sense to me. A False Dominant is a person persuaded against her deepest inclinations into assuming the mantle of the Dominant in order to gratify the Submissive – who is of course both a 'False Submissive' and in all probability the 'True Dominant'. According to the theory, the True Dominant in a relationship of this type is the person who engineered it in

---

5. *A Gallery of Nudes.*

the first place, no matter what appearances may dictate at any given moment.

My darling, cast your mind back to the moment our relationship began. Who was the instigator, you or I? Did you manœuvre me into taking charge, or did I simply take charge? Which of us two was it who first sensed the hidden nature of the soul opposite, realised that it meshed exactly with one's own, and unleashed the sequence of events that now holds us firmly and joyously enclasped?[6]

Relationships of this level of complexity clearly do not depend upon a single element. Pain, hitherto the supposed sole *raison d'être*, is revealed as only one of a cocktail of considerations, mental, physical and atmospheric, which together form the flagellant experience. Indeed, it comes later rather than earlier in most scenarios, and is dependent for much of its quality, even for its legitimacy, on its sequential ancestors.

To understand how flagellation works, we must therefore put aside – for the time being – all other questions, including that of pain, and examine instead the first, all-defining link in the chain: the scenario.

---

6. *The Queen of the Grove*, pp. 116–17.

8

THE SCENARIO

All the world's a stage . . .
William Shakespeare, *As You Like It*, vii, 139

We live in an age which is called democratic, and whatever else it may truly be, or stand for, democracy is the enemy – the classic opponent – of hierarchy. Since dominant-submissive relationships, temporary or permanent, require hierarchy as a *sine qua non* (you don't generally chastise your equal), those who mine real life for sample scenarios are unlikely to strike pay dirt. For so successful has democracy proved – especially since the spectacular defeat fifty years ago of one great rival, fascism, and the no less spectacular (if so far less bloody) recent collapse of the other, communism – that, in the civilised West, convincing everyday examples of hierarchical relationships based ultimately upon physical dominance are becoming increasingly difficult to find.

The near-abolition of physical sanctions in schools, their total abolition in prisons or as a judicial penalty, the tightly guarded exclusiveness of the world's remaining harems, the abolition of slavery, the elimination of feudal nobility, the quasi-extinction (except for the wealthy) of domestic service, the conceptual annihilation of the ancient rights and duties of husbands . . . one by one, the traditional settings and *dramatis personae* have been swept away. Settings for conventional seductions have also suffered serious attrition: the modern couple cannot afford the honeymoon suite, are not allowed to light a log fire because they live in a smokeless zone, avoid cornfields because both suffer from hay fever and one of them is allergic to pesticides, and dare not make it on the moonlit beach for fear of armed muggers.

Dominant-submissive couples seeking to create convincing miniature worlds in which their games may acquire some depth are therefore obliged (1) to reinvoke the past in some form, (2) to exploit a contemporary situation or (3) to create an outright fantasy.

The selection of one of these categories, and the subsequent empirical refining of a satisfactory scenario within that category, may well depend in turn on participants' alter-ego ambitions. If a submissive male sees himself as a naughty schoolboy, then for him an ideal scenario is the old-tyme classroom, with his partner automatically cast as the Stern Schoolma'am or Governess. If he prefers to envisage himself as a recalcitrant slave, then the punishment room or dungeon[1] is the place to be, with his partner transformed into an implacable, authoritarian – yet self-controlled – dominatrix. Where the need for outright fantasy or role play is less overt and all-encompassing, the dominant-submissive couple may find delight and fulfilment in domestic discipline scenarios, without costumes, apparatus, props or *noms de fouet*.

Most dominant-submissive couples and individuals find themselves more or less at home within one or the other of these basic scenarios. There may be many practical reasons. For example, teacher-and-pupil events are less likely to involve either restraint (bondage) or very severe castigations, since these are not in context: whips and handcuffs are also not likely to be used, for the same reason. So if the passive partner is uneasy about being tied up, or does not wish to be treated with undue severity, or desires to feel that he or she is being corrected rather than tormented, then either the pedagogic or the similarly controlled domestic discipline scenario is likely to be an instinctive first choice.

---

1. It should be made clear that this rather frightening word is simply 'SM-speak' for any room fitted out for the administration of punishment. Most 'dungeons' are suburban back rooms transformed (probably temporarily) for the purpose.

Cultural familiarity is another reason for choosing one or the other of these relatively 'authentic' scenarios: we are all acquainted with examples of domestic or pedagogical authoritarianism, and many of us can remember when demonstrations of disapproval from these quarters were likely to be accompanied by physical punishment. Even when one has no direct experience of such events, our culture is still replete with such scenes (see chapter 1). Physical discipline is still very much part of our tradition, and its imagery, if not the actuality, is alive and well and being renewed night after night in many anonymous, pleasant homes around the Western world.

Scenarios may be 'one-act plays' – self-contained events with their own rules which take place at ordained intervals but are otherwise discreetly embedded within a 'normal' lifestyle – or they may be extended to cover much longer periods: weekends, holidays, even lifetimes. They may involve couples or larger groups. Many people who are attracted by domination and submission become such passionate devotees that the practice steadily makes its way to the forefront of their public selves. Here it is hard to say where the scenario stops and real life begins, and certainly an exhibitionistic and promiscuous element (by no means confined to flagellationists) may be involved – as in the case of the rubber-clad revellers in nightclubs. Some, like the writer and academic C.S. Lewis, who spent the middle part of his life meekly and apparently happily under the thumb of his partner – a relationship that was thought, by some of Lewis's intimates, to have a flagellatory or at least disciplinary element – and the great Australian composer Percy Grainger, who lived and dreamed of whipping, are unsuccessful in concealing their proclivities. Others, like the nineteenth-century poet Algernon Swinburne and the mid-twentieth century dramatist and producer Kenneth Tynan, hide them from the world at large but make no secret of them among their friends and acquaintances, who are so numerous that it amounts to the same thing. Still others, like T.E. Lawrence (of Arabia), are reasonably discreet but, in the end, not discreet enough; and others, like William Gladstone,[2] three times Prime Minister of Great Britain, keep it a dark secret throughout their lifetimes, confiding their feelings and fancies only to private documents – which also usually turn out to be not discreet enough.

Use of the word 'scenario' implies a construct: something artificial, if not arch, full of pitfalls for the self-conscious – at least until the lines have been learned. It is important to realise that for many who are attracted to domination and submission it is this aspect of their lives which is natural, even real, and the rest which is bizarre and outlandish. They feel perfectly at home in their private hierarchical world of obedience, discipline and penalty, and alienated by the egalitarian late twentieth century which persists in knocking vulgarly at their windows. They cannot change the world, and are usually wise enough not to try; instead, they do their best to shut it out.

HOME, SWEET HOME

'But how do you put it into his mind?'

'As a joke to start with. Find fault with him on some account. Suppose that he's unpunctual. Then you can say, "Next time you are late I shall have to whip you." Watch how he reacts. If he seems to relish the idea, if he says, "Oh, you wouldn't do that, would you?" you'll know he's nibbling. "Oh, yes I will," you'll say, "and it won't be a laughing matter, I can promise you." . . . Then one day you will produce a whip, or a birch – there's a lot to be said for a birch. It stings rather than bruises; you show it to him and say: "Do you see this? This is for you next time you're late. One stroke for every minute." As likely as not he will be late on purpose.'

A Spy in the Family

---

2. These revelations concerning Gladstone's private life only came to light in the 1960s.

The crime may be venal (lateness, untidiness, forgetfulness) or more serious (insolence, disobedience, telling untruths). It may be real, or something made up on the spur of the moment ('That's the third time you've forgotten to call me "Mighty One" since dinner . . .'). The dominant *dramatis personae* may be the couple's real, everyday selves (the lover, the spouse), temporarily transformed into authority; or for the purposes of the exercise they may go further and assume different personalities – the Stern Aunt, Wicked Uncle and Severe Stepmother are all popular choices – possibly donning special costumes to do so. But the setting is always the same: one's ordinary home life in all essentials (give or take the rearranging of an item of furniture or two), with an added ingredient of physical punishment.

Domestic discipline is probably the least pedantic of the main scenario types, for although formality, even ritual, may be involved, the fundamental nature of the setting allows much more ad hoc variation. It lies very much at the disciplinary as opposed to gratificatory end of the scale. That is, what takes place – the entire event from start to finish – has a 'moral' purpose: the correction of a fault. It is proper, ineluctable and ultimately beneficial, and always parental in style, for even when spouse corrects spouse as spouse (or 'employer' corrects 'servant'), the corrector has temporarily placed him- or herself *in loco parentis*. The older, or wiser, or more authoritative, chastises the younger or more immature as a single, discrete, self-contained act; before returning, after a suitable interval and observing all necessary 'decompression' rituals, to his or her real self.[3]

The actual place of castigation need not be specified overmuch, so long as it conforms to the domestic ideal: though of course there are traditional locations for the physical correction of sins within a family context: the bedroom, the study, the boxroom, and, in North America, the traditional woodshed.

---

3. This, of course, may be one and the same, since for many couples who enjoy this type of relationship, it is a continuous affair, and therefore as real as can be, though they may still conceal all evidence of it from everybody else in their lives.

As into the woodshed Elizabeth went
To atone for a moment's domestic dissent,
She spied out an object that could cause her some pain,
She spied out an object that looked like a cane.

Why it looked like a cane to her gaze was because
A cane was the actual object it was—
And swung at the end of her father's stout arm
It looked like a cane that could do her dire harm.[4]

Few of us have woodsheds or even boxrooms, and in most cases
the bedroom will be the chosen venue, not least because it is also
the ideal location should the act of discipline transmogrify, in
due course, into the act of orthodox love. It is also the most private room in any house and therefore an ideal place to store or
conceal any punitive objects or other impedimenta (including
costumes) which may be called into use. Appropriate instruments of chastisement include the hairbrush (back of), the
slipper and, most of all, the palm of the hand – very much at the
'humane' end of the range, as we shall see in due course, though
canes, paddles, straps and even riding crops may also be
involved, since these more severe implements are still within the
domestic context.

It may surprise many readers to learn that systems of mutual
domestic discipline – with spankings for misbehaviour given
from adult to adult – have been seriously propounded in the
past as valid ways of settling arguments and misunderstandings
between married couples. In 1930s America, Mrs Dorothy
Spencer, an ordinary housewife, produced just such a scheme
and publicised it widely.

The idea of a modern spanking is to administer punishment
when it is needed – then make up and forget the whole incident. In this way, every disagreement is effectively closed

---

4. P.N. Dedeaux, *The Woodshed*.

before it has time to ferment into serious discord – to grow into hatred or an indifference which even a great crisis may not be able to heal.

The couple that has every difference out when it arises is not likely to build up an antagonism that can be settled only in the divorce courts.

Also, modern spankings and whippings, correctly administered, tend to improve dispositions, increase domestic happiness, create a much more desirable spirit of unselfishness, and eliminate much other unpleasantness.

The operation of the Plan calls for unselfish devotion to high ideals. It calls for willing submission, and the loyal obedience to a co-operative system of beneficial discipline.[5]

She had clear ideas about the scenario to be adopted:

When a spanking is to be given, the wife is directed to go to her room and get ready. This means she is to undress and wait up in her room until her husband comes up to discipline her.

She must not argue about the matter – beg to be let off – or show any sign of resentment. She must obey without a word. When her husband enters the room there should be no delay in carrying out the discipline.

It is best not to say a single word during this period.

The wife should quietly place herself across her husband's lap – after he seats himself on the edge of the bed. Holding her in place, in the age-old spanking position, he begins spanking her. His duty is to do a thorough job – taking the utmost pains to do it right.

The spanking over – and still without speaking – the husband should let his wife up, then quietly leave the room.

It is the wife's duty – after dressing and drying her tears (if the spanking has provoked any) – to go to her husband, then

---

5. Dorothy Spencer: *The Spencer Spanking Plan* (c. 1936).

129

thank him for administering the discipline, and kiss him.[6]

Since Mrs Spencer ardently proclaimed herself (and her husband) followers of her plan, it is a charming picture that presents itself as a result of reading these passages. But this was no one-way relationship. In a passage addressed specifically to husbands, she declared:

> Remember, when you sign a Spanking Agreement with your wife TWO THINGS HAPPEN. You gain the right to *spank* her – she gains the right to *whip* you. It is NOT a one-sided affair! American women are too independent in spirit to approve of any System that does not give them EQUAL RIGHTS and PRIVILEGES.[7]

In fact, somewhat more than equal, as the differential between spanking and whipping implies. In fact she uses the latter term in the age-old generic sense: whips as such are out.

> Under Spencer Rules a girl or woman can be spanked with the palm of the hand only. No other spanking agency can be used – not even a light strap or ruler. [On the other hand] Men are to be whipped. A light leather strap, a wooden paddle or ruler can be employed to administer the punishment with [*sic*]. Wives must use extreme care, however, not to cut the flesh, raise welts or injure the recipients in any way.[8]

What could be more humane, or have a higher motive? And all with a proper regard for the sensibilities and capacities of the weaker sex! But for all its author's concern that brutality should be avoided, and that such affairs should be fundamentally loving in character as well as egalitarian in spirit, the Spencer plan never caught on in a big way (so far as anyone can ever know),

---

6. Ibid.
7. Ibid.
8. Ibid.

almost certainly because of its egalitarianism. Although individuals may indeed switch from mode to mode, such changes of character usually take place with different partners. Two-way discipline with the same partner works against the flow of hierarchy that is a vital part of dominant-submissive relationships, consensual or otherwise. But whatever her personal proclivities, as a citizen of the world's then-largest democracy Dorothy Spencer had little choice but to build the national political credo into her plan. Alas, at the time the Spencer doctrine was first propounded – as now – American women were indeed 'too independent in spirit' to accept the licensing of male-over-female situations, even on a spasmodic and reciprocal basis. Similarly, in 1936 the self-image of US manhood was at an apogee of masculinity, and American gentlemen were unlikely in the extreme to accept an arrangement that allowed their wives to wallop them on the bare bottom with a leather belt for, say, driving at a speed greater than 40 mph – one of Mrs Spencer's *bêtes noirs*.

Nowadays it might be a different story – at least so far as American men are concerned.

THE HAPPIEST DAYS

Soon the world had a fifth quarter, called School, presided over by an omnipotent deity called Miss Farrow, who knew everything, and who was so supremely great that you never realised her smiles might be intended for you, and who on terrible occasions wielded the cane upon such small boys as dared to be naughty. That cane was much more to be feared than any possible smacking Mother might give.

C.S. Forester, *Brown on Resolution*

Few modern Westerners have ever been permitted inside an authentic harem; most of us have never been part of a household where domestic servants are employed; but all, or nearly all of us have been to school, and, in the West, as everywhere, the classroom is the place that most of us first come to associate with discipline, particularly when based upon the sanction of corporal punishment. If schools as the term is generally understood have been in existence for, say, 2,000 years, then it is only in the last 1 per cent of that time that schoolteachers have begun to abandon (or have been deprived of) their ancient privilege and duty to administer physical correction to the lazy, the inattentive, the badly behaved and the tardy.

For many if not most of us, the schoolroom has always been, and remains – despite what educationalists might prefer to think – a place of foreboding and anxiety. Decorating classrooms with infant art to brighten the atmosphere is to acknowledge this in the most telling way; like piped music in the dole office, or TVs in prison cells, a cosmetic face-lift to conceal the hard fact that the subject's presence amid all this creative endeavour is not to the smallest degree optional. Moreover, as he early learns to recognise, the schoolchild's role can never be any other than subordinate. In recent years schools have learned to put on a happy face, so to speak, but although a few of the more traditional pedagogic techniques are falling out of use, the coercive note is never very far below the surface and will easily be uncovered by those of individualistic or irritant bent who persist in scratching at the surface of order, or who simply do not wish to be part of the proceedings at all. School remains a place of discipline, and although sanctions and 'disincentives' have changed somewhat (evolved, as educationalists would claim), as a concept, and an everyday event, punishment remains firmly on the agenda.

School is a classic hierarchy: it compels attendance and obedience, and attempts to compel loyalty; it exerts discipline by means of reward and punishment; it frequently allows – or, more often, compels – those within its walls to wear special clothing proclaiming their status; and it arranges its ranks and the transmission of power in the classic feudal pyramid (principal, deputies, senior staff, staff, senior pupils, junior pupils). All this is held somehow to be effective training for the democratic way of life, but in fact impresses the opposite social principle – hierarchy – on the youthful mind.

There are many arguments for compulsory schooling, nearly all of them ultimately economic; and as much to be said against it, principally, but not exclusively, from a libertarian viewpoint. However, such as the system is, Western society has been committed to it for well over a century, with no sign whatever of imminent change. Indeed, the contrary is true: since the triumph of economic imperatives over all others (otherwise known as the Industrial Revolution) the rulers of countries who have accepted this hypothesis have prudently taken thought for tomorrow's prosperity by ensuring that as many as possible of their future citizens spend the most vital part of their lives in a world fundamentally harsher, and certainly more hierarchical, than anything they will subsequently encounter. No wonder the imagery of the classroom is so potent, its very symbols – desk, blackboard, ferule – instantly and universally recognisable. Is it so strange that, for some, the memory lingers on?

If one were to make a judgement based exclusively upon a scrutiny of the smaller display advertisements in journals like *Forum*[9], then the school scenario is perhaps the most popular of all in the British flagellant's world. These ads are almost always placed by 'professionals', for most of whom all scenarios are necessarily much the same. For a professional to continue to prosper in the face of so much competition (there are a lot of display ads in *Forum*) she must regulate her menu to attract a clientele. To judge by the number of 'stern schoolmistresses' offering their services – either directly or via a 'chatline' – a very great number of male passive flagellants actively wish to pass time being treated, and possibly dressed, as naughty schoolboys, and are prepared to pay for the privilege.

One should beware of such a judgement nonetheless, since it is based on the marketplace and on no other research. Here a distortion may well have crept in, because, of all scenarios, the classroom is perhaps the most difficult to set up and maintain. It is pedantic and equipment-rich and can seldom be discreet. For

9. A long-established and, *sui generis*, respected British sex magazine.

this reason it is extensively featured by the pro community. Nobody else can acquire, store and maintain the infrastucture.

This can be minimal or, as we shall shortly see, elaborate and authentic to the level of an art form. Few 'schoolmistresses' go so far as to furnish their disciplinary environments with globes of the world, though some have acquired blackboards and chalk, a good few go in for caps and gowns[10], and probably a desk or two[11], with writing materials (for there may indeed be a period of 'writing' before the big moment arrives), pens, ink and rulers (the latter possibly serving a secondary purpose). And of course there will be instruments of physical chastisement appropriate to an old-time schoolroom: the cane, the strap, possibly the birch rod.

> Ten minutes after you enter my classroom a sense of security returns. You soon realise: here is someone who will keep a very close eye on me, make sure I do my best and punish me if I don't. You find yourself sitting up straight, concentrating and enjoying the peacefulness that comes when someone else is absolutely in charge and all you have to do is be obedient and do your best.

> I should here make it clear that moderation and leniency are shewn where necessary. If a pupil has not received corporal punishment since schooldays long ago, or if, as often happens, she is someone who has never been punished but is drawn by the thought of punishment, then care is taken to

---

10. In Britain, schoolteachers traditionally wore academic gowns and mortarboards. At my own school, forty years ago, masters certainly wore gowns, as did prefects, but I never saw a mortar-board in my life outside the pages of comics like *Dandy* and *Beano*, and the covers of Billy Bunter books. The image, however, remains incomplete without this curious item of headgear – so potent a symbol that in England it still serves as an 'instant graphic' for 'school' or 'teacher'.

11. The more enterprising and craft-conscious 'doms' take the trouble to acquire real school desks (at auctions, etc.), since these generally have the patina of use and are instantly evocative of the *milieu*. Problems can arise when a very large male client is invited to seat himself at a desk made for a human being of approximately half his dimensions. Hoping to be diminished by the experience, he finds himself instead swelling to Brobdingnagian proportions. This can spoil things for those with no sense of humour.

ensure that the discipline is fair and appropriate. On the other hand, for those pupils who are able to receive the cane, and deserve and need firm handling, strict, hard punishment is freely given.

No one is ever punished for ignorance in my classroom, only for laziness in the matter of learning corrections or forgetting the rules. This fairness is especially necessary with those girls who were born after the end of the 1950s and who have had slack and casual schooling rather than an effective formal education. I once had to teach a girl the alphabet because she had received so little education!

Let me summarise what happens when a pupil comes for a lesson. You arrive and are given a short interview. You are then taken to the schoolroom and the rules of the classroom are explained. These you are expected to repeat to me. The lesson begins. Work such as a spelling test and mental arithmetic are given in the first lesson. You will not be punished for initial mistakes, but you are expected to remember the rules and shew respect and to learn any corrections before you are tested. The punishments are given at the level which I believe to be appropriate for the girl concerned and may vary from person to person in severity.[12]

As the above passage (which is an authentic deposition) makes clear, the school scenario can appeal to male and female alike; the primary difference being that while the masculine version of the fantasy is (almost) always heterosexual, the feminine equivalent, while adhering every bit as precisely to the pre-war boarding-school atmosphere[13], and invoking corporal punishment

---

12. *Sweet Retribution*.
13. As defined, for most of them, in the schoolgirl fiction of that and later periods, an entirely English literary genre which has no equivalent in other cultures and, together with pony books, still forms a central part of the middle-class Englishwoman's dream childhood. Such books are very numerous, have abundant charm, and are full of kindly dominance and sweet submission (albeit with the use or threat of the rod barely to be found).

even when most girls' schools of the target period seldom if ever employed it, is more often centred upon its own sex.

When women do a thing, they do it properly. The story of St Bride's, an establishment operated a few years ago in the Republic of Ireland, drawing its exclusively female clientele from professional women able to afford both the fees and a lost week or two on the wild and remote north-west coast, is one of the most remarkable of recent years, and was the subject of a series of newspaper exposés in the mid-1980s. (The author of the above-quoted passage was one of the moving spirits behind that enterprise.) This is not the place to tell the full story – if indeed it can ever be told – but it may be worth mentioning that, in the view of many of those who attended, both the schoolroom and the atmosphere were entirely, utterly authentic; rows of genuine school desks, a peat stove, high mistress's desk, blackboard, chalk, exercise books, slates – and the cane. 'It was like stepping back a hundred years in time,' records one correspondent.[14] 'It was all absolutely perfect – immaculate. Within about half an hour I felt like a fourteen-year-old from an Angela Brazil story.' Except that Miss Brazil's stories for Edwardian English schoolgirls barely mention the subject of corporal punishment.

As for the latter, the ladies who conceived and ran St Bride's remain adamant that this was never the central point of the exercise (as it would most likely be for men). It was the atmosphere that was all-important, 'not merely a classroom, but a whole world'. If corporal punishment was used (and my sources affirm that it most certainly was), the newspapers were never able to prove it conclusively; even so they managed to spoil the ladies' opening day, at which the local mayor officiated. As for the locals of the tiny fishing village of Burtonport, they were seemingly well aware of the essence of what went on up the hill, but, in the manner of the Irish, were entirely tolerant of the eccentric ladies and indeed rather liked them.

The experiences of male aficionados of school discipline are

14. Deposition made to the author.

seldom so refined, and it can be difficult to maintain the atmosphere in the light of certain commonly encountered inadequacies.

> The problem with most professional schoolma'ams is that they are professionals first and 'schoolma'ams' a long way second, if at all. I don't like to be a snob or make myself out to be superior, because I am not, in any ultimate sense – far from it – but I am far better educated than any professional 'headmistress' I ever met and can't keep a straight face some-times. One once told me, during some sort of written 'test' I had to undergo, 'You ain't spelled that proper – bend over!' I burst out laughing, which more or less brought the session to a close there and then. Atmosphere is the really vital thing, since after all you are trying to recapture the kernel of your childhood, to cast yourself back in time. It's difficult at the best of times and needs all the help it can get.[15]

The nature of the school scenario is control – and calm. Whatever may happen in real life, and some fiction, there is no question, within this world, of peremptoriness, injudiciousness or assault. The 'teacher' does not lose her temper – the disci-plined atmosphere extends to her, too. Like domestic discipline, events proceed at a measured pace. The 'pupil' enters the class-room, possibly dressed beforehand in appropriate garments. He or she is seated at a desk or table, and 'tested' on such skills as spelling, maths or geography. It hardly needs to be stated that this preliminary is a mood-inducing interlude, which also usu-ally plays another part – the furnishing of a 'reason' for punishment. The correction of the fault then follows . . . and so the long day wears on, until the client's time is up.

Although almost all school-based scenarios are one-to-one events (in which case the 'schoolmistress' is more properly a 'governess'), there are some pedagogues *manquées* who are so

---

15. Deposition made to the author.

devoted to the idea, usually because they themselves have been touched by this same passion, that they go much further and, like the ladies of St Bride's actually set up 'adult schools', very much like the role-playing holidays in which participants may act out an Agatha Christie-style whodunit in a suitable country house, or spend a week living as an Iron Age farmer, or a day as a Civil War soldier. These entirely respectable activities have many passionate devotees (especially, for some reason, the last-named) and are widely considered to add charm and originality to the recreational scene.[16] While the law has no objection to people playing at mass slaughter by means of sword, pike, musket and cannon, or to the simulation of a homicide, it takes strong exception to people seeking to recapture (or exorcise) what was for them the essential note of their schooldays – an experience, be it remembered, that the same law compelled them to undergo.

There are therefore very few 'adult schools' in being at any one time, and again with the exception of St Bride's, premises are not usually permanent and the 'school' is therefore peripatetic.

At the time of writing the longest-running of these 'adult schools' is the Muir Academy, based in Herefordshire and usually operating in the general region of England's south-west. Established in 1988, it is the brainchild of a lady I shall call Prudence[17], whose husband, 'Guy' takes care of all logistic matters. 'Schools' are held about eight times a year and last two or

---

16. A curious phenomenon of recent years has been the appearance of Victorian schoolroom tableaux in places like museums of childhood, heritage museums, etc., around the country. Many of these establishments set up 'schools of yesteryear' in which visiting children may dress in Eton collars, pinafores and button boots to play at being a schoolchild of long ago. All of these make some reference to caning or strapping, though in deference to the politically correct, these staged events are hedged about with dramatic circumlocutions which obscure the full impact of the original experience. For example, the 'schoolmistress' will smack the edge of her desk rather than the child's hand with the cane or strap. If those who stage such scenes imagine this lessens children's interest in such matters, I respectfully submit they are mistaken.

17. Her 'stage name' is Prudence Prim, Ph. Dom., MCP. Readers may decode these abbreviations for themselves.

three days. They are therefore 'boarding schools'. Classes range from six to a dozen persons, of both sexes[18] (with a 3:1 male-female ratio). Everybody dresses the part: short trousers and blazers for the 'boys', gymslips for the 'girls'[19] and cap and gown for the headmistress. There are desks, inkwells, exercise books and all the proper school equipment.

Prudence recalls:

I had always wanted to go to boarding school as a real child. As an adult my fascination for CP naturally centred around school-style games. So it followed that the ultimate school fantasy (as an adult) would be to go to boarding school. I began searching through any CP literature I could find in the hope that something of the kind existed somewhere. I could find nothing, except a report (in a Sunday paper) about some ladies in Ireland who were running a boarding school for young ladies only [St Bride's]. Unfortunately at the time, much as I wanted to, I did not have the resources to go all that way.

I confided all this to my boyfriend, who is now my husband, who asked me why I didn't start my own school. It wasn't quite what I had in mind, but with his help and encouragement I did just that. Like most things the Muir Academy started small, with just two male pupils. In the early days I was not just the teacher, but the cook, secretary, bursar – the lot! It was hard work, and I could not have succeeded without the help of my husband, but most of all it was fun.

As Miss Prim, the headmistress, has grown, matured and developed in the years since her creation I have developed an insight and understanding of the CP scene over a much wider field than I had before. This had naturally been centred around my own desires. Now I understand the

---

18. Or rather, all three sexes, since there is a regular contingent of 'boys-who-would-be-girls'.

19. And 'boys-who-would-be-girls'.

needs of others and how to help them fulfil their fantasies I get a lot more pleasure from my own.[20]

The cost of such a weekend compares to that of a three-star hotel. Muir Academy 'pupils' fall into two categories: regulars, who come back again and again, and occasionals.

They come from all walks of life, from those with high-powered jobs with a great deal of responsibility to factory workers with mind-numbingly boring jobs; and of course housewives and househusbands. Once in the academy they are all equal. The common bond that binds them together is love of role-play, especially in the school scene. There is no upper age limit so long as you can cope with the excitement, and are twenty-one or over.[21]

In the United States, with a longer tradition of 'liberal' education than the British, the school scene is less in demand, though many individual dominatrixes offer a scenario broadly based on the same principles, with the all-American paddle[22] replacing the all-British cane. But there is no American tradition of school uniform, so this particular dimension of the schoolroom world is wholly absent from US practice.

UPSTAIRS, DOWNSTAIRS

The relationship of mistress and maid is more like a family relationship. The purpose of the mistress is to protect and cherish the maid. To look after her. The purpose of the maid is to love and serve her mistress . . . it is a fact of life that some people are happiest to serve and be protected, and other people are happiest to rule and protect . . .

---

20. Deposition to the author.
21. Ibid.
22. See Chapter 11.

Discipline may take many forms . . . from a basic minimum acceptable in a civilised society, to the very strict regime preferred by some mistresses and maids (and let us be clear from the very beginning, when a maid enters a strict household, she does so because that is what she chooses and prefers).

When the Wind is Free

The practice of chastising domestic servants was once considered perfectly normal. Samuel Pepys records that he whipped a maid with a birch 'broom' for delinquency[23], and no doubt well into the last century there were masters and mistresses of households who followed his example, long after it became nominally illegal, by means of a little judicious blackmail – the threat of being 'turned off without a character' (sacked without a reference) was a nightmare in Victorian Britain, which of course had no system of social security. But certainly within the last century and a half householders have had no such rights: for most people alive today, even domestic service itself is a curiosity from the past. Very rich people still have maids, and occasionally mistreat them[24], and there are many middle-class families who employ nannies (a vastly different species from the legendary dragons of yesteryear), but the idea of giving, say, a twenty-one-year-old Swedish au pair a spanking for staying out too late, or failing in her duties, is preposterous (even if some employers wish it were not).

Nonetheless the servant scenario enjoys considerable appeal. It is, after all, one historically authentic way in which one might be at another's beck and call and subject to discipline. Substantially, it is a variant of the ordinary domestic discipline

---

23. *Diary*, 1 December 1660.
24. A fairly recent case to appear before the British courts concerned two Saudi Arabian princesses, domiciled in London, who terrorised, starved and whipped (with electric flex) their Filipino maid. Knowing no English, the poor girl had not known how to ask for help. The two princesses were fined substantial amounts.

scenario, with the employer *in loco parentis* and the servant in the role of the delinquent child. It might be said that this is a favourite of those who desire to be treated in the manner of a child without having to assume a juvenile persona.

Even more, and remarkably, it is a popular way for those (usually males) who desire to use the freedom afforded by fantasy actually to change sex.

'Are you interested in the position?' She asked, looking directly at me. i was most conscious of Her eyes; they seemed to be examining the innermost corners of my mind . . .

'Position?'

'Yes, christopher, the vacant maid's position.'

'Maid position!'

'Why yes. I have found that young men like you are very suitable, after proper training of course, to serve as a Lady's maid. Here, let me show you something.' She reached into a closet and took out a classic black satin French maid's uniform trimmed with white lace and held it up against me. 'Definitely suitable for you. In fact, you have lovely legs that I am sure would be enhanced by stockings and proper high heels.'[25]

This, it must be conceded, is a variety of flagellationism that must appear almost self-evidently 'perverted' (if harmless); the grown man, dressed as a French maid, being ordered about and now and again soundly thrashed by a woman.[26] In fact, like the

---

25. *A Lady's Sissy Maid*. The use of lower-case personal pronouns for the (male) narrator and upper-case for the woman is a convention of 'femdom' (female domination) literature. 'Sissy maid' is an American term.

26. A famous instance of this peccadillo was publicised during the trial (for procuring) of Dr Stephen Ward, during the Profumo affair of early-sixties Britain. Various call-girls gave evidence of flagellationary parties, at which an unnamed man played the role of a French maid, though wearing a mask. He is believed to have been somebody very important, but although various candidates have been put forward, he remains unidentified to this day (possibly because of the libel laws).

boys-who-would-be-girls of the Muir Academy, it represents a blending of two distinct desires: the wish to be within a disciplined environment (with the appropriate penalties) and the desire to do so in the clothes of the opposite sex. It is almost exclusively male. This is a subject to which I shall return, since in its various forms (and there are several distinct ones) it plays a considerable part in the flagellant fantasies of a great many men. For now, let me stress that the male maid does not wish to pass as a woman, or even greatly to resemble one externally: he dresses as a female because he has been *required* to do so, 'against his will', for reasons which may vary from a supposed need on his part to be made to empathise more strongly with women to simple caprice on the part of the 'mistress'. So widespread is this fancy that, at time of writing, a 'school' for such 'TV maids' (or 'sissy maids') is flourishing in New York City, very much on the lines of the Muir Academy, but with training in hoovering, dusting, drinks-serving and cooking replacing algebra, spelling and arithmetic. In fact the Muir Academy, responding to a perceived demand, also offers limited courses of similar type, as Prudence confirms:

> We do have maids and maid training, but they are in the style of a school maid. No frilly French maid uniforms as worn by useless maids, only fit for decorating a shop window. The maids here wear real maids' uniforms, be they male or female, and they work properly on real domestic chores.[27]

There is another, less often encountered, variant of this scenario in which the 'domestic servant' takes an active (dominant) part in a flagellationary event. Victorian and Edwardian nannies and governesses of the traditional type were, of course, employed within a household (while not being quite classed with the rest of the servants, if they could help it), and these two classes of

---

27. Deposition to the author.

female most certainly had the right to correct their juvenile charges physically. But these punishments should be classed under domestic discipline and school discipline respectively. However, it was also not uncommon, in the last century and perhaps later, for the task of whipping a naughty child to be given to ordinary (albeit specially selected) servants. An obscure novel by the English mid-century novelist Mrs Henry Wood supplies the prototype:

Lady Lydia was in a silent passion: she, to do her justice, believed in this instance that Tom was guilty. When did she not believe him guilty of anything he might be accused of? Had Jarvis brought her a story that Tom had drunk the Severn dry she would have given ear to it.

Baby though he was, or only little removed from one, she hated him with a bitter hatred. The fear of Sir Dene had not let her entirely crush him; but she was doing her best towards it in a quiet way, always working for it safely and silently.

'Wicked, crafty reptile!' cried Lady Lydia, her eyes blazing with light. 'Poor dear Otto, poor inoffensive boy, riding without thought of treachery, must have his pony startled and his life endangered by you! Take him, Dovet, and whip him. Whip him well.'

Dovet seized Tom by the hand to bear him off to punishment. It came pretty often, this chastisement, and Tom neither might nor dared resist. On trying to resist once, the whipping had been redoubled: in Dovet's hands, a strong woman, Tom was not only powerless but conscious that he was so . . .

Tom took his punishment with tears and sobs; not loud but deep: if he had made much noise Dovet would have treated him to a double portion. She kept an old thin leather slipper for the purpose, and whipped him soundly . . . he was put to stand, by Dovet, in the corner of the room, his face to the wall. Leaning his head against it, he cried

144

away the smarting pain, and finally cried himself to
sleep.[28]

The above passage, while distressing (and intended to be so), is
nevertheless extremely rich in flagellant imagery – the mistress's
eyes 'blazing with light'; the culprit 'not only powerless but conscious he was so'. The same scenario is hardly better illustrated
in a deliberately erotic novel of exact contemporaneity:

'How dare you, child, behave to me with such disrespect?
Stand up, take your hands out of your pockets, and repeat
your hymn.'

'I won't. I'm too big to be made to say verses like a baby.'

'You won't! Is that proper language to me? Now listen,
Kathleen, for I'm in earnest. I warned you yesterday that, if
this occurred again, I would make Stiles whip you. She is
willing to do so and has the rod prepared; beg my pardon
and say your hymn, else I shall ring the bell and bid her
fetch it.'

'I don't care. I won't say such silly stuff, and you need not
try to make me, for I *won't* do it.'

'Will you beg my pardon?'

'*No!* – whip indeed! I'll slap Stiles well if she dares to lay
a finger on me.'

'Tush, child, that is the rankest nonsense, Stiles will have
my orders for what she does, and you'll find she won't be tri-
fled with. O Kathleen, you have never been punished yet,
you don't know what it is to be whipped with a birch rod.
Think of the disgrace, the pain – and what it will cost me to
see you beaten, and not able to interfere consistently with my
duty as a Christian parent? Must I ring? Stay, it wants five
minutes to nine; I will give you till then to think better of it.'

So saying, she laid her massive gold watch upon the table
where it could be seen by both. The rebel flung her Watts into

---

28. *Dene Hollow* (1865).

145

the corner, folded her arms, and seated herself, legs up, on the window stool. The short frock scarce covered her lolloping legs, and she faced the old lady, who, recalling the different manners of the day, shook her head and sighed remorsefully.

A pause ensued big with the fate of Kathleen Kennedy. Had the maid been tender-hearted as the mistress, the upshot would have been of little moment, but such was far from being the case. Only lately emancipated herself from birchen rule, Miss Stiles gloried in the acquisition of the right end of the rod, and the privilege to whip a lady. A gentleman would have pleased her better still, but Hedworth was out of the question. While binding the branches of the stinging birch and visiting the rod when made, she had pampered her fancy with visions of reddening flesh, kicking limbs and shouts of pain under the cuts inflicted by herself in requital for sundry slaps bestowed on her by Kathleen, who, by the way, might have contended with an elephant. Stiles stood five feet ten in her stocking soles; 'Granny's Grenadier' Hedworth called her; her will was strong, her arm muscular and brawny . . .[29]

This version of the Upstairs, Downstairs scenario is not widely popular, being rather difficult to arrange, but for some passive flagellants, the idea of being chastised by a servant (at the orders of another person) has undeniable poignancy.

THE CONFESSIONAL

Thrice three times upon Candlemas-day,
Between Vespers and Compline, Sir Ingoldsby Bray
Shall run round the Abbey, as best he may
*   Subjecting his back*
*   to thump and to thwack*

---

29. *The Romance of Chastisement*, pp. 22–23.

Well and truly laid on by a bare-footed friar,
With a stout cat-o-nine tails of whipcord and wire
                              The Ingoldsby Legends

The idea that confession is good for the soul is very ancient: penance and absolution are later, purely Christian additions. This transaction once lay at the heart of Western religious practice, but in the fifteenth century, the collection of impulses and theories collectively known as non-conformism broke out in the form of Lutheranism, Calvinism and related doctrines, most of which vehemently denied the necessity of intermediaries (priests) for any purpose whatsoever. Europe was plunged into a ghastly war – not yet quite ended – and when the dust had settled the greater part of the continent and its larger offshore islands had divided into two camps: non-conformists (Protestants) in the north and (Ireland excepted) the west; the faithful (Roman Catholics) in the south. Only in the Catholic lands did the practice of confessing one's sins continue wholesale[30]; it has all but disappeared from the tradition of the Protestant countries, along with rosaries and Hail Marys.[31] The Roman Church persists in the system of penances, and many of these remain corporeal (how could it do otherwise, when so many of its early saints achieved canonisation chiefly by prolonged and extreme mortification of the flesh, with chains and metal scourges and devices to cause pain at every single moment of the day, and to prevent sleep at night; to such an extent that some of them undoubtedly died of it?).

---

30. The notably lesser interest in domination and submission shown by Mediterranean (i.e., Roman Catholic) cultures may well be due to the continuation of the custom of ritual confession, penance and absolution in everyday life, to a dwindling but still substantial degree. This fundamental Christian ritual, essential for the doctrine of redemption from sin, clearly also fulfils other criteria: it is hierarchic, humbling, and involves the willing acceptance of punishment imposed for one's own good.

31. Except in those cases where, for various historical reasons, both forms of Christianity co-exist on roughly equal terms within the borders of a single state, e.g., in the United States, France and Switzerland.

Nevertheless the urge to tell all is, or can be, a form of healing in its own right – the basis of much successful 'therapy' is the simple ability of the therapist to listen. With the introduction of the penance motif as the sole means for obtaining absolution, the transaction becomes more ambitious and complex. A dynamic and corollary have been set up: if you do such-and-such (penance), you will be cleansed from sin (for the time being); but if you do not, you will remain in a condition of sin (forever). More to the point – the essence of the non-conformist objection – the position of the third party within the equation has been changed: from being a confidant he or she has become a judge, not only hearing the confession but pronouncing the penance and bestowing forgiveness. Even more significantly, this plot actually requires the culprit to initiate proceedings – one of the few legitimate ways in which a submissive may do so yet remain submissive.

Since Christianity has been in existence priests have heard confessions, and for nearly as long they have pronounced penances. One really cannot say how long they have exploited this advantageous position to obtain personal (and highly sinful) gratification, but the systemisation, at a very early date and by various hands, of the corporal punishments that might be allocated in penitential contexts suggests a keen general interest in the topic that perhaps exceeded the requirements of simple guidance to priests. There were rules, and rules within the rules, constantly revised and subject to considerable local variation. It is probably safe to say that the tradition of penitential flagellation was kept alive by the monastic communities during Europe's Dark Ages; and since what few children were educated in those days were taught by monks, these holy men kept the tradition of the pedagogical rod alive as well.

This long association of cowl and lash has generated two distinct and even opposed flagellatory traditions with appropriate scenarios. One is 'righteous' – private and proper confession and penance. The other is its hooligan opposite: anti-clerical, libidinous, orgiastic, not to say occasionally satanic, quintessentially de

Sade (or Hellfire Club) and therefore eighteenth-century in style. In fact or fiction, it is probably the most determinedly depraved scenario of all, an approach which is said to lead to disappointment in most cases (at least, one hopes so). And it is difficult to stage.

WHOLLY OWNED

In the final hours of the night, when it is darkest, when it is coldest, just before dawn, Pierre reappeared. He switched on the bathroom light, leaving the door to it open; thus, a square of light was thrown upon the centre of the bed where O's body, slender and curled up, made a small mound under the blanket. This Pierre snatched away, in silence. As O was lying on her left side, her face towards the window, her knees somewhat bent, it was her white flanks reclining on black fur that met his gaze. He removed the pillow from under her head; politely, he said: 'Would you please stand,' and when, helping herself by holding on to the chain, she had reached her knees, he took her elbows to aid her the rest of the way up; she faced the wall, her forearms and her elbows were flushed against it. The illumination cast upon the bed was faint, since the bed was black, and while it made her body visible, his gestures were not. Without being able to see, she guessed he was lessening the length of the chain and refastening it by another link so as to keep her upright; by the pressure on her neck she felt the chain go taut. Her naked feet rested flat upon the bed. Nor did she see that, at his belt, instead of the leather whip, he was carrying a black crop similar to the one with which she had been struck earlier but struck only twice, and they'd been flicks rather than cuts she'd received at the pillory. Pierre's left hand settled upon her waist, she sensed the mattress give a little, for he had put his right foot on it to give purchase, he was bracing himself. And then, at the same moment, O heard a whistle in the gloom, and she felt an atrocious blaze rip across her flanks, and she yelled. Pierre plied the crop with all his might. He did not wait for her screams to sub-side, and four times over began anew, taking care to deliver the blows either above or below the spot he had been work-ing over previously, so that the pattern of welts could be distinctly seen.

Pauline Réage, *The Story of O*

We now come to the most widespread, and, dare one say it, pop-ular of all flagellant scenarios: slaves and their masters or mistresses. Slavery is such an emotive word, evocative of ancient atrocity, that one must remember that in the ancient world it was not necessarily a despised state (though of course it could be); nor was it necessarily permanent, since faithful service might be rewarded with manumission, a certificate of freedom. In fact, in the later Roman, Mongol and Chinese empires, slaves often rose to become powerful in the state's affairs, even to com-mand armies. Although brutal or foolish owners of slaves might indeed behave as they pleased – being property the latter had no human rights – in practice physical punishment was rare enough, since by damaging the slave one was damaging one's own goods.

This is indeed the essence of the slave's condition: to be the absolute property of the owner. Under such an arrangement, be it malign or benign in style, the subordinate abdicates all respon-sibility for his or her actions; becomes the servant, child, plaything, full-time victim of the dominant. It is a deliberate (since of course here the 'slavery' is entirely voluntary) rejection of the civic rights hard won over the last two centuries in most Western countries: and no doubt those who had the winning of them would be the first to label such inclinations 'perverse'.

In one sense slavery is an extreme form of childhood: the polit-ical conditions are so nearly identical. The owner enjoys, and exercises, on a regular basis, all possible rights over the slave, short of serious injury or death (even in historical slave-owning societies these ultimate sanctions were often subject to some form of higher authority). These certainly include physical punishment. But other factors – dress, posture, permitted modes and times of speech, even bowel movements – may also be under the control of the dominant, as the following remarkable manifesto confirms.

BASIC ETIQUETTE FOR THE SLAVE

These ground-rules must be insisted upon by the Superior and obeyed from the start or else the slave is to be rejected as unfit material for manipulation.

One: He will at all times address the Superior as 'Mistress' or 'Master'. You may require him to use a variation on this title such as 'Divine Queen Goddess', 'Father Confessor', 'Supreme Being', as you like. He may not use the possessive pronoun, i.e., he may not say 'My Mistress' as he is the one owned.

Two: He may never present himself at full height but remains below the waist or knees of the Superior on his knees or belly. Enjoin him to keep his little paws to himself, at his sides or behind him. No other pose is acceptable.

Three: He may open his mouth only to answer direct questions, fetch, or receive dispensations. If he absolutely will irritate the Superior's ears he must ask permission to speak, which is in itself an act of disobedience.

Four: The slave ought to be compelled to appear in some form of humiliation-wear you have chosen. Standard humiliation-wear is the underwear of the opposite sex and will do until you designate a special role for him such as hooker, or baby, when he will be dressed accordingly.

Five: If he is employed as maid, try to relieve yourself of the bother of constantly ordering his inept person about by training him to anticipate your wishes. He will of course be punished for assuming too much, for trying to make his uselessness indispensable.

Six: Impress the slave that he ought to submit gratefully to your orders, whims and cruelties, that an incredibly fortunate intervention of fate has bestowed upon his pathetic life a purpose he would never have realised by himself. That the Superior considers him material amenable to manipulation ought to be a source of joy, for most slaves are so essentially worthless it is a waste of time trying to make anything of them.

Seven: Hammer it into his pea-brain that he has no will but to do as the Superior commands him to do. The Superior may delegate this authority to another whom he must obey as unconditionally as he would the beloved Superior in person. For the Superior knows best what the slavish soul needs, and unless he puts his full trust in her influence he will remain a craven dog without a home.[32]

An important point about 'modern slavery', exemplified by the above passage, which, incidentally, was written by one of New York's better-educated 'doms' – is that it is more broadly 'masochistic' than other forms of flagellationism. The use of the rod of punishment is part, but only a part, of an overall scenario that pursues the domination-and-submission theme into all available areas of human interaction. There is a further important distinction between this and other scenarios: the Dominant is not required to be just or caring (the for-your-own-good motive); may

---

32. *The Correct Sadist*, pp. 17–18.

indeed, perhaps should, be tyrannical and capricious, even (as above) contemptuous. In the slavery scenario, there is no immediately obvious moral note, no greater good or higher purpose being exalted by servitude, humiliation and unremitting discipline. What is being gratified is one person's desire to surrender completely to another – and, in an ideal match, the other person's desire to dominate and oppress at will, without censure or legal penalty.[33] Since of course the slavery condition is ultimately voluntary, it may at least be admitted that such relationships require, from the submissive, an extraordinary amount of trust.

This scenario, thought to be typical of flagellationism, is in fact one of those crossroads where several peccadillos rub shoulders. A 'slave' may be made to dress in clothing either transvestite or fetishistic (or both); may be tied up or otherwise restrained for long periods (bondage); may be whipped, verbally humiliated, or even urinated over: all these activities are designed to reinforce the nature of the relationship, which is absolutist.

This woman who shaped the direction of my inner life employed some means which for me were more decisive than the indubitably violent, but also transient, pain of the whip. To give you only one example. She would wind a rather heavy steel chain around me which I had to wear against my bare body day and night and to the lock of which she alone had the key. If she wanted to punish me for inattentiveness, she would pull the chain around me tighter for a day so that the pain finally became almost unbearable. She also liked to have me kneel for hours on the sharp edge of a wooden plank and especially to ride it; above all, she would lock me up for the slightest infraction. During the vacation season probably not a day went by in which I was not locked up in a tiny dark cell for five or six hours, wholly unclothed

---

33. Though legal penalties will still apply if the dominant goes too far – needless to say, the law recognises no such bargain.

and without being able to make a move, since she either chained my stretched out arms to the ceiling of the cell, or locked me up crammed tight. Often, when she went to sleep, she also tied me to her bed for the whole night, and I was forced to stay there in one spot for ten hours, motionless. Today my blood still runs hot and cold when I recall the smile that hovered around her eyes and mouth during such scenes. In this way, however, she very soon brought me to the state that she desired and to which I myself was irresistibly drawn by an innermost compulsion. I carried out her wishes, which at first I often resisted, at a mere wink of her eyes. Indeed, I tried to anticipate them and tried all the harder to carry them out to her full satisfaction. . . . Finally, things went so far that the littlest thing in my life, every step that I took, every movement that I made, every word that I uttered was occasioned by her will, so that my own will was wholly excluded. She punished the least inattentiveness sharply and pitilessly, and not once did she ever take back or soften a punishment once pronounced . . . She had so trained my body that, even if I were not wearing the chains on my naked body, it would not have been possible for me to bare it before another person without becoming deeply ashamed. I was wholly her own, nothing else without her.[34]

But just as by no means all historical slave-owners resembled Simon Legree[35] or Ann Palmer[36], so there are slaves and owners whose relations may be on an altogether more kindly basis – even if flagellation is involved. A little-known dramatic work by

---

34. Letter from Dr Eugen Beyer to Edith Cadiveç, 26 March 1926 (*Confessions and Experiences*, pp. 276–77).
35. The fictional (but authentic) wicked slave-owner of *Uncle Tom's Cabin*.
36. 'The White Witch of Rose Hall'. In the late 1820s Mrs Palmer inherited, under mysterious circumstances, the Jamaican plantation of Rose Hall, near Montego Bay, and thereafter ran the estate with legendary cruelty and notable employment of the whip. She was murdered in a slave uprising of 1834 and to this day her name is *obeah* (taboo) in Jamaica.

the Victorian poet Algernon Swinburne captures this relationship exquisitely.

Frank: I have bled for your sake some twenty times a month, Some twenty drops each time; are these no services?

Imperia: I tell you, if you use me lovingly, I shall have you whipt again, most pitifully whipt, you little piece of love.

Frank: God knows I care not. So I may stand and play to you, and you kiss me as you used to kiss me, tender little side-touches of your lip's edge i' the neck.

Imperia: By my hand's hope, Which is the neck of my Lord Galeas, I'll love your beard one day; get you a beard, Frank; With such child's cheeks.

Frank: Madam, you have pleasant hands, What sweet and kissing colour goes in them, running like blood!

Imperia: Ay, child, last year in Rome I held the Pope six minutes kissing them before his eyes had grown up to my lips. Alas!

Frank: What makes you sigh still? You are now so kind; the sweetness in you stabs mine eyes with sharp tears through. I would so fain be hurt. But really hurt, hurt deadly, to do good to your most sudden fancy.

Imperia: Nay, live safe, poor little red mouth. Does it love so much? I think when schooltime's off then thou wilt be no such good lover. Dost thou know, fool Frank, Thou art a sort of pleasant thing to me I would not lose for ten kings more to kiss? Poor child! I doubt I do too shamefully to make thy years my spoil thus: I am ashamed. Would not thy mother weep, Frank, cry and curse that an Italian harlot and dyed face made out of sin should keep thee for a page, to be kissed and beaten, made so much Her humour's jesting-stock, so taught and used. As I do here.[37]

The slavery scenario is more overtly fantastical than others (for what could be more fantastic than slavery in this day and age?) and the suspension-of-disbelief element is correspondingly higher. As a result more excesses – of taste and style as well as punishment – occur within its considerable ambit. A great deal of nightclub SM takes this apparent form. For example, it is by no means uncommon for the more celebrated 'doms' to be accompanied, in their public appearances, by personal 'slaves'. More often than not these gentlemen will graciously be allowed to pick up every one of the bills, and may indeed have been selected on this basis (a curious and not entirely creditable inversion of the traditional mistress-slave relationship). The difference between him and the classically put-upon sugar daddy is surely only one of degree.

---

37. *Laugh and Lie Down*. In later life Swinburne became of the most notoriously public of all flagellomanes. This unfinished three-act comedy was written while he was still at Oxford, probably in the year 1860. It is especially interesting because (at least, to judge by the vast amounts of dreary 'floggerel' he later wrote) his version of the *œuvre* is more usually notable for its homophiliac nature – the dominants in *Lesbia Brandon* and *The Flogging Block* etc. are exclusively male – whereas at this earlier stage it is clearly, if passingly, heterosexual.

9

LORD AND MASTER

. . . And all the men and women merely players.
William Shakespeare, *As You Like It*, vii, 139

Although in an earlier chapter I presented the several components of the flagellant experience as if they were serially and
causally connected, as in all human activities there is a degree of
lateral blurring and in some situations it may be hard to say
which stage (if any) is the true parent of another. To a considerable extent this is true of the relationship between the scenario
and cast of characters, since while the latter may be indeed
derived from the former, it is also possible that the reverse may
be true – for example, that a particular dominant's desire to play
the schoolmistress (or a submissive's wish to be treated as a
naughty pupil) itself dictates the schoolroom scenario, rather
than the other way about. The two are closely related and each
imposes constraints of context upon the other. (Even apparently
minor details – for example, a particular instrument – may serve
as the initial entry point to a scenario, and contextually dictate
nearly everything else about it. One might call such scenarios
fetish-driven.)

Context is vital in all works of dramatic intent. If, in an otherwise conventional country-house thriller – all tweeds, tennis
courts and locked gunrooms – the killer is revealed, when
unmasked, as a shape-shifting extraterrestrial, the reader may
conclude that context has slipped somewhat. In orthodox
courtship, the Romeo who shows up at Maxim's for the seminal
dîner à deux wearing latex underpants and a gas-mask – and

nothing else – will be left in no doubt he has made an error of context. And the husband who deems it appropriate to clothe himself Waffen-SS-style – boots, steel helmet and Iron Cross, Second Class – in order to administer a mild and voluptuous domestic spanking to his wife is also, we may feel, missing the point a trifle. Context is an iron mistress, and those who flout her dictates had better possess the strength of character – or the style – to carry the thing off. Which is not to say it cannot be done.

The *dramatis personae* of any flagellant event are more limited in the number of available roles than a stage play. At its simplest, and most usual, it is a duet: dominant and submissive. However in the more complex set-pieces and fantasies the cast may expand. There may be a witness, 'accidental' or otherwise; perhaps more than one. The witness may take a more substantial part in proceedings, by acting as an assistant (the flagellants' equivalent of group sex). There is a considerable number of variations on this third-party theme, each with its own particular nuance; yet they do not really affect the central drama, which, as in orthodox courtship, is ultimately one to one.

Some of these hierarchical personæ are rooted in distinct historical periods: the Slave-Master is a nineteenth-century plantocrat, the Schoolmistress is the early twentieth-century model. Her sibling, the Governess, is derived from mid-Victorian times (although the two sister archetypes were once virtually indistinguishable). Many well-known submissive personæ are also associated with particular periods, fanciful or otherwise: the classical/mediæval Slave or Pageboy; the early twentieth-century Schoolboy or Girl, the richly dressed androgyne of the *fin de siècle*, the undutiful 1920s French Maid brought to book. Others are of no particular temporal derivation, or such a confused one that it amounts to the same thing: the Naked Slave; the Bad Girl; the Naughty Boy; the Rocky Horror Transvestite Nun.

It is important to restate what has already been said in an earlier chapter, that the degree of realism in such situations may vary greatly, depending on the commitment of the participants.

The hypothetical husband who smacks his wife across his knee every now and again – with her consent, maybe even at her suggestion – as an enjoyable preliminary to lovemaking, is only pretending, *pro tem*, to be an authoritarian. He is acting a part, just as she is – in their everyday lives they may well behave entirely differently – and the success of the production will depend to a very great extent on their suspension of disbelief, itself enabled or crippled by the quality or otherwise of the available thespian skills. A temporarily submissive female may require a very great effort of will to convince herself, even on the most fleeting and insubstantial level, that a very short man with a squeaky voice who keeps mispronouncing the Words of Power is actually a confident and capable superman, whose jaw is firm, whose word is law, whose intentions are not to be flouted, and whose iron-muscled thighs constitute an altar on which all sins will be washed clean. That it can be achieved at all is probably due to the overmastering qualities of fundamental sexual desire. ('Close your eyes and imagine he's Sean Connery.')

Similarly, for an otherwise obliging passive partner to forget or fluff the appropriate responses can result in a deep and immediate sense of anti-climax for the would-be dominant. The 'culprit' who giggles excitedly as she's hauled across her lover's lap for 'the hiding of your life', or who murmurs 'Mmm . . . that's nice!' as her knickers are peeled down to her knees, may be responding both honestly and intuitively, but it is also possible that she has not studied her lines properly, or worse, does not even realise what may be required. Nor is there any easy ad hoc way to correct matters, since there are few equivalents of the actor's prompt that do not run the risk of breaking the spell.

I found myself in the middle of a beautiful, gilded and well lighted room. I must admit I was astonished at what I saw there. A man and a woman, apparently his mistress, were sitting at one end of the room near each other. What made it so odd was the man, none too young, was dressed in a child's coat of a pinkish colour and a bonnet of the same style. The woman was tall with large, dark and fiery eyes. Her hair was the color of ink with pearl strands and flowers running through it. She wore a foreign dress of cerise taffeta with golden spangles. From her exotic beauty and the weirdness of her head dress, one might almost have imagined her to be the Sultana of Constantinople. I sat down quietly without saying a word, for a moment not having the slightest idea of how to address them. Both got up. The man spoke first, assuming a childish and lisping voice. 'Good day,' he said. 'Good day, nurse, good day!' I saw my part at once. 'Yes, my children,' I replied. 'Here I am. And how are you today.' 'Really, nurse,' he exclaimed, 'you did well to come and keep Rosette quiet.' 'Nurse,' cut in the lady, quickly, 'Johnny is at fault, not I.' 'Nurse,' he continued, 'because she is taller than I she steals all the cakes and the jam tarts from me.' . . . I listened to all this as serious as a bishop; it is fatal to laugh. I made the little boy approach me in the centre of the room. 'Little rascal,' I said, 'come nearer. What have you done with all your money and who has eaten up my jam?' 'He, nurse,' exclaimed Rosette. 'He ate the nut jam.' 'Over here,' I said, 'in this little corner.' He followed me as though ready to weep, into the space between the bed and the wall. I made him kneel and took off his breeches. Under my apron I had two stout birch rods, one of which I laid on the bed. With the other, after I had lifted his coat and listened to him say the most amusing things, I gave him a dozen strong blows. 'Nurse, oh nurse,' exclaimed the lady who was on the other side and could not see very well, 'if you do not spank Johnny before everyone in the middle of the room, it won't do.'[1]

As every good actor knows, the effectiveness of the performance increases with commitment. Method acting involves intense preparation and fanatical concentration, with the object of doing

---

1. *A Lady of Quality.*

as much as possible to conceal – from himself no less than anybody else – the actor's real personality, so that the role he is playing fills the vacuum: he *becomes* the character. The danger lies in departing too far from reality in pursuit of realism. The man who 'becomes' an irate, punitive husband with such success that the severity of his slaps actually begins to exceed the mutually agreed limits has overdone things. The ideal lies in holding back in this important area while, in every other respect, striking a convincing note.

Then there are those relatively rare situations where the scenario is not a construct, but the real thing – or nearly. In other words, little or no acting is taking place: the transaction is genuinely, or mostly, punitive, and wholly painful. Here the archetypes come fully to life.

Disciplinary characterisations, therefore, fall mainly into two opposed but complementary groups: dominant and submissive; two modes: active and passive[2], two genders: male and female, and a variety of related personæ which may be adopted more or less wholesale, adapted, or ignored altogether. Even though these are, in the main, exactly what the lay reader might expect, given the scenarios in question, there are nevertheless considerable differences of style and nuance, and a surprising amount of regular migration from one persona to another.

Building a disciplinary personality to accord with the desires (which may never have been formally defined) both of one's partner and oneself can be a long and complicated process, more likely achievable by those in happy long-term relationships than by those given to one-night stands – which is a sound argument against promiscuity, in this as in all other areas of lovemaking.

Finally, although I have attempted roughly to systemise the

---

2. These do not necessarily correspond exactly to dominance and submission. Many events of this type take a form where the submissive initiates proceedings and may indeed occupy the driving seat throughout – in all respects save the most apparent one. The call-girl-client relationship is an excellent example of this kind of false submission.

range of classic disciplinary archetypes, chiefly by dividing them, as seems logical, into male and female (and beginning with the former), in this, as in all matters flagellatory, things may not be what they seem. What I define are roles, nothing more.

Flagellationism is not specific to hetero- or homosexual love, nor do gender-constrained dress codes always prevail. In no other field of human activity is there such freedom to move between genders and personalities, but it can be confusing at times for the voyeur.

THE NO-NONSENSE LOVER

Infuriated by her barbarous response to his advances, Michel grabbed her by the nape of the neck and jerked her forward with such force that she lost her balance and fell face down across his knees.

'You must be taught how civilised people behave toward each other,' he said.

While he held her head down by the back of the neck she was helpless, for all her kicking. He pulled up her skirt and under-slip to reveal a rump clad in almost transparent rose-pink silk. Her struggles became more frantic and her hands were pulling at his fingers to release herself. When that failed, she scratched at the back of his hand with her nails.

'Ah, would you!' he said, gripping all the tighter and wrenching her flimsy underclothes down to expose the pale skinned cheeks of her bottom.

'You behave like a badly brought-up child and you will be disciplined like one,' he said loudly.

He raised his hand and smacked her hard.

Anne-Marie Villefranche, *Plaisir d'Amour*

It is probably safe to say that in his ideal form this persona is the most popular male dominant of all amongst females of submissive inclination and neo-Gothic taste. In addition to possessing the usual romantic aces (good looks, wealth, style, a tragic background, an unruly comma of black hair falling over the right eyebrow), this fellow is also, when pushed (deliciously, he may have to be pushed quite hard), pretty unreconstructed. For 99 per cent of the time he will be a perfect gentleman. Driven to the brink, he is transformed into a masterful, expert and sensuous smacker of bottoms. But although he enjoys this duty, he never loses control, errs on the side of mercy, and once the final smack has been delivered, reverts to his former smooth, ironic self (which is not to say that he might not first take advantage of the erstwhile culprit's condition to convert one form of passion into its close relative). He is Lord Byron, Mr Rochester, John Wayne – and James Bond.

> He stood away and held her at arm's length. For a moment they looked at each other, their eyes bright with desire. She was breathing fast, her lips parted so that he could see the glint of teeth. He said unsteadily, 'Honey, get into that bath before I spank you.'
>
> She smiled.[3]

Goaded or provoked, he will warn once, and then act. And it will hurt – but not too much: that would never do. For he is neither a bully nor an obsessive, and for him the flagellation is only nominally a punishment; its prime duty is to serve as a catharsis, its secondary purpose is aphrodisiac. In other words, he is safe (a not unimportant consideration if you happen to be a submissive female). He is unlikely to favour any weapon other than his own hand, though slippers, hairbrushes or even rolled-up newspapers cannot be ruled out, if they are available (submissive females who incline towards other weapons are therefore obliged to stock the scene beforehand). His chosen position for the culprit is traditionalist to a fault: across the knee, the most intimate of all

---

3. *Doctor No*, p. 155.

postures. He is not likely to make a meal of it, or to impose extra penances or humiliations, though when it comes to preparing the culprit for punishment, he will certainly attenuate the process, as a lover might. He will maintain an air of cool amusement throughout. Afterwards, not even his tie will be crooked.

Our man walks a thin line between lover and parent, and will expertly and sensitively migrate this way or that as his senses tell him. Whenever he chastises without sex (he never does so without affection), he crosses the line from one persona to another. When the necessity for a parental manner has passed, he will become a lover once more.

This is a role many men would love to play. Few enough ever get the chance – or are sensitive enough to recognise it when offered, or bold enough to take advantage, or expert enough to do so effectively. The loss is not theirs alone.

THE STRICT FATHER

'I said eat it,' said Rob. He took a spoon, chopped some of the tagliatelle and held it to Pia's mouth. Pia kept her lips shut and breathed through her nose. 'Eat it.' With his other hand Rob gave Pia a sharp slap on the back of her head. It sent her forward against the spoon with such a jerk that she opened her mouth. The spoon went in. As Rob took it away he too was breathing hard. 'Now swallow.'

Pia looked at him with her small black eyes and spat out the tagliatelle. As with everything she did, the spit was direct and it landed on the tablecloth in a stain of tomato and gravy. Caddie gave a little hiss of terror, and Rob lost his temper.

He jerked Pia out of her chair and, in a second, she was face downwards across his knee. He turned up her skirt, showing her little rump outlined in snowy white briefs edged with lace. 'You asked for it; you shall have it,' said Rob, and, before all their eyes, he gave her a good spanking.

Hugh and Caddie sat too shocked to speak; Fanny was

white to the lips, only Giulietta watched with amusement in her eyes as if this were entirely natural. At last the sound of slaps ceased and Rob lifted Pia off that powerful knee.

Rumer Godden, *The Battle of the Villa Fiorita*

By no means all women believe that fathers who spank are monsters from the pit, but enough do, and in any case such approaches are under heavy fire from the social engineers. As we have seen (in chapters 2 and 3), spanking is out, and particularly so when it is the male parent who does the spanking, since males are more likely than females to derive gratification from the act, and are therefore considered more likely to administer spankings specifically in order to enjoy such sexual excitement. Does this cap fit? Despite the generic male-hatred that underpins so much 'politically correct' thinking, the latter part of this viewpoint is not, in my view, entirely without justification, for – I speak as one of the tribe – males in general do react more immediately than females to situations with sexual potential, are considerably less responsible, and much more ruthlessly self-centred. The dangers, such as they are, are certainly greater where males are involved in the active role.

Nonetheless the authoritative father-figure remains a powerful archetype in the imaginations of many women who already incline, unfashionably perhaps, to heterosexual submissiveness of one flavour or another. Older males are indeed more likely than callow youths to have developed the aura of power and command which so many submissives, not only females, find compelling. The ruthless use of personal power can be a powerful aphrodisiac, and what more expert way to demonstrate it than to give the uncompliant junior female a sound chastisement when she needs one? However, for the submissive whose impulses are specifically flagellatory (rather than generic) the Strict Father is not absolutely required to 'take advantage' afterwards. Indeed, for him to do so would be a violation of the trust given from 'child' to 'parent', and possibly out of context. He is godlike, a patriarch, possibly a tyrant, certainly authoritarian, and his punishments are, or can be, severe; but their motivation is never overtly sexual, and as a result he is seldom unjust. In real life he would be unbearable: but much sexual fantasy is unconcerned with real life, and the nice young man who is sufficiently adept to don the mantle of Grim Old Bastard when required, and who wears it well, may find that the change of character does not always pass unappreciated.

There are several sub-variants of the Strict Father persona, of which the most popular is the Old-Fashioned Employer. Manner and style are nearly identical, with the chief variances being setting and, of course, motive. The culprit has committed a serious lapse, which normally would entail dismissal, but she's been a good employee in other ways, so just this once . . . It's probably safe to say that this is a fantasy favoured by employers rather than employees, and without doubt it has been tried on in real life by employers, many times.

THE UNCLE FROM HELL

After supper came those terrible two dozen with the tawse. The tawse is a Scotch instrument of punishment, and in special favour with Scotch ladies, who know how to lay it on soundly. It is made of a hard and seasoned piece of leather about two feet long, narrow in the handle and at the other end about four inches broad, cut into narrow strips from about six to nine inches in length.

Alice had never seen, much less felt, one.

She was commanded to bring it to her uncle, and had to go for it naked – not even a fan was allowed! How could she conceal the least of her emotions? Oh, this nakedness was an awful, awful thing!

She brought it, and opened her book and knelt down and said:

'Please, uncle, give me two dozen with the tawse for being ashamed and trying to cover my nakedness, and for my disobedience.'

166

'Across my knee.'
'Across— your— knee.'

The Yellow Room

By contrast, the Strict Father's demonic sibling, the Uncle from Hell, is expected to take the fullest possible advantage of any temporary disciplinary authority that may have been granted to him. He is Sir Jasper Foulfellow of Victorian melodrama, and well known to students of erotica due to his many appearances in famous works of the period. Frank Harris, as well as the narrators of *My Secret Life* and *A Man with a Maid*, are classic wicked uncles, each a middle-aged rake with a seemingly enormous bank balance, apparently infinite leisure, prodigious sexual vitality and the ethics of a cruising tomcat. Although he can pose as a man of principle and a father-figure, whenever opportunity allows he twirls his moustaches and transmogrifies without hesitation into an unprincipled satyr. In many versions he is an unprincipled satyr from start to finish. He usually triumphs in the end.

This may appear to be a disturbing fantasy (some real uncles, and indeed real fathers, do indeed behave in this way), but in fact is not quite what it seems: its spirit is Dionysian and lustful, its main purpose to legitimise a change of mode, so that what begins as a quasi-judicial (i.e., non-sexual), parental chastisement may evolve into something more culminative when and if the appropriate moment arrives. The submissive therefore experiences two events in one – all 'without her consent', which removes from her shoulders any responsibility for the dastardly double deed. Whipped and violated she may be, but she is still 'innocent'.

THE SCHOOLMASTER

'Do you know why you are sent to school?'
'Scalding father.'
'No; you are sent to learn to read and write.'

'But I won't read and write,' replied Jack sulkily.

'Yes you will: and you are going to read your letters now directly.'

Jack made no answer. Mr Bonnycastle opened a sort of bookcase, and displayed to John's astonished view a series of canes, ranged up and down like billiard cues, and continued, 'Do you know what those are for?'

Jack eyed them wistfully; he had some faint idea that he was sure to be better acquainted with them, but he made no answer.

Mr Midshipman Easy

If young Jack Easy had been better read, even though he had never been to school, he would have been well aware of schoolmasters and the ancient peril they represented, and would have behaved more circumspectly. In the folly of his youthful ignorance he chose another course and suffered accordingly. Until very recent years, such has been the traditional fate of all save a very few lazy, tardy, disobedient or insolent schoolboys. The Dominie with the Rod is one of our most terrifying social archetypes; and not without reason. The immature mind, often incapable of comprehending what is really meant by prison, or even death, can usually visualise without difficulty the shame and pain attached to a beating. Until very recent times this sanction may be said to have been the chief dread of all children, particularly so when administered in a schoolroom, usually in public, by an adult male in the full flower of his authority and physical strength. School punishments, of course, have also been administered by women, and may be feared even more for that very reason, especially by boys (I shall deal with this in a later chapter); but without doubt the classic image of the pedagogue is male, if only because until only two centuries ago, this was – dame schools aside – almost exclusively a male profession.

Here is also probably the one disciplinary persona which needs little or no elucidation. We all know what a schoolmaster is: the type is surprisingly constant across cultures and epochs. A man, grave and learned, no longer young, faces a roomful of juveniles,

probably, but not always, boys. His demeanour is severe and formal, theirs is rigidly, unnaturally attentive. His discourse may
have something to do with this, but more likely the pupils behave
as meekly as they do because of the rod of punishment which will
be somewhere at hand, usually visible, maybe in the pedagogue's
grasp, possibly hanging from a hook awaiting the moment of its
next employment. In old Islamic, Chinese and Japanese prints it
will be a length of bamboo or rattan; in European woodcuts and
lithographs of similar vintage it will be a bush-like birch rod; in
twentieth-century English school-story illustrations it will be a
cane with a crooked handle, or a strap with a forked tongue, or
possibly an old gym-shoe lying on a desktop. The ferule is the
Schoolmaster's staff of office, his divining rod, his magic wand.
With it he can perform miracles; or, at the very least, enforce his
will. It is the rod, his willingness to use it, and his authority to do
so, granted by the community at large, which make him such a
figure of fear. Without it he is nothing, or nearly nothing.

Master Stockwood opened the register and drew a deliberate
line through Adam's name: at that moment it had the final-
ity of a death sentence. Then he turned to Nicholas and
commenced the homily which invariably preceded a flogging given outside Corrections, and as invariably contained
promises of eternal damnation if the culprit did not mend
his ways. In church, similar comminations, being spread
over the whole congregation, could be disregarded: in the
schoolroom, addressed to him personally, they alarmed
Nicholas considerably. He tried to shut his ears and his
mind; and was so far successful that he was half-taken by
surprise when the birch-rod was presented for him to kiss:
almost with relief he pulled himself together, knelt, and
touched his lips to it.

'Untruss,' said Master Stockwood, and stood up.[4]

---

4. *The Player's Boy.*

Here we see the Tudor pedagogue from which the archetype surely took its modern form in action; a learned man, perhaps even in holy orders (a legacy from the monkish educational tradition of the early Middle Ages), and both devout and responsible, using Holy Writ and long tradition to guide him in all matters of his craft – in other words, a frequent and unpitying wielder of the birch on his pupils. Throughout the centuries which follow, this archetype varies but little. He is Oliver Goldsmith's village schoolmaster, Washington Irving's Ichabod Crane, Fielding's Doctor Thwackum, the erudite and whimsical (therefore all the more terrible) Matthew Busby of Westminster School, the upright and devout Thomas Arnold of Rugby, nobly and unselfishly birching his flock towards salvation. In later years, he dispenses with the antique birch rod in favour of the more efficient and long-lasting rattan cane, but thrashes no less often and has lost nothing of his hereditary power and terror. He is the urbane and deadly Mr Bonnycastle, the beaky-faced martinet Samuel Quelch of the Billy Bunter stories, or the deputy prep-school headmaster Archibald Dunbar, to whose care ten-year-old George Curzon found himself committed, in 1869.

> He executed all or nearly all the punishments, whether by spanking on the bare buttocks or by caning on the palm of the hand or by swishing on the posterior. I remember well all three experiences. He was a master of spanking, though he used to say that it hurt him nearly as much as it did us. I remember that it was at about the fifteenth blow that it really began to hurt, and from thence the pain increased in geometrical progression. The largest number of smacks I ever received was, I think, forty-two. But comic to relate, I still remember the delicious feeling of warmth that ensued five to ten minutes later when the circulation had been thoroughly restored and the surface pain had subsided . . . with the birch he never gave me beyond ten or twelve strokes – and that for

some peculiarly grave offence – in his bedroom at night.[5]

This passage is notable for its complete lack of self-pity: 'comic' and 'delicious' are not feelings one normally associates with despotisms (although Dunbar, Curzon reported, was 'detested' by the majority of the boys, he had favourites, of whom Curzon was one). In fact both the archetype and the actuality were, slowly, beginning to be humanised. The Schoolmaster need not inevitably appear in the form of a frightening, thickly bearded tyrant king. He was growing younger, becoming far less remote, perhaps more like an older brother. This new pedagogue understood boys and their code of honour and respected it where he decently could. He was, or could be, a pal. But, like the fictional Mr Rose (of *Eric, or Little by Little*), he nevertheless remained the Schoolmaster and still, where necessary, wielded the cane. Yet although the latter hurt just as much as it ever did, it was now resented less than ever before, at least in fiction, solely because of the new bond of affection between master and pupil – unthinkable at any earlier period. An obscure short story by Roland Pertwee from a 1930s *Strand* magazine exactly captures this new, quasi-fraternal relationship:

It is the primary duty of a commander never to accuse on suspicion, but only upon established evidence. Byno dropped a pencil, stooped to recover it, and, in the fraction of time occupied in doing so, the villainy of Toby was unmasked.

As noon struck Byno dismissed his class, but added the rider:—

---

5. *Curzon*, p. 11. This episode in the early life of the future Viceroy of India has been almost entirely overlooked in favour of the slightly earlier (in fact immediately preceding) but vastly better-known period when young Curzon, together with his brothers and sisters, was under the charge of the most notorious of all real-life cruel Victorian governesses (see chapter 10). Young George therefore experienced unusually tough luck, even for a child of his class and era; though it seems he did not resent Mr Dunbar as he did Miss Paraman. No doubt it was all a matter of style.

'With the exception of Norman, who will remain.'

The rest filed out impressively and in silence. The door closed. Addressing Toby, Byno said:—

'You know why, of course?'

'Yes, sir.'

'And you know what it's worth?'

'Six, sir.'

'On the other hand, Norman, I could cancel your leave during "Half."'

'Half' was the half term break, and Sylvia would be coming down— and— oh, lor!

'Couldn't you make it eight, sir? My sister is coming down, and it would be frightfully difficult to explain.'

Byno mused over it.

'I'll fog the negative, sir, I swear I will.'

'That would be a pity,' said Byno. 'You exercised quite a lot of trouble and ingenuity to get it, and I might be glad of a copy. Still, rules are rules.'

'What about ten, sir?' Toby suggested.

Byno released one of his rare smiles.

'This isn't an auction room, Norman, and no doubt six will suffice.'

'Thank you, sir.'

'This is your first whacking?'

'Yessir.'

'Well, what do you think? Shall we get on with it?'

'Yessir.'

So Byno whacked Toby, dispassionately, but with zeal. Toby had had plenty after three. He pinched his nose very tightly to stifle emotion. The rest came and went. Presently it was over. Toby rose and did up his braces. Neither the man nor the boy made any further comment upon the business.

This is almost certainly the closest the Schoolmaster has ever got to a sympathetic public image; and for many – schoolmasters included – it remains the ideal variant of the archetype.

Perhaps surprisingly, the Schoolmaster is not greatly in demand within heterosexual flagellant scenarios, almost certainly because relatively few female submissives are emotionally involved in its dynamic. Unlike the United States, where the tradition is firmly the opposite, in Britain co-educational or mixed-sex secondary schooling is a relative newcomer: almost everybody over, say, forty years of age attended a school where the pupils were exclusively of one sex while the staff were nearly so. Since that time the complex contingencies of mixed-sex education have tended to level down all forms of discipline, not just the physical kind.[6] That dedicated and expert disciplinarian, the Schoolmaster, has been deprived of his main tool of trade, physical power over his pupils, and as a result is on his way into oblivion (accompanied by many other formerly authoritative male archetypes). In any case for a male teacher to apply physical punishment to a girl pupil has, throughout my lifetime, been a risky undertaking for the schoolmaster, and many who have done so, whatever their motives, have come to grief in the courts. Such was not always the case:

Mr Davis gave a portentous 'hem', and said, in his most impressive manner—

'Young ladies, you remember what I said to you a week ago. I am sorry this has happened; but I never allow my rules to be infringed, and I never break my word. Miss March, hold out your hand.'

Amy started, and put both hands behind her, turning on him an imploring look, which pleaded for her better than the words she could not utter. She was rather a favourite with 'old Davis', as, of course, he was called, and it's my

---

6. In theory, the introduction of mass co-education into Britain in the 1960s might have meant that girls would henceforth be disciplined in the same way as boys had always been. In practice, it resulted in boys being treated more like girls – caned a lot less frequently and a good deal less severely than before, and eventually – thanks to the Sex Discrimination Act as well as gradually spreading abolitionism – not caned at all. So matters stand.

private belief that he would have broken his word if the indignation of one irrepressible young lady had not found vent in a hiss. That hiss, faint as it was, irritated the irascible gentleman, and sealed the culprit's fate.

'Your hand, Miss March!' was the only answer her mute appeal received; and, too proud to cry or beseech, Amy set her teeth, threw back her head defiantly, and bore without flinching several tingling blows on her little palm. They were neither many nor heavy, but that made no difference to her. For the first time in her life she had been struck . . .[7]

This persona often takes a role in homosexual flagellant encounters of the traditionalist sort. The Victorian poet Algernon Swinburne is surely the classic example of a passive male fixated on the image of the authoritative, birch-wielding schoolmaster. At Eton, he would of course have encountered the most fearsome surviving form of the archetype. But today many older archetypes are passing away, or transforming into figures of fun, and the favoured 'dom' persona of most modern homosexual SM submissives wears not a scholastic gown, but a leather jacket bedangled with chains, leather trousers and intimidating boots.

For a few women the Schoolmaster (or his close relative, the Tutor) remains a fascinating if distinctly old-fashioned personification of male power. He too is a close relative of the Strict Father: the rod he applies (with reluctance) to his fair pupil is energised and directed only by a stern and sad sense of duty – it is for her own good – and each time he wields it her affection and respect for him grow. The famous mediæval story of the monk-philosopher Peter Abélard and his pupil, the nobly-born Héloise, defines this relationship to perfection.

Your lessons are, Master Abélard, priceless in all things Fransh; that is how I think; and your pupil, Master Abélard,

---

7. Louisa M. Alcott, *Little Women*.

how does she think? Proving herself worthy of your
attention is not that so? If not, Master Abélard, you must
punish her. A little touch of the birch on our hinder parts . . .
good for all of us, especially the young. A thing they know
well in convents is the value of— a touch of birch about the
buttocksh. Ishn't tha' so, Master Abélard? Am I not right?
Maybe the taste of it lingers in my niece's mind or elsewhere, and maybe not, for good accounts always came from
the convent; and good pupil wants no birching.[8]

Abélard accepted this *carte blanche* and whipped his pupil –
and, like the modern British schoolmaster facing charges of
indecent assault, though for rather different reasons, later
wished he had not.[9] Perhaps his is not, after all, the happiest
example.

THE TASKMASTER

'Did you order my horse?' shouted Randolph in an angry
voice.

A frightened expression appeared at once on the woman's
face.

'No sah, I didn't. I quite forgot dat yo' tole me to order de
hoss,' she answered, in a faint voice, glancing deprecatingly
at her angry master.

He flew into a violent passion – he was a most violent
man – the veins of his forehead swelling, and his eyes
gleaming with rage.

'Oh, you forgot, did you!' he exclaimed. 'I'll teach you to
forget my orders.'

Rushing at Dinah, who stood cowering, he seized her, and

8. *Héloise and Abélard.*
9. He whipped her; fell in love with her; eloped with her; and was recaptured
and gelded by her vengeful relatives. Héloise was put into a convent and spent
the rest of her days there.

sitting down at the end of the sofa, threw the great big woman across his knees, just as if she had been a little girl.

Dolly Morton

Here is almost certainly the most objectively unsympathetic of all male dominant archetypes, a thoroughly bad man, violent, cruel and even brutal. He is no gentleman, to say the very least. Not for him the judiciousness of the Strict Father or the Schoolmaster, nor the purposeful and ultimately gentle efficiency of the No-Nonsense Lover. He is an urbane, middle-aged, immaculately ruthless slave-driver, whose most famous fictional prototype is Sir Stephen in *The Story of O*, but who has role models throughout history, particularly in the last century, when the plantations of the southern USA were staffed by such creatures, called 'overseers', whose job it was to ensure that all those who laboured in the cottonfields did so to the limits of their capacity and beyond. If they failed, the whip or paddle would be employed without mercy, both to punish slackness and *pour encourager les autres*.

He is the male equivalent of the Slave-Mistress (see chapter 10), but in his original incarnation lacks her capacity to show occasional warmth towards those within her power. In fact, so decidedly unpleasant, if not downright dangerous, is the prototype that in his fantasy incarnation he is more often than not humanised to a considerable degree, naturally without relinquishing his essential ruthlessness and inflexibility, which remain his most attractive qualities to those of submissive disposition.

It was not one man who entered the garden, but a group of three. Yet two stood back in deference to one who advanced alone and slowly. In the tense silence, Beauty saw his feet and the hem of his robe as he moved about the circle. Richer fabric, and velvet slippers with high upturned curling toes, each decorated by a dangling ruby. He moved with slow steps, as if he was surveying everything carefully.

Beauty held her breath as he approached her. She squinted slightly as the toe of the wine-coloured slipper touched her cheek, and then rested upon the back of her neck, then followed the line of her spine to its tip.[10]

In one respect only does the Taskmaster resemble the Schoolmaster: that is, in being a preferred dominant archetype of male homosexual submissives. Perhaps the generally stronger tastes of males accounts for this, since there is little or no subtlety in the persona. He simply orders done that which he wants done, and if he is not obeyed promptly and efficiently, will use the whip. He may well use it in any case.

10. *Beauty's Release*, p. 37.

10

THE LADY
WITH THE LASH

Ah! Luckless he, and born beneath the beam
Of evil star! it irks me whilst I write;
as erst the bard by Mulla's silver stream,
Oft, as he told of deadly dolorous plight,
sighed as he sung, and did in tears indite;
For brandishing the rod, she doth begin
To Loose the brogues, the stripling's late delight;
And down they drop; appears his dainty skin,
Fair as the furry coat of whitest ermilin . . .

But ah! what pen his piteous plight may trace?
Or what device his loud laments explain –
The form uncouth of his disguised face –
The pallid hue that dyes his looks amain –
The plenteous shower that doth his cheek distain?
When he, in abject wise, implores the dame,
Ne hopeth aught of sweet reprieve to gain;
Or when from high she levels well her aim,
And, through the thatch, his cries each falling stroke proclaim.
William Shenstone, *The Schoolmistress.*

The conviction, among many of both abolitionist and feminist
opinion, that the physical disciplining of children by means of
the rod is a specifically male villainy, is not, to put it mildly,
founded in historical fact. As long as women have had charge of
children they have whipped them, in the home and also in

school. And if in general (and *The Rainbow* excepted) the Schoolmistress has not been guilty of the excesses of pure violence that call to mind Messrs Busby, Udall and Keate, she has frequently deployed a great deal more finesse, and her chastisements produce, for boys particularly, an almost infinite amount of humiliation: her distinct intention. Here lies the power and longevity of this truly formidable archetype, one of the most enduring of all flagellatory personæ.

But surely this humiliation is only the equivalent of the shame experienced by a female pupil physically punished by a man in front of boys? Certainly the pedagogues of both sexes of the seventeenth, eighteenth and nineteenth centuries birched the bare bottoms of both sexes without regard for dignity. But females benefited much earlier from the move towards propriety; and by the mid-nineteenth century it was increasingly rare for girls to be whipped by schoolmasters at all, let alone on their bare bottoms in public: they were still whipped, of course, but usually in private, and nearly always by their own sex.[1] For boys, no equivalent considerations obtained until much later.

The feminine archetype differs from her male colleague above all in the degree of refinement she introduces into punishment. What she lacks in physical strength she makes up for in a sense of ceremony, as the young Samuel Clemens (Mark Twain) discovered on his first day of school.

My school days began when I was four years and a half old. There were no public schools in Missouri in those early days but there were two private schools – terms twenty-five cents per week per pupil and collect it if you can. Mrs Horr taught the children in a small log house at the southern end

---

1. The classic literary example is Miss Scatcherd's birching of Helen Burns in *Jane Eyre*. This punishment was inflicted on the back of the neck, but at Cowan Bridge School for the Daughters of Clergy (the model for Lowood), girl pupils were birched on the more usual place, and it is likely that Miss Brontë bowdlerised this excoriation in order to conform to contemporary rules of propriety.

of Main Street. Mr Sam Cross taught the young people of larger growth in a frame school-house on the hill. I was sent to Mrs Horr's school and I remember my first day in that little log house with perfect clearness, after these sixty-five years and upwards – at least I remember an episode of that first day. I broke one of the rules and was warned not to do it again and was told that the penalty for a second breach was a whipping. I presently broke the rule again and Mrs Horr told me to go out and find a switch and fetch it. I was glad she appointed me, for I believed I could select a switch suitable to the occasion with more judiciousness than anybody else.

In the mud I found a cooper's shaving of the old-time pattern, oak, two inches broad, a quarter of an inch thick, and rising in a shallow curve at one end. There were nice new shavings of the same breed close by but I took this one, although it was rotten. I carried it to Mrs Horr, presented it and stood before her in an attitude of meekness and resignation which seemed to me calculated to win favour and sympathy, but it did not happen. She divided a long look of strong disapprobation equally between me and the shaving; then she called me by my entire name, Samuel Langhorne Clemens – probably the first time I had ever heard it all strung together in one procession – and said she was ashamed of me. I was to learn later that when a teacher calls a boy by his entire name it means trouble. She said she would try and appoint a boy with a better judgement than mine in the matter of switches, and it saddens me yet to remember how many faces lighted up with the hope of getting that appointment. Jim Dunlap got it and when he returned with the switch of his choice I recognised that he was an expert.[2]

Another refinement lies in the requirement for the punished

---

2. *The Autobiography of Mark Twain.*

culprit to thank his mistress for her late efforts on his behalf, as evidenced in the early nineteenth-century doggerel:

> Flip-'em, flap-'em over the knee
> Say 'Thank you, good Dame, for whipping of me'[3]

Punishment on the bare bottom was, of course, a devastatingly humiliating sanction. Even to threaten or refer to it produces huge feelings of shame:

> A teacher in second grade, saying to a pupil – a sullen boy, larger and taller than the rest of us – when he dropped a pencil and often when nothing had happened at all, 'Your father should take you across his knees and pull down your pants and give you what for!' Said in a light voice, ominous as a nightmare in its sweetness; once a week an uneasy wave of titters set off to lap across a hushed room, twenty-eight seven-year-olds bending their heads over their desks with a shame as inexplicable to them as it was pervasive.[4]

While to receive such a correction is, of course, the ultimate schoolroom terror.

> Me and a girl called Edna Whitfield were both called out by Miss Swinton. We both got up from our desk and stood in front of her. It was four or five minutes from home time. Miss Swinton said to us both that our handwriting was very bad, [and] that she was going to smack our bare bottoms. She told us both to stand facing the wall until the class was dismissed . . . I could see Edna Whitfield shaking and her face was pale. She was already sobbing. After the class was dismissed Miss Swinton called Edna to her. She sat on a chair, and she put Edna over her knees. Then she lifted Edna's

---

3. Quoted by Cooper (*HOR* Introduction).
4. *9½ Weeks*.

frock up, and she took her knickers down. Then she began to smack Edna's bare bottom. Afterwards she was told to stand facing the wall.

Then it was my turn. When I got there she started undoing my trousers. She took them down and put me over her knees. Then she began to smack my bare bottom, and tears came in my eyes. I felt my bottom stinging. When it was all over she put me off her knees . . . It was now half past four and the teacher made me stand facing the wall with Edna, and we were both still crying. It was half past five when the teacher let us go home.[5]

There is more than a hint of premeditation in the above episode – such considerations adding sharply to the flagellant's *frisson* (that he or she is the object of *very* special attention). Since it is supposed, by some, that when schoolmistresses have applied corporal punishment, they have invariably done so only at very short notice, as a last resort, or in despair – these factors naturally tending to exculpate the whipper – such planning ahead seems 'out of character'. Surely no woman could be so keen to punish that she actually devotes forethought and prior preparation to its execution? Special ceremonies, special punishment rooms, a range of weapons to suit every culprit's physiognomy . . . these trappings are surely specific to the male fantasy, as far removed from the essentially kindly and gentle nature of woman as can be, though one may note that in both *The Rainbow* and *My Brilliant Career* the attractive young *fesseuse* uses a weapon deliberately selected beforehand. However, unwelcome though it may be, on many occasions there is documentary proof of a quality of refined connoisseurship to rival if not exceed that shown by even the most dedicated male disciplinarians. The following episode – which

_____

5. Letter to *Janus* (spanking magazine), 1980. Unlike the majority of material which appears in this and similar publications, this particular anecdote has, in my opinion, the ring of truth.

is a genuine memoir – makes this point with considerable acuity.

I was invited to tea by the directress . . . After we had gone over all the details of the daily instruction program, we came to the question of discipline . . . 'And now,' she continued in a tone of great solemnity, 'it is my painful duty to explain what happens when they come before me. Since the founding of our orphanage in 1851, according to regulations, corporal punishments for serious infractions have been administered solely by the directress, and the instrument of punishment has always been the birch rod. A visit to the directress, therefore, is always viewed by the pupil as a sign of the greatest reward and likewise of the severest punishment. This has been the will of the founders. Therefore you must know that if you lead a girl into my office, she will inevitably receive a birching. This is administered to her exposed bottom, after she has been ordered to unbutton her bloomers. Little girls under ten are punished with willow soap rods; for the older ones a birch rod soaked in salt water is used. I always administer the punishment alone, without an assistant.

'After the teacher has registered her complaint with me, she leaves the office and the culprit remains. And now I shall show you how and where the punishments take place. My office is on the second floor, and adjoining it is a small room which in the beginning was set up as a punishment area. Please come with me.' . . .

We climbed the stairs and entered the office. From [here] a small door leads to the punishment chamber. It is very small and cramped, partially slanting under the roof. A skylight with six panes occupies this slanting part of the roof. The floor is covered with a thick rug, and a felt curtain hangs over the door!!! Below the window there is a sofa-like piece of upholstered furniture which in our language we call a 'puff' [pouffe]. Approximately in the middle of this item of furniture two leather straps are attached, whose function is obvious. A chair and a low closet in the corner complete the room's appointments.

The directress opened the closet and showed me her rods: a few small willow soap rods and many birch rods in different sizes, which were being softened in a tall jug of salt water, so as to be in constant readiness . . .[6]

The hallmarks of this archetype, then, are these: she operates within a formal, controlled atmosphere; she is judicial and calm; and her punishments, if generally speaking less physically severe than those of her male colleague, are considerably more humiliating, due to the considerable degree of refinement that is above all her stock-in-trade.

Her stereotype (not quite the same thing) is unmistakable and crosses many national boundaries: in caricature form she is tall, thin and angular, with a small bust, slim waist and sombre, conservative, very well-tailored clothes; invariably immaculately dressed. She may well wear spectacles or pince-nez, and her hair will be scraped cruelly back into a bun or chignon at the back of her head. She may be of any age; and is more likely to be a Miss than a Mrs. She is virginal in manner; if she ever had a lover, he was killed in the war (any war), and she has never again shown any inclination to tread the primrose pathways of love.

The Schoolmistress is the supreme professional. Her erudition and intelligence are formidable; her memory is extraordinary; and in all respects she is a model of precision. But hers is not a warm public personality, due, perhaps, to the exigencies of having to deal with small human beings *en masse*; though in private, perhaps after a whipping, or when doling out praise rather than penalty, when the circumstances more closely resemble those in which her sister, the Governess, operates, she can occasionally warm up to an unexpected degree, giving the

---

6. *Eros: The Meaning of My Life.*

recipient of blame or praise a fascinating glimpse of her depth of character.

She is not loved, alas, but instead commands a degree of respect that can nearly amount to the same thing – especially with the hindsight of later life.

THE GOVERNESS

It was close upon four o'clock, at which hour we always broke up for a run in the garden for an hour . . . I had done nothing with my task – Miss Evelyn looked grave.

'Mary and Eliza, you may go out, Charles will remain here.'

My sisters, simply imagining that I was kept in to finish my lessons, ran into the garden. Miss Evelyn turned the key in the door, opened a cupboard and withdrew a birch rod neatly tied up with blue ribbons. Now my blood coursed through my veins, and my fingers trembled so that I could hardly hold my pencil.

'Put down your slate, Charles, and come to me.'

I obeyed, and stood before my beautiful governess, with a strange commixture of fear and desire.

'Unfasten your braces and pull down your trousers.'

I commenced doing this, though but very slowly. Angry at my delay her delicate fingers speedily accomplished the work. My trousers fell to my feet.

'Place yourself across my knees.'

Anon., *The Romance of Lust*[7]

If any single archetype of either sex epitomises the flagellant passion, surely it is the Governess. Even more than her sibling, the Schoolmistress, whom she closely resembles, she stands for

---

7. Gibson (*TEV*, p. 273) also quotes this passage, describing it as 'one of the most acute I have come across'. On this point at least I agree with him.

refined, intimate, humiliating and occasionally excruciatingly painful corporal punishment administered to juveniles. Because the world she rules is a small one, she is able to set her own rules, and to enforce them virtually free of supervision. No one interferes with her: she is mistress of her closed world, and she wields the rod with refined enjoyment, unconstrained by any tiresome bonds of propriety, practice or regulation that may be set upon her sister in the public schoolroom. In fact, she is a concentrated version of the Schoolmistress (instead of thirty pupils, she has at most two or three) and as a result even more terrifying – and fascinating.

Historically, she has longer antecedents than her sister archetype: governesses have plied their trade since Roman times, if not earlier, long before women kept school to any general extent: the French word *gouvernante* may be dated to the fifteenth century. She differs in being found almost exclusively among the wealthier environments, as the employee of a great family, or at least a substantial middle-class one, retained especially to teach and discipline its scions until the boys reached an age where they might be sent to school and so escape her regimen (though probably encountering one even more tyrannical). Girls conventionally remained under her sway until they were of marriageable age.

There are in fact two versions of the archetype: the first, illustrated by the above passage, is the subject of this section; the second is its direct opposite. In recent years feminist scholars, anxious to see in the classical governess a dispirited, exploited, underpaid, socially snubbed victim of rampant patriarchalism and rigid class conventions, have produced studies to this effect. And beyond doubt much of what is written there is true enough – governesses were very often badly treated and viewed as little more than servants, and far from having virtually unlimited authority over their pupils, were themselves at the mercy of rowdy, under-disciplined brats who, in the eyes of the parents, could do no wrong. But the two images are by no means mutually exclusive. A governess who resented the circumstances of her employment might well take it out on her charges where she could get away with it, and in any case there is evidence aplenty, quite apart from the astonishing staying power of the flagellatory persona, that many governesses, for this or other reasons, were fearsome and indefatigable wielders of the rod of punishment.

I make no apologies for quoting here the famous passage concerning the most notorious of all Victorian governesses and her approach to child-rearing, since it virtually encapsulates all that a tyrannical governess might do, given the temperament and of course the freedom of action.

She persecuted and beat us in the most cruel way and established over us a system of terrorism so complete that not one of us ever mustered up the courage to walk upstairs and tell our father or mother. She spanked us with the sole of her slipper on the bare back [i.e., bottom], beat us with her brushes, tied us for long hours to chairs in uncomfortable positions with our hands holding a pole or blackboard behind our backs, shut us up in darkness, practised on us every kind of petty persecution, wounded our pride by dressing us (me in particular) in red shining calico petticoats (I was obliged to make my own) with an immense conical cap on our heads round which, as well as on our breasts and backs, were sewn strips of paper bearing in enormous characters the words Liar, Sneak, Coward, Lubber and the like. In this guise she compelled us to go out in the pleasure ground and show ourselves to the gardeners. She forced us to walk through the park at even distances, never communicating with each other, to the village and to show ourselves to the villagers. It never occurred to us that these good folk sympathised intensely with us and regarded her as a fiend. Our pride was much too deeply hurt.

She made me write a letter to the butler asking him to make a birch for me with which I was to be punished for lying and requesting him to read it out in the Servants' Hall. When he came round one day with a letter and saw me standing in my red petticoat with my face to the wall on a chair outside the schoolroom and said 'Why, you look like a Cardinal!' I could have died of shame.[8]

Miss E. (or V.) M. Paraman, governess to the blue-blooded Curzon family in the middle of the last century, thereby takes centre stage as the very model of a malevolent martinet. Reading the above passage, one may identify, among other sanctions, flagellation of several kinds, including spanking with both slipper and hairbrush and flogging with a birch rod; 'petticoating'[9]; a truly baroque version of the fetch-your-own-rod-my-boy gambit favoured by Mark Twain's Mrs Horr; isolation, and even bondage.

Miss Paraman's is the most famous example of a real governess living up to the flagellant archetype; many others are known, and frequently quoted. In case there should remain any doubt that governesses could and did behave in this way, whether or not as a form of oblique revenge upon their employers, I offer the following passage, which to the best of my knowledge has never been quoted elsewhere.

'Mademoiselle's' great qualification was that being Alsatian she could teach two languages for the price of one. She had a red face and very long greasy hair that descended to her ankles, and which in the process of braiding she coiled several times around her neck. She might conveniently have hanged herself in this fashion, but unfortunately she did not. Peter and I . . .were given entirely into her keeping, morally, spiritually and physically . . .

Five years of appalling torture ensued . . . Mademoiselle had an affinity with all that was dull and dreary. The books that she provided were worn, brown, discoloured, underlined. The print was small, the covers torn; their musty

---

8. *Curzon II*, p. 20.
9. See chapter 12.

smell created an atmosphere. When we did not know our lists of words she pinched us cruelly on the arm. So hard and so often did she pinch that sometimes I wished I could change into Peter's place so that the other arm might have a turn, for it is very painful to be pinched repeatedly on a bruise that is already blue and pink and green . . .

In the second year of the reign of Mademoiselle, the scene changed from London to a lodging-house at Eastbourne . . . Before leaving us our mother expressed a pious hope that we might be speaking fluent French on her return. This hope produced a grievance; Mademoiselle considered that it reflected upon her prowess as a teacher. She said that I never knew my lessons nor seemed to take an interest; if we could not yet speak French it was no fault of hers. I was lazy, stupid and obstinate, a discredit to any teacher. She was tired of my sullen unreceptivity and resolved to beat it out of me. Peter also should be beaten, but not as hard or often. Boys she considered less hateful than girls. Peter did not look so sullen, he was more bearable. Accordingly at the first provocation I was ordered to my room and told to undress. I did so, wonderingly. Mademoiselle called in the housemaid who stood inertly and said:

'Fancy now! And you being such a naughty little girl, who'd ha' thought it?'

I am not sure which I minded most, the beating with a wooden spade or the indignity of being seen with no clothes on by the housemaid. A latent class consciousness was bitterly aroused.

Another day Peter was beaten with the wooden spade, but his punishment was for some offence of mine. This represented another effort on the part of Mademoiselle to drive the wedge between us. Peter, who knew my agony of mind, tried not to cry, so that I would not think he was being hurt . . .

Every morning we did our lessons in the wood, and this was preceded by a systematic ritual: as soon as we had arrived at the habitual spot, Mademoiselle picked up a stick and hit it against the nearest tree trunk to prove whether it was brittle or not. If it withstood the test she then threw me to the ground holding me up by my heels, and proceeded according to habit. This, she explained, was in order that I should know my lessons.[10]

So much for the historical picture – or a portion of it. One may feel that no fantasy could do justice to the objective reality of a Miss Paraman or a Mademoiselle, and indeed the standard persona found in erotic literature from the eighteenth century to the present day does not greatly differ from it – except in one regard: the fictional Governess is usually a good looker. Here at least she differs sharply from the Schoolmistress, whom convention requires to be no such thing.

Mr Lovel saw before him a tall young woman in her mid-twenties. A brunette with a very white skin, she wore her dark, almost black hair in a plain style, parted from forehead to crown and drawn smoothly back to a chignon at the nape of her strong, graceful neck. Her brow was well-shaped and intellectual; the nose was straight, short, and full of energy, the mouth rather small, with thin lips, the chin quite prominent. Everything in her face and pose denoted decision and force of character; but her glance, reserved, serious, even academic, could not conceal the soft brilliance of her deep grey eyes. She wore a tight-bodiced dress of plain black silk with a full skirt falling from a bustle and coiling around her feet – a costume that revealed a superb bust, a slender waist and well-muscled hips.[11]

The above passage, from the most famous (and certainly most literate) erotic novel dedicated to the species, contains every single

---

10. *Nuda Veritas.*
11. *HM*, p. 7.

one of the necessary codes: the unnaturally pale skin, the chignon, the thin lips, the sombre clothing and the fine figure. She is very nearly supernatural; but as it turns out she is human enough, being subject to strange passions. And it is to fulfil these, and for no other reason, that she has selected her profession.

But although she can be a terrifying martinet to no lesser degree than the Schoolmistress, she may also display another side: caring and compassionate. It does not prevent her doing her duty, of course – it would take an incoming asteroid to do that – but it does mean that, every now and again, she will explain, in velvet tones, the rationale behind the imminent event, in order to make it clear to the recipient of her attentions that what is about to happen is in his own interests and does not mean that she dislikes him – quite the contrary:

> She looked at him for a moment with absolute impassivity, her eyes glowing. 'I must, Richard,' she said. 'It is for your own good.' For the first time she seemed moved, her voice shaking slightly. 'You must be punished. I have decided upon it. And do not expect ever to soften or divert me, Richard,' she said, her tone becoming suddenly harsh. 'You do not know me yet, I'm afraid! I am very strict, and I do not change my mind. And you, you need a firm hand over you, as your father said – do you remember, Richard? Well, my hand will be firm, you need have no doubt of that. Come, now.'[12]

This mixture of sweet and sour is absolutely central to the flagellant experience in its most refined form. At the very least it removes all brutality from the punishment: it may even be said to add depth, complexity, grace and – for some – charm.

Nevertheless, the term 'governess' has, in recent years, lost some of its original meaning and image. Since, more than any

---

12. Ibid.

other term (except possibly dominatrix), it is a single word which stands for a single woman willing to administer corporal punishment to a single recipient, it has to some extent been hijacked by the professional community: a governess, as understood by those who read the classified ads in *Forum* or a hundred other magazines in all parts of the Western world, may well turn out to be a female dressed in a black corset and black thigh boots wielding a horsewhip. A client attending the premises of one of these ladies will not be instructed in Latin, Greek, algebra or any other academic subject. He will simply be tied up and walloped. Miss Paraman would scarcely have approved.

THE NANNY

Let every nurse have license free and large
To scarify her juveniles in charge
And make each nursery, in its form and rule
A real Preparatory Flogging School
The Rodiad

If flagellation is a passion experienced by both sexes and many cultures, with many of the archetypes thus far discussed in common, then the Nanny is a peculiarly English phenomenon (though her ancestor, the Nurse[13], is found worldwide). The classic nanny ruled children of pre-school age, usually of a single household, from infancy to the time they were handed over to the governess (or were sent to school). She had no academic skill, and was not required for educational purposes: she was there to teach nursery disciplines, and to care for her charges in all manner of ways, including the most intimately physical. She was *in loco maternis*.

---

13. The original meaning of this word is a children's nurse (i.e. mother surrogate) rather than medical nurse.

Nowadays nannies are likely to be young women specifically trained and qualified for the task, and, following the teachings of the Norland Institute, are extremely unlikely – even if permitted by the employing parents – physically to discipline their charges. The nanny of Victorian and Edwardian times, however, operated under no such restraints, as Jonathan Gathorne-Hardy makes clear in his definitive work *The Rise and Fall of the English Nanny*, and as many personal memoirs corroborate. If given to tyranny – and though many were not, many were – her field of operations was even more comprehensive than that of the governess, since in addition to controlling all everyday aspects of her charges' lives, she was also responsible for their inner selves; in other words, their bowel movements. Since at one end of the scale there is a distinct link between the flagellatory and the excretory, the Nanny sits astride this particular conjunction – indeed she defines it – to no less an extent than the natural mother, and in many cases without the compensating attribute of genuine maternal love.

> There she stood, a tyrant in her white starched apron, filling the lavatory with fear and misery. After . . . hours of trying I would shuffle off the lavatory seat. Nanny would peer into the bowl. Nothing![14]

The Nanny may in fact be quite young (teenage girls have traditionally been trusted with the task of caring for very small children). She has other, closely related, incarnations: the Babysitter and the (hospital) Nurse. The latter is not usually associated in reality with corporal punishment – though enemas and humiliating manœuvres in the bathtub are a distinct speciality of the persona – but the former has already acquired an impressive pedigree, at least in legend, as an ad hoc smacker of small bottoms, especially in the United States where babysitting has been a social habit for far longer than anywhere else. If

---

14. *The Rise and Fall of the English Nanny*, p. 263.

she operates in a private capacity outside the home, it will be as a childminder; though since in the UK these women are obliged to be registered with the local authority, they are unlikely to apply corporal punishment, even to the mildest degree, to badly behaved children.

Her appeal is above all to that variety of flagellant who prefers the most intimate and juvenile styles of punishment – enemas, over-the-knee spankings – and is therefore dubbed 'infantilist'.

MAMMA MIA

In the erotic orientation of the woman to the child her motherliness operates impersonally as a sovereign, shaping force of the primordial female instinct. For the woman the rearing and the care of the child is a pleasure-accented erotic and sexual act which fills out her whole life. She loves when she rears. She loves when she punishes, for her seeming cruelty is but a higher degree of her tenderness . . .

My education of young people free of sickly pampering produced the phenomenon that my erotic will to power vouchsafed me the highest and most beautiful fulfilment as mother and educator. The punishment of children had an exciting effect upon me without my seeing something special therein. The erotic backgrounds of these seemingly enigmatic actions lay hidden in the depth of my instinctual life. The instinct to motherhood with its consequences and its will to power is a natural fact which lies beyond all moral evaluation.

The typical sexual component of the woman and, at the same time, the different goal of the male and female Eros lies in motherhood which, since primordial times, has constituted the metaphysical dimension of femaleness.

Confessions and Experiences

More bottoms have been smacked by natural mothers than any other class of human individual. This does not mean that all mothers smack – far from it – but nonetheless it is likely that nearly all 'debut spankings' have been received from this quarter. And since the time span of the natural mother's generally accepted physical authority over her own offspring precisely corresponds to early childhood – when, as nearly all authorities agree, personalities are shaped and characters formed for good or ill – it may fairly be supposed that, if deviant tendencies *are* produced as a result of childhood mishandling, as many allege, then mothers are more responsible than anyone else.[15]

It is a curiosity of history that so many great soldiers were, as boys, notably whipped by their mothers. Napoleon Bonaparte, T.E. Lawrence (of Arabia) and Bernard Montgomery are but three examples. It is certainly arguable that had they not been so disciplined they might not have become soldiers at all, which many will hold desirable in its own right. But what will these cynics say of the remarkable Australian composer Percy Grainger, whose mother administered corporal punishment until well into his teens?

Percy was brought up by his mother according to a very strict black-and-white philosophy of reward and punishment. The rewards were the trips to the Dandenongs, pony rides, tramcar hopping, being allowed to go sailing or to make model boats (in which he especially delighted). The punishment was simply the whip. If he misbehaved or neglected his piano practice his mother would beat him

---

15. This belief, absolutely central to the abolitionist case, is curiously suspended when the supposed influence of the British public schools is discussed. These institutions are often held to be directly responsible for the nurturing and growth of the British-style flagellant passion: boys were apparently free of all such tendencies until the moment of their arrival at Greyfriars. I suggest that parents who sent their boys to these schools were likely already to be believers in corporal punishment, and since boys typically began their secondary schooling at eleven, by the time they arrived at Greyfriars they might, via domestic influences, already be well set on the path. Almost all flagellationists date their first realisations of 'the passion' to their very early pre-school lives.

severely. This form of corporal punishment continued until he was fifteen or sixteen. Perhaps the most curious aspect of this regime was not the nature or vehemence of the punishment, but the fact that whilst Percy did not have any particular liking for being at the receiving end, he never for one moment bore any resentment towards his mother for it.[16]

In Grainger's case – as in all others mentioned thus far, including the most self-pitying of them all, Rousseau – it simply cannot be said that these men's lives were enfeebled or crippled by this treatment; on the contrary, of each it may be claimed that he was in his own way a genuinely great man, without whom humanity would have been the poorer. Nor, with the exception of Montgomery, did the maternal punishments in childhood appear to affect later relations. Therefore, while it cannot reasonably be claimed that childhood whippings at the mother's hands evoked greatness in later life (though there are many who would promote just such an idea), it is equally difficult, in these cases at least, to prove the opposite: that 'abuse' rendered the remainder of the subject's life futile and barren or indeed damaged it in any discernible way.

The Mother is the most central of all dominant archetypes. Here at least is one everybody can recognise; more than an archetype, a divinity.[17] She is the oldest of all deities, the central religious icon of nearly all ancient faiths, with a thousand names and a variety of aspects, many of them young, beautiful, warm and benevolent (Isis, Venus, the Virgin); others awe-inspiring (Minerva, Artemis); a third aspect wholly terrible (Hecate, Kali, the Morrigan). She is the central human creature, the hub of the

---

16. *Percy Grainger.*
17. The archetype is a popular one in depicted art: as Venus/the Virgin the young mother chastises Cupid/Jesus across her knee in the most famous of maternal punishment postures (in French the over-the-knee posture is often called *à maman.*). This theme has been explored by artists from mediæval times to the present day.

family, the vector of all life on earth. Nearly all dominant female personæ are ultimately derived from her.

> The woman, by her nature, is much more closely bound to the child than to the man. She can sexually dispense with him, but not with the child. For the man the sexual act exhausts itself with the animal sexual act, whereas for the woman it is the point of departure to sexual action. In motherhood nature has given her a continuation of the love-process and a heightening of her instinctual life. The more highly organised woman considers the nature-willed sexual union between man and woman as a soulless animal act utterly devoid of spirituality, whose justification she recognises only when it serves the preservation of the species. For her, erotic and sexual spirituality begins with the sublimation of the natural urges which frees the human being from all animality and leads to the spirituality of the highest bliss.[18]

It is rare for the Mother to appear as a flagellatory persona in her own right. Instead, motherliness permeates many other female dominant archetypes. Even the conventionally pitiless Slave-Mistress, stroking the hair of the newly punished boy slave, momentarily displays this quality. When a Schoolmistress or Governess speaks quietly and sincerely to a pupil of his faults before thrashing them out of him, she is temporarily *in spirito maternis*. The Nanny is clearly so, nearly all the time, though on a lower level. Only the Institutional Dame or Matron (see below) shows no softer side, though in this she is but reprising another (and the grimmest) of the ancient personalities of the Mother – that of Hecate, the terrible dame in whose ancient and withered loins any juices of maternal tenderness dried up long ago. This implacable aspect of the eternal female caused Havelock Ellis to reach perhaps the most contentious of all his conclusions concerning love and pain.

---

18. *Confessions and Experiences*, pp. 82–83.

In that abnormal sadism which appears from time to time among civilised human beings it is nearly always the female who becomes the victim of the male. But in the normal sadism which occurs throughout a large part of nature it is nearly always the male who is the victim of the female. It is the male spider who impregnates the female at the risk of his life and sometimes perishes in the attempt; it is the male bee who, after intercourse with the queen, falls dead from that fatal embrace, leaving her to fling aside his entrails and calmly pursue her course. If it may seem to some that the course of our enquiry leads us to contemplate with equanimity, as a natural phenomenon, a certain semblance of cruelty in man in his relations with woman, they may, if they will, reflect that this phenomenon is but a very slight counterpoise to that cruelty which has been naturally exerted by the female on the male long even before man began to be.[19]

The same quality is less sombrely touched upon in a French novel of the 1920s.

The boy had answered his mother back. She was in the yard, and became very angry. It was obvious he was going to get a terrible punishment!

His mother dragged him into the house, into the dining room, where we were talking. She held him under her arm and took his trousers down in no time at all. She really did it quickly!

And then she spanked him! How she spanked him! But she didn't hurry in the least. She didn't say a word, although she was in a real rage, a cold rage, and the more she spanked the more she wished to spank. You should have heard the slaps! She was a big woman, and as strong as a horse.[20]

---

19. *Psychology of Sex*, Pt. 2, II, p. 128.
20. *Paulette Trahié.*

The most public of all forms of corporal punishment, of which most of us have witnessed at least one example in our lives, is the ad hoc smacking administered to the fractious or disobedient child in, say, the supermarket by its furious mother. The archetype lives on.

CRUELLA DE VILLE

> *To look at her majestic figure*
> *Would make you caper with more vigour!*
> *The lightning flashing from each eye*
> *Would lift your soul to ecstasy!*
> *Her milk-white fleshy hand and arm,*
> *That ev'n an Anchorite would charm,*
> *Now tucking in your shirt-tail high,*
> *Now smacking hard each plunging thigh,*
> *And those twin orbs that near'em lie!*
> *They to behold her di'mond rings,*
> *Ev'n them you'd find delightful things!*
> *But above all, you'd love that other*
> *That told you she was your Step-mother!*
> *Then handing you the rod to kiss,*
> *She'd make you thank her for the bliss!*
> *No female Busby then you'd find*
> *E'r whipt you half so well behind!*
> *Her lovely face, where beauty smiled,*
> *Now frowning, and now seeming wild!*
> *Her bubbies o'er their bound'ry broke,*
> *Quick palpitating at each stroke!*
> *With vigour o'er the bouncing bum*
> *She'd tell ungovern'd boys who rul'd at home!*
> *Madame Birchini's Dance*

Wicked Stepmothers and Stern Aunts are sub-archetypes of the Mother and share most, if not quite all, of her attributes. Both operate at one remove from natural motherhood. It is of course disputed that stepmothers as a class have deserved the truly awful press they have always had (Snow White's stepmother supplies the fictional prototype). It is pointed out that there have been – and continue to be – genuinely horrific stepfathers, though it is not clear why the abundance of one should necessarily preclude the existence of the other. A tyrant or disciplinarian who might conceivably, if illogically, make an exception for her own flesh and blood (Cinderella's stepmother for the ugly sisters), might not inevitably feel the same constraints with a child she had in some way inherited. And where, as is wholly conventional in stepmother stories, the incumbent stepchildren are seen by the newcomer as a positive inconvenience, not to say encumbrance, then discipline might well be replaced by vindictiveness.

Whatever stepmothers are or have been in reality, the archetype is that of the Mother, but drained of all human kindness. She may or may not be motivated by malice (it is not strictly necessary that she should be): it just seems that way to those at the receiving end, which is to say that her discipline is so strict and cold that malice may be suspected even when it is not present.

The Stern Aunt, on the other hand, is a mellower – but only slightly – figure. After all, she is still related by ties of blood. Nonetheless she is usually formidable; maternal, yes, but with more than a touch of other personæ – say, the Institutional Dame – when necessary. Bertie Wooster's Aunt Agatha supplies the best-known non-flagellatory literary example: she has the knack of turning Bertie 'inside out with a single glance'. (This schoolmistress-like power of command is an essential attribute of the Stern Aunt.) The brace of aunts who oppressed the early life of the writer Saki (H.H. Munro) with frequent applications of the birch are a good example of the archetype achieving objective reality. Less strict than stepmothers, aunts are stricter than natural mothers in the main: without the bonding between mother and child to get in the way, as they see it, they are generally more objective about a particular young person's requirement for discipline.

Come in, young man, and close the door behind,
Please comprehend that smirks won't get you very far.
Your bad behaviour has been lately on my mind,
I find I've failed in duty to your dear Mama.
Two years you've been here; and in all those months
I've never scolded you, nor used harsh phrase;
—I've told you, boy, don't look at me askance!—
It's time you saw the error of your ways.
Because my regimen has been too kind
You fancy that this means I'm always weak.
What I intend may somewhat change your mind
For now and then I turn the other cheek.[21]

There is a sub-persona of the Aunt; a younger, more openly erotic version. Let us call her the Seductive Aunt. In a way she is the direct equivalent of the Wicked Uncle – she is certainly amoral – since she is by no means matronly and may in fact be exceedingly attractive. She is lustful and Dionysian, and exploits her situation (of authority) for all its worth as the senior and more experienced partner in a delightful and prolonged game.

At the hour prescribed, Willie knocked at his aunt's door, and receiving no reply, entered, bolted it behind him, and stealing to the bed-side, found her immersed in slumber . . .She lay on the broad of her back, the bedclothes on account of the heat half flung off, her chestnut curls strewing the pillow. The vermilion lips, a little apart, were wreathed into a smile ill becoming the stern purpose of the preceptress. Can she be really asleep – her eyelids seem to see him?

'Aunt, it's six o'clock. Please get up and whip me.' No response. Slipping his hands beneath her night dress, he tickles her bosom lightly to awaken her.

---

21. 'An Aunt Does Her Duty' in *A Guide to the Correction of Young Gentlemen*.

'Naughty boy, I told you what I'd do.' She rose in seeming wrath, went to the wardrobe, and drew forth – even the old Cupid correctors. These she laid upon the bed, undid the brace buttons, and opened the front of his Russia ducks. Unwilling to expose him in the position in which he then stood, she did not suffer the continuations to descend more than a few inches; without removing the sustaining hand, she lectured him for some time in guarded terms such as the nature of his offence required. The lecture ended, she let fall the ducks, and led him, shuffling but nothing loath, to the stool where he had first suffered, on which she seated her-self . . . She now removed the ducks altogether, and made other necessary preparations . . .

This she did, turning the boy slowly and deliberately round the while, stern necessity obliging her now to expose without reference to position. Seizing her victim by the waist and leg, she hoisted him on to the altar of her lap, arranging his position there by sundry pulls and pushes.[22]

She is the Older Woman, said to be the dream partner of many men; and the male passive is her toyboy. In real life she would be locked up, but in fantasy scenarios she provides an excellent and convincing way in which authority, hierarchy, discipline and erotic love may be blended together with the female in the position of power.

THE INSTITUTIONAL DAME

'Yes,' said Cunigund soon afterwards, 'only a few years ago Helen, whom I have just punished, would have got the birch in the morning. Every little domestic fault that I could put a stop to summarily with a few stripes was then punished in that manner. In the early morning I have gone along . . . to

---

22. *The Romance of Chastisement.*

the bedside of a culprit and, while she was held down by her comrades, have given her a proper thrashing. And then there was order, great order, far better discipline than at present; therefore I was always glad to do it, and I gave such satisfaction that I was often called into the men's quarter to give the birch to some big lad, sometimes sixteen or seventeen years old. Ah! I delighted to lay on the stripes on a naughty boy's trousers, and I always thought then of the wise Solomon and Jesus Sirach, who order us not to spare the rod on wicked children, particularly boys. You'd hardly believe it, girls, how I did lay into them! Then as now the public was allowed to be present – for what have lads like that to show? . . .

'But, oh, you should have seen, children, how the great ladies, who never fail to be present at great "Welcomes" and "Farewells", how they rushed into the hall when it was announced that the "Welcome" or "Farewell" was to be given with birch to a lad . . . Oh, how often would one or other of them come and shake my hand, leaving in the palm of it a bright piece of money, and how often did I hear them say: "Yes, today good Cunigund has done her work downright well; wherever did she get her strength? Yes, she delivers her strokes as if they were measured with a compass, and the marks on the skin look as if they had been traced with a ruler!"'

Nell in Bridewell

Not all women are motherly. Some never appear to possess this quality in any measure at all; in others, sadly, it withers early, often as a result of other disappointments. They become – or so it seems – altogether heartless. Because they wish to be avenged upon the world (or a portion of it), or are naturally drawn to personal power – or both – historically they have gravitated into those 'enclosed worlds' where women have always been able to wield unusual authority, licensed to do so by the greater and yet more powerful world of men beyond the walls, but within their own domains near-absolute mistresses over a great many subordinate souls.

Schoolmistresses enjoy a measure of this power, and there have been many times when due to the general gloom and rigidity of regime it has been impossible to distinguish between school and corrective institution, or school and orphanage: it is also true that many orphanages have been considerably less repressive places than contemporary schools, due to the kindness and expertise of those who cared, in the best sense, for waifs and strays. Even so, in the general perception, orphanages and children's homes remain chillier and more unkind places than even the worst private schools; and as for corrective institutions, these represent the very end of the line, the ultimate terror.

Most of these institutions have historically been staffed by women of the type mentioned above, as well as equivalent males. They are usually called superintendent, directress or simply matron. Conventionally middle-aged, they are usually uniformed, often buxom, and they wield the rod with ferocity and little discernible pity. The dreadful Cunigund from *Nell in Bridewell* supplies the prototype, but historically, as we know from personal memoirs from all strata of society, as well as occasional court cases, women in charge of children within an institutional setting very often behave in tyrannical ways, with corporal punishment very much on the agenda. The actress Shirley Anne Field was brought up, as an orphaned child, in just such a place run by just such women (the cane was kept in the chimney). So was Noele Arden, incarcerated during the twenties in a girls' approved school[23] called St Christopher's at Great Crosby, a few miles north of Liverpool. The place was, needless to say, fully as harsh as in all the worst tales: girls were made to scrub the outer yard with pieces of half-brick till their fingers bled. When Arden and another ten-year-old absconded for a day to the nearby city, they were handed back over to the authorities

---

23. Correctional institute.

by, consecutively, the other girl's mother and the local police, who were 'sympathetic'. On return to St Christopher's:

> We were taken before the whole school, and there we were stripped to knickers and vests, then put across a chair, had our knickers pulled down, and were caned across the back-side. Needless to say, I kicked and screamed and was taken to the detention room. This tiny room had no furniture at all, only a mattress on the floor. The window was . . . covered with thick wire mesh; but had the added security of iron bars across the outside. I screamed for ages, but no one took any notice as this room was at the very end of the school, and no one really bothered how much noise you made. Because I played up I was put on a bread and water diet.[24]

The most astonishing real-life example this century of an insti-tutional dame wielding spectacular – we might say outrageous – physical authority over the opposite sex is Mrs Beatrice Fry. The wife of the famous cricketer C.B. Fry, together with her husband she managed (her husband remained nominally in charge) the training ship TS *Mercury* in the period before, during and after the First World War.[25] By all accounts she was an implacable dame of the most terrifying kind, though in her ultimate value system (and appearance) she seems far more masculine than feminine, which removes her slightly from the general run of the archetype. Nevertheless she behaved, on one level, like the most insensitive and tyrannical school matron or nanny, routinely inspecting boy cadets' pyjama bottoms after reveille in order to search for evidence of masturbation. It seems that not one boy dared, or was ever discovered – her regime was hard enough already.[26] Once she had taken over the full-time management of

---

24. *A Child of the System.*
25. The privately run training ship system was more or less the equivalent of the American military academy.
26. Cadets were aged from ten to fifteen.

the establishment, the incidence of public canings rose sharply. These were inflicted in the harsh way then commonplace in the Royal Navy when young seamen were to be punished: in full view of all, with the offender bent (as was traditional) along the breech of a gun – a ceremony that in Nelson's time was called 'kissing the gunner's daughter'.

Beating was the punishment for a wide range of offences. Merely being a nuisance was enough to earn a trip to the gun. For boys who were caught stealing there was no escape, but they were so hungry that they still took the risk, looting the vegetable garden in which their more fortunate predecessors had worked their own plots. Running away was considered the worst offence, so that the boy who most feared the regime was the prime victim of its severity.

Beatie [Mrs Fry, no pun intended] decided who was to be flogged, 'awarding' – her word – up to twenty-four strokes . . . In 1921, for example, No. 1766, J. Isaacs, was awarded twelve strokes across the gun 'for being a General Nuisance'. After breakfast the ship's company marched to the gymnasium and were formed into lines to witness punishment. Meanwhile, Boy No. 1766 was conducted to a changing room where he was made to strip naked and then dress in a pair of thin white cotton trousers. When he entered the gymnasium he walked past his assembled shipmates and mounted the gun platform. He stood facing the gun, the barrel pointing away from his midriff like a huge steel phallus. Behind him and to his right was [First Officer] McGavin, a clipboard in his hand bearing a piece of paper. 'Sharkey' stood to his left, holding a thick, almost inflexible cane with decorative twine wrappings at its extremities.

McGavin read out the charge and the number of cuts. The greater the punishment, the more likely it was Beatie would be present, standing by the main entrance, looking across the heads of the boys to see that it was done. 'Sharkey' ordered the boy to bend over the gun, and on the order 'Carry on!' from McGavin he struck with all his might.

The instant the blow fell 'Sharkey' would decide if his victim could stand the rest without flinching. Often he could not, and the man laid aside his cane and with short cords tied the boy's ankles to rings on the platform, and his wrists to the gun-carriage. 'Sharkey' then took up the cane and continued his work . . . McGavin dutifully ticked them off on his fly sheet, and Beatie watched impassively.[27]

Mrs Fry therefore preferred to ordain and witness these savage and wholly indefensible beatings rather than inflict them herself; it cannot be for want of strength, for she was a powerful woman, able to shovel tons of coal if there was nobody else to do it, or row a thirty-two-foot whaler all by herself. Later on she recruited her stepdaughter Sybil to aid her in her duties; in this she no doubt sensed a kindred spirit, for Sybil immediately took up the disciplinary task with flair, decreeing many floggings across the gun in her own right.

Beatrice Fry was decorated with the Order of the British Empire in 1918. Her funeral in 1938 was attended by the upper echelons of the Royal Navy, and Admiral Sir James Somerville[28] read the oration.

This version of the archetype is therefore altogether grim, implacable and pitiless, as befits an avatar of Hecate. There is no love in her. She scares a culprit out of his wits before thrashing him: he is immured with her and there is no escape. Justice – a shining quality of the Schoolmistress, an archetype who can otherwise resemble her on occasions – is not a factor in her punishments: their only purpose is to ensure that her will prevails, and if there is a greater good in view, it is not readily apparent to those under her sway.

The School Matron is a slightly softer version of the same

---

27. *The Captain's Lady*, pp. 114–15.
28. C in C Mediterranean Fleet during the early part of the Second World War.

archetype. Here, maternal feeling of a kind may be present to some degree. Nevertheless there are many anecdotes of hairbrush-wielding school matrons; and an equal number of women, it seemed, who while nominally providing the mother-figure in a boarding schoolboy's life, nevertheless, like Mrs Fry, lost no opportunity to have him excoriated whenever it was felt necessary. Not, it must be said, that this was always resented:

> Under 'Miss Jane' . . . the House maintained to the full its position as the best House in Eton. Hers was a splendid character; an unusual compound of the best of feminine and the best of masculine characteristics. A thorough Judge of boy nature, she knew unerringly who to trust and how to trust, and she was seldom, if ever, deceived. She loved her boys with her whole heart, she gave them her entire confidence, she was unflinchingly loyal to them in their difficulties and their scrapes, so long as they were frank and honest with her, although she never hesitated in her approval of a flogging when a flogging was deserved; and so she set up in the House an atmosphere of truth and honour which pervaded it throughout.[29]

Jane Evans (1826–1906) succeeded her sister Annie and her brother-in-law Samuel in running Evans', one of the famous dame's houses of Eton College, in the middle part of the nineteenth century. These are, and were, halls of residence – what other schools might call houses – and the Evans sisters were, each in her turn, house mothers. It must be made clear that both were beloved and respected; even though both, particularly Miss Jane, ordered beatings whenever necessary without a moment's compunction. Here are some extracts from her diaries of the period 1878–90.

Boys very tiresome, throwing water out of the window.

---

29. *Annals of an Eton House.*

Handed them over to the Captain [senior boy of the house] and they were caned.

After dinner went into House, and found B. and S. and H. having a comfortable pipe. Handed them over to their Tutor [for a birching].

G. very naughty: came in through his window, which is close to mine, and I never heard him. Sent him to the Head Master. Saw him make a good score [G. was soundly flogged].

Lowers [junior boys] very noisy; want squashing. Lowers caned.[30]

It was not only the dames at Eton who were appreciative of the merits of corporal punishment. The maids who did the housework in the dame houses might also put in their oars. Martha Ihams, who retired in 1896, was once called a liar by a boy. 'I told Mr Evans, and he got swished; and after early school he meets me on the stairs and says: "You got me something this morning; thank you." And that was that.'[31] James Brinsley-Richards reported that after his first flogging, one of the maids taunted him: 'Give you five cuts, did he sir? Well, I think you got off cheap.'[32]

The archetype therefore ranges from the essentially kindly (though rod-friendly) Jane Evans on the one hand, to Beatrice Fry or even Cunigund on the other. Its appeal at the former end of the scale is relatively easy to discern, being a close relative of the Nanny, with more than a hint of Stern Aunt. It is more difficult to see the attraction in being at the mercy of creatures like Beatrice Fry or Cunigund, of whom truly little or nothing may be

---

30. Ibid.
31. Ibid.
32. *Seven Years at Eton.*

said in mitigation. Nevertheless it is this quality of implacability, perhaps the single most distinguishing feature of the Dame, which appeals: faced by such a terrible manifestation of opposed willpower, one can only submit and hope against hope for mercy. The Dame is therefore a 'crash course' in submission, the headiest of all tonics; by no means for the faint of heart.

THE SLAVE-MISTRESS

Another day or two and she would take possession of this body, solely hers by right of purchase and contract. She would teach this living, breathing, piece of property new duties, new obligations, new ceremonies. Particularly the latter she intended to develop to their utmost magnificence. Soon she would begin to expand the secret luxuries her inner nature craved, to revel in the invention of fanciful apparel, address, formulae, the precise method of bowing and bending she would require from her slave. The commonplace rituals which preceded, accompanied and followed the girl's past whippings should be made much more elaborate, as befits her real status of slave . . . And all these plans would be crowned with the laurel of her slave's unfaltering devotion, the quality of which would be further enriched by the girl's ecstatic happiness in her lot. For she would be intensely happy in her bondage, she was certain.

Modern Slaves

If the subject of the above passage were a genuine sadist, the happiness of the slave would be a strong disincentive. Historically, slaves were not required or expected to be happy. But in the flagellant scenario which styles itself upon this estate, the inner bliss of the slave – his or her delight in becoming the 'property' of a superior being – is the most important single dynamic. If real slavery was slaver-driven, then its voluntary modern counterpart is slave-driven. The resulting buyers' market has produced an absurd situation – sometimes irreverently referred to as 'dom wars' – in which many professional female slave-mistresses find themselves actually competing, in some cases rather bitterly, for a by no means infinite number of client-slaves willing to spend serious money on their hobby.[33]

The archetype is considerably more glamorous and potent: she is Messalina, the Queen of Babylon, She-Who-Must-Be-Obeyed, Cleopatra, Countess Elizabeth Bathòry, Catherine the Great or Mrs Ann Palmer of Jamaica: goddess, queen and tyrant to those under her sway. Her justice, such as it is, is the unfathomable justice of a higher being. The only law is Her will, that is to say, Her whim. She is always addressed in capital letters, on one's knees and with lowered eyes, and always with careful, trembling respect. She can do absolutely anything She wants (in theory), and against Her decisions there is no appeal.

Perhaps because of her essential amorality, She is more flexible than many of the other personæ and may, if She wishes, and at different times, display flashes of each of their specific qualities. She can be motherly, even nannyish for a moment – then a second later She has been transformed into the most terrible Dame that ever walked the earth, Her ferocity barely human, *la belle dame sans merci* indeed. But most of the time She is regal, calm, authoritative, dominant without domineering: it is an understood thing that Her will be done, and that is all that counts.

This is necessarily a compact involving an enormous degree of trust and – on the part of the slave-mistress – deep understanding:

> If this trust the slave proffers is taken lightly, as it may be by the prostitute 'playing the game of S&M' one assumes the risk of aggravating his guilt intolerably. The masochist trusts that the Superior has the power to elicit his hidden desires, help him express them, and remove the guilt from them:

---

33. It may be guessed that the potential number of slaves *manqués* is very much higher, but many men are discouraged or repelled by the very idea of transactions with prostitutes and therefore, where their wives are unsympathetic, keep their inclinations to themselves.

that the Superior accepts, and perhaps even approves of his masochism. Only the true Superior is capable of inspiring this, while the play-actor will in the end be found sneering at the slave as 'sick'. . . .

I am always amazed when this trust is given to me, a complete stranger. I feel nothing but respect for the bravery of the masochist in submitting to his desires, in my care. Even the inexperienced Master or Mistress can assure themselves against the delicate problems that arise in the sado-masochistic exchange by rigorously maintaining the appearance of a true Superior, and working continually on perfecting its truth. The voice need not be raised, or angry, but cool and even and emotionless. The gait is graceful, slow and assured. Dark and concealing formal evening clothes are never unintimidating; severe unadorned styles being more imperious than the flashy. All coarse easiness of manner must be eradicated. She is a flawless lady, and a highly moral creature.[34]

In my opinion, there is more compassion and comprehension in this single passage than in all the works of all the great behaviourists put together. Sadly enough, what its author firmly excludes – a domineering manner, unsuitably flashy clothes – actually represent the norm of professional dominatrixes, who while pretending to dominate are openly pandering to the more banal masculine fetishes (flawless ladies, not to mention highly moral ones, do not receive gentlemen in their bedrooms while wearing black corsets and latex thigh-boots), and are thereby giving the game away at a fundamental level. Nevertheless the Down-Market Dominatrix has become the new icon of flagellationism in the mind of the public – to whom she does not look awe-inspiring at all, only silly. Since, however, there remains the undeniable fact that she is being paid, and paid well, to dress and act thus, it is her clients who, at the end of the day, appear even sillier.

---

34. *The Correct Sadist*, pp. 119–20.

11

A Choice
of Weapons

A tree there is, such was Apollo's will,
That grows uncultured on the Muses' Hill,
Its type in heaven the blest immortals know,
There called the Tree of Science, birch below.

Henry Layng[1]

Considerable, not to say exceptional, importance is attached,
within many flagellant scenarios, to the type of rod employed by
the dominant. The selection of swishing birch or whippy cane;
cruel crop or homely carpet-slipper; hairbrush, wooden spoon,
ruler, carpet-beater or silver-mounted paddle made of vulcanised
rubber and embossed with the dominant's initials – or the rejection of all of these in favour of the palm of the dominant's own
hand – can provide much of an event's focus for many individuals. In the flagellant scenario, the rod of punishment is far, far
more than a device with which to hit people: it is a sceptre of
lordship, a magic wand and a sword all together. Settings and
personalities aside, if there is any single prop which can stand
for the event as a whole it will be the rod.

There are many reasons. Firstly, and most obviously, corrective
implements range, in overall severity, from the very minor, almost
token, to the ferocious; even, in some circumstances, dangerous.

---

1. From *The Rod,* a poem in three cantos (early nineteenth century). Layng (or
Laing) was a Fellow of New College, Oxford.

It is easier to be lenient with some types of instrument – the palm of the hand being perhaps the best example, though all flat implements share this benign quality to some extent.

Secondly, they vary in effect, by which I mean the quality of the stroke: a broad-soled slipper produces a markedly different feeling from a more slender weapon such as a cane, while an implement made up of several switches (like a birch rod) or thongs (like a martinet) is a kind of hybrid of the two, though with physical resonances of its own.

Thirdly, they require, from the dominant, different levels of expertise, by which I mean, above all, precision. It is extremely difficult to miss the target with a flat implement such as a paddle or slipper: on the other hand, the skilled use of a cane or crop – which are in any case much more severe weapons – requires a golfer's or tennis-player's eye, since far greater accuracy is called for and a stroke that lands where it ought not can do damage, or at the very least produce the 'wrong' effect. Moreover, the longer implements – canes, birches, martinets and some straps – curve in flight and, being to greater or lesser extent flexible, wrap around the target on impact (this effect is particularly noted with straps) unless measures such as changing position or point of aim are taken to avoid it.

Fourthly, context dictates the weapon as it does so much else. At its most basic level it may simply be a matter of posture. A dominant who desires to punish the submissive across his or her knees in the age-old parental position will be better advised to use palm, slipper or hairbrush than to attempt to wield a cane: the latter implement is generally far too long to be used at such close range. Conversely, if the style of the chastisement requires the culprit to make formal submission – by bending over, for example – then the choice of weapons immediately increases (though this posture itself suggests the use of the stricter implements) and nearly any may be put to effective use.

But context also works in a more specific way, with certain implements being closely, even totemically, associated with specific scenarios. For example, the hairbrush is a purely domestic implement, and while canes and birches may also be found within the home, they are more frequently encountered in schoolrooms. Straps may be found nearly anywhere, while the equestrian over-tones of riding crops and dressage whips are more properly associated with those dominants who control 'slaves' rather than 'pupils'. These rules of association are not rigid: a slave-mistress may well use a cane, though if she does it is likely to be of the straight-handled type rather than the traditional curved-handle English school cane, which sends the wrong visual signals. And in recent years some blurring has taken place, so that the martinet, a many-tailed short whip like a miniature cat-o'-nine-tails, once exclusively associated with European (particularly French) domestic and pedagogic discipline, now appears in the red-taloned grasp of many a corseted American or English dominatrix; while the paddle, so definitively associated with the American approach to corporal punishment in both school and home, is now nearly ubiquitous. Finally, the birch rod, the most ancient of all symbols of corporal punishment[2], has now dropped almost entirely from use. In America it was long ago eclipsed by the pad-dle in school and home, and has never been part of the SM scene. In Europe, its ancient home, it has hardly fared better – almost cer-tainly because of all rods of punishment, the birch has the shortest life and is in addition the most time-consuming and complicated to manufacture. There is also the problem that for those who live in cities, there is simply no access to suitable trees.

Lastly, there is the minor but still significant aspect of pose value: a cane or crop may be put to valuable ongoing use by the more theatrical type of dominant – tapping the boot, pointing for emphasis, tickling the subordinate where he or she might not normally expect to be tickled, or administering spur-of-the-moment incentives. It is more difficult to cut a dash with a wooden spoon or a rolled-up newspaper.

---

2. Magistrates in the Roman Republic were preceded in procession by two 'lic-tors', each carrying a *fasces*, an axe bound in birch rods, to symbolise the magistrate's power of ordaining capital or corporal punishment.

Some dominant-submissive partnerships rejoice in this rich variety of *ferulae* and over the years collect one or more examples of each type. (These obviously pose something of a security problem.) Other dominants would not dream of using anything so innately vulgar, as they see it, as a purpose-built chastisement implement, and prefer to improvise from domestic weapons of wholly innocent primary purpose. But nearly all of them have a cane tucked away somewhere.

THE PALM

She raised her gloved hand and brought it down with a resounding slap upon my quivering bottom. I could not endure it. The kid-glove stung my tender flesh, but the childlike character of the chastisement stung my soul. I lashed out with my legs trying to kick my feet free from the delicate fetters of my drawers. But the frills clung about my toes, and caught on the high-heels and diamond buckles of my shoes.

'It's abominable,' I cried, 'to treat me like a little girl.'

But the kid-gloved hand rose pitilessly again and came down heavily upon naked and helpless flesh. I moaned, I plunged, I writhed upon Miss Priscilla's knees. I kicked, I strained impotently at the ribbons which bound my hands.

Miss High Heels

Gloved or not, the palm of the human hand is certainly the oldest of all flagellatory weapons and to this day remains the favourite for administering spankings. (The definition of the latter word once exclusively implied use of the flat of the palm, though it has now been extended to include any flat-surfaced weapon.) It is the most intimate of all rods, and has the shining merit of being always available; it is also the most flexible in terms of harshness, since any quality of punishment, from a few light taps which barely pinken the skin to truly epic smackings, may be administered, though the hardest hand-spanking is unlikely to approach, in severity, even a moderate castigation with something essentially sharp such as a cane or crop.

Like the birch, its effect is seriously compromised by even a single layer of clothing, so the bare hand is nearly always applied to bare skin (and traditionally in the across-the-knee position). The only serious qualifier to its use is, of course, the fact that, as the smacking progresses, the build-up of stinging heat is two-way; and though the palm is thicker-skinned than the buttocks, a natural limit is still imposed by the dominant's own capacity to endure pain. This moment may arrive farcically early if a delicately nurtured female attempts to hand-spank a male whose prior experience of much severer rods has transformed the skin of his bottom into a material rather tougher than leather. Here indeed a glove might come in useful.

THE SLIPPER

I dislike all prolonged punishments, such as sending to bed, shutting up in a room, and depriving a child of its usual food, as I think they are injurious to the health, and really do very little good. I object to the rod as unfeminine, so, up to ten or twelve years old, I whip all my children, boys and girls alike, with my slipper; it punishes quite as much as a birch, and leaves no marks behind. I make it a rule never to whip a child at the moment, but wait until I am calm and collected.

Letter to *The Englishwoman's Domestic Magazine* (1868)

Like the palm, this implement – one of the homeliest – is generally associated with domestic discipline (the 'slipper' used in English schools is usually a rubber-soled gym-shoe); and, also like the palm, has ad hoc merit, since almost any item of flat-soled footwear can be so employed. A special slipper might be kept for punitive purposes, but at a pinch, whatever the dominant is wearing at the time (high-heeled boots excepted) may well be suitable for instant impressment.

Lady C— opened the window, and broke off some slender sprigs from a myrtle which grew outside, completely spoiling the bush by doing it. In a few moments she had them bare of leaves, and tied together with a blue embroidered garter, with silver fringe, which lay upon the floor.

'Too short to be of much use,' she said; 'but we'll try. Come, my lady, kiss the rod.'

And my lady knelt and did it, laughing all the while; and then Lady C— pinned up her chemise all round, and gave her a good whipping across her knee. Not with the myrtle, though – it proved too brittle, and broke off in little twigs with every blow. Lady C— was at no loss: she didn't let go of my lady; but put up her great ugly foot, and whipped off her slipper. Such a slipper! It had done duty at more than one ball, and was all frayed and soiled at the edges . . . I think I can see that old woman now, flourishing that old pink shoe; and I could see the expression of my lady's face, that she did not relish being touched with it. My lady had beautiful firm flesh; her skin, though dark, was clear and smooth, and every stroke of the pliable slipper raised a deep red mark.[3]

Normally the slipper is held by the heel, and the flat sole is applied. Its effect is very like that of the palm of the hand. As a result most slipperings fall very much at the mild end of the discomfort spectrum and may even not hurt at all.

In the common room one morning the headmaster reported an occasion when corporal punishment meted out by him had been 'hardly as dreadful as it ought to be'. He had found it necessary to correct, with the aid of a slipper, a tendency by one dormitory to become noisily conversational before the first gong. Finding the proceedings somewhat lengthy and pausing to take stock and rest his arm he had discovered

---

3. *Recollections of the Use of the Rod.*

that each victim had rejoined the queue and was coming round again for further correction.[4]

Though the slipper is not normally regarded as a severe weapon, this depends to some extent on its size, weight and flexibility, and on the material of which its sole is constructed: cork, wood, leather and rubber are all commonplace.

THE HAIRBRUSH

Those nursery spankings, where the female hand
Softly insistent and severely bland
Imparts to tender skins a crimson blush;
Those merry smackings with a smooth-back'd brush[5]

The back of a hairbrush is another domestic implement *par excellence*. Specifically a weapon of the boudoir, like the slipper, any flagellatory role it has is secondary to its primary function. If wielded with gusto, it can be a severe weapon, due to its rigidity and weight. Above all, it is a supremely ladylike weapon, used by nanny, mother or stern aunt, and also in English boarding schools, by matron – and others:

The VICTIM fetches a hairbrush from her washstand, gives it to the MONITOR and bends over her knee. The MONITOR slowly raises the VICTIM'S nightie to the waist and, even more slowly, pulls down her knickers. The other girls gather round to watch the spanking. It takes place in slow motion, with the VICTIM ritualistically wriggling as each blow falls. The girls count in unison. We should feel that this is a kind of tribal ceremony – the sacrifice of the willing victim. As the MONITOR spanks, it might be a good idea to project on the

4. *Whimpering in the Rhododendrons.*
5. *Squire Hardman.*

backcloth a moving close shot of the VICTIM's bottom. The counting grows louder and the pace increases. At about the count of ten, we hear electronic 'take-off' music, possibly like the sound used by the Beatles in 'A Day in the Life'. As this sound and the spanking reach a climax, we

BLACKOUT[6]

THE PADDLE

For very serious offences there would be what were known to us as 'public spankations'. Of these, there were only two during the four years I was at the school. The first took place after a weak assistant master had entirely failed to control a prep. which gradually dissolved into a general, anarchic rag. Everyone was wondering why the master was apparently doing nothing. In fact, he was taking names to report to Mr Stow. After evening prayers that night three of the principal offenders, picked at random, were told to come up to the front and take down their trousers. They were then beaten hard with the fives bat[7], before the eyes of the whole school.

The Day Gone By

Sports equipment aside, the true paddle or tapette is a purpose-built implement – or rather, a family of implements, so widely does design and construction vary – intended to introduce technical efficiency into flat-impact forms of corporal punishment. In this specialised arena it stands at the opposite end of the severity scale from the palm of the hand, which it otherwise resembles. In early American schools such implements were called Jonathans. The French name is *tapette* (literally 'smacker'). There is no direct British equivalent.

---

6. Stage direction from *Oh! Calcutta!* (Kenneth Tynan); one of the openly flagellatory scenes that were often cut as the production moved around the world in the early 1970s.

7. A fives bat resembles a table-tennis or Jokari bat.

In 'tone' and style it is wholly American – modern, technically efficient – and for well over a century it has been the standard implement used in US schools, and a serious rival to the palm, hairbrush or leather strap in domestic corrections. In its ultra-severe form it was feared on the cotton plantations of the Antebellum South, and in many adult corrective institutions as well until more recent times. In somewhat lighter vein, it has also come to be associated with 'hazing', or initiation cere-monies, in many American colleges, female as well as male.

At its simplest a paddle is an artificial human hand: a flat oval or rectangular piece of wood or hardened leather with a stiff handle (table-tennis bats serve very well). Both the striking area and the handle may be of any size, though with monster paddles the build-up of air resistance underneath the descending blade may seriously compromise the effectiveness of the stroke. For this reason many plantation owners had their paddles pierced with a number of small holes to allow free passage to the air, reduce the 'ground effect' and so increase severity.

In recent years the paddle has been a highly successful American cultural export. By many couples it is preferred to the cane or the narrower straps, since unlike those weapons it does not leave weals, but a profound reddening over a much broader area. Excessive use of a heavy model will produce bruising, but it is practically impossible to cut the skin. Nonetheless it is ptoentially by far the most severe of all what may be termed spanking weapons, and the complexities of its construction have stimulated a good deal of dissertation from those who wield it. The following three examples of expertise are drawn from the United States, France and Great Britain respectively:

A good paddle ought to have some inner structure, a rein-forcement of plexiglass, metal or leather. Paddles come long, thin or round. The former permits the Superior to concen-trate on small areas, while the round ones elicit an all-over glow. The unreinforced paddle is suitable for light punish-ment, but I consider the hand more precise and intimidating in that case. One paddle I used with excellent results was of thick leather reinforced with rubber, long, thin and bifurcate. This 'slapper' made a terrifying noise when striking home, and acted as a cross between a paddle and a whip, allowing one all the sinuosity of attack that a whip provides, along with the heavy-handedness of a paddle.[8]

There are many other instruments which one should not ignore: for example, table-tennis racquets, flat rulers and all other easily manageable wooden flat surfaces. (Avoid plastic objects, even when they appear solid: if they break they can suddenly be transformed into dangerously sharp blades.)[9]

The sound of the paddle's impact is the most tremendous *whack*! – in this respect at least it is the most awesome of all implements of correction. At the same time its effects, though extreme at the time, rapidly fade, so that a culprit who is literally dancing from foot to foot after a liberal application – a curious phenomenon, which I have seen again and again – will, an hour later, be found sitting down with little or no difficulty.[10]

There is only one problem with this excellent implement: it has no obvious purpose other than that for which it has been manufactured, and is therefore a give-away.

THE STRAP

'You get them to put their cuffs over their wrists so you don't injure their wrists when you belt them. Then you put the belt over your shoulder and line yourself up. Keep your leg out of the way because it's pretty painful and you look

---

8. *The Correct Sadist*, p. 33.
9. *Je Dresse Mon Mari.*
10. *A Guide to the Correction of Young Gentlemen*, p. 66.

stupid if you hit yourself. You don't use an enormous amount of movement from the shoulder – you just let the weight of the belt follow through. And you hit them.'

A Scottish Schoolmistress[11]

The punishment strap remains a favourite implement among the Celtic fringe of the English-speaking nations, with Scotland and Canada (the latter perhaps because of its Scottish connections) leading the way. For some reason it has never been popular in continental Europe, though the *ferula* of Roman pedagogues (in origin, as etymology implies, a stalk of giant fennel and therefore a switch or cane) frequently took the form of a thong of leather or rawhide. In an equestrian society suitable lengths of leather would always be available, and the question of durability surely played a part. A person appointed to do more than the usual amount of thrashing (schoolmaster, slave-driver) might well prefer the permanence and portability of such an instrument: giant fennel does not grow everywhere, while a strap may be coiled up and put in the pocket.

It can be improvised readily: in times gone by, from a scrap of harness-trace, a razor strop or a leather belt of traditional sturdiness. But for at least two centuries it has been the favourite official instrument of scholastic discipline north of the Anglo-Scottish border, and it is in Scotland that this thrifty instrument has secured its lasting fame.

'Taw' is an old Celtic word for thong. Take a few feet of spare harness, double it so that has two tails, and you have a pair of taws, or 'tawse', as the word has evolved, losing its plurality if none of its fearsome reputation. Though in fact in both Scottish and Canadian schools for most of this century the instrument has traditionally been applied to a culprit's open palm, it can, of course, be applied elsewhere as well.

---

11. Scottish schoolteacher Valerie Thornton, speaking on BBC Scotland's *Current Account* TV news magazine (1981). She was demonstrating how to apply the tawse (colloquially known in Scotland as 'the belt'). Readers will be relieved to hear that the object of her demonstration was a desktop.

The strap is a hybrid implement which may vary in shape to a considerable extent, from very wide to very narrow, tailed or otherwise, and sometimes with a stiff handle. It is usually made of leather, though a century ago the Canadian educational authorities deployed New World technical know-how and produced an even more fearsome variety made from hard rubber backed with canvas (vegetarians at least ought to approve).

There is an undeniable mystique attached to the strap. An official model from Scotland or the north of England (where it was also much favoured by schools, though it has now fallen entirely from official use) is today a collector's item. Much lore has been published about how they should be made – the quality of leather, and so on – all the way down to the embossing of the maker's name and the symbol that stood for the grade of severity of the finished article. Two main kinds were in use. One was broad and flat and fairly wide; the other was thin, cruel and bifurcated into two slender tails which gave it something of the effect of a short whip – the famous Lochgelly pattern tawse, a true descendant of the Roman thong, and widely regarded as the most painful incarnation of this ancient weapon.

The thinner the striking surface of a strap, the faster it will move through the air for the same output of force and the more painful will be the result. Moreover, the added flexibility of the thinner straps will produce a lashing or wraparound effect unless extreme care is taken. The broader straps are more like paddles in their effect; less flexibility and a more diffused blow put them at the milder end of the severity scale. Length may vary, from fifteen inches up to three feet (the latter is almost impossible to aim and control, and in any case far too severe).

WHIPS, CROPS AND MARTINETS

The whip – which can entangle, choke and even wound – is technically a most fascinating 'weapon': it should taper from butt to tip, and when it is shaken a wave of motion runs along its length. Energy cannot be created or destroyed; the mass of the moving section decreases with the taper as that wave moves from the butt, but the energy $\frac{1}{2}MV^2$ must stay the same and so the wave velocity increases. If the whip tapered perfectly to a point, the very tip would ultimately travel at infinite speed (ignoring relativity for a moment); even in this imperfect world, it does move faster than sound to produce the whip-crack. This high velocity also means that the tip can flick through skin to leave lash-wounds.

War in 2080

Largely for the reasons advanced above, the true whip is not a suitable instrument for the discipline of man or beast, let alone flagellatory fun and games. Deadly weapons (and for once 'weapon' is the *mot juste*) like the historical Russian knout, of which one stroke could kill, may have pose value: luckily the longer ones are almost impossible to wield in a confined space. In other words, they are either ridiculous or dangerous, and in either case should be eschewed entirely.

But many instruments may be called a whip: anything with a lash or lashes, for example, is usually so described. Crops and riding switches are often also termed whips, even though at the lengths usually encountered they are semi-stiff like canes. The longer and thinner an equestrian switch becomes – for example, a dressage whip – the more its overall flexibility increases, the more it begins to resemble a true whip, and the more potentially dangerous it is in use.

The riding crop is an instrument of the former class, and one greatly favoured by dominatrixes, since it is capable of great returns of severity for the expenditure of minimal effort. Moreover, it is an elegant weapon with considerable ancillary pose value.

She posed before him, a long and thin riding-crop in one hand. She stood arrogantly, legs apart, head back and her fists on her hips, glaring down at him.

'Now, you swine – it's time you found out what happens to scum like you! Straighten your back! Stop drooping like a bag of rubbish!'[12]

In many respects the crop resembles a cane, but is even more flexible, and may well have a heavier, if shorter, shaft. In the past crops and riding switches were made from whalebone, a substance noted for its astonishing combination of density and flexibility. These days 'doms' – and riders – must make do with nylon or plastic-cored crops. 'Keepers', the squared-off leather tags at the business end, or short supplementary whipcord lashes are optional.

Generally speaking, the multi-tailed varieties like the 'cat', the monastic discipline and their little sister, the martinet, are less likely to lacerate than other kinds of whip. The lashes, often flat ribbons of leather, fall in a body, often entangled, and may even hinder each others' effectiveness: the stroke of a martinet is seldom an elegant fanning out of all nine leather strips into a broad catchment area, but all too often a heavier smack as they arrive in a body. Lashed implements are also difficult to use accurately (in both azimuths). For this reason, while they can take severe heavyweight forms – the naval cat-o'-nine-tails is the most notorious example – the lighter grades are not regarded as seriously punitive weapons, though they look well in fetish catalogues.

Rose had taken from the cupboard two instruments of flagellation. She placed one on a seat near the arm-chair and held the other in her hand. [This was] a martinet or cat o' nine tails, but of a kind that would have been of no terror to a naughty boy. While the wooden handle was bound round with soft leather, the six leather thongs, about a foot long, were covered with crimson velvet.[13]

Those inclined to accept the alleged Englishness of this particular

---

12. *Blue Angel Nights.*
13. *Two Flappers in Paris.*

vice may profitably contemplate the spectacle of the French nation (who originally made the allegation) methodically disciplining their children for over a hundred years with the martinet, a highly specialised instrument. Refined into its modern form by a Major Martinet, of the French military academy St Cyr[14], who desired (apparently it was his life's work) to develop an implement suitable for punishing officer cadets on their bare bottoms with logical consistency, it was taken up by many generations of French (and other European) parents, and even achieved a fleeting popularity in America, though it has seldom been seen or used in the British Isles. For the English, it was probably not precise enough. Besides, they already had something much more effective of their own.

THE CANE

He approached the bed and shivered slightly. On the silk coverlet, beside the pillow, the governess had left a cane whose end was split and beginning to fray – that cane, he knew it only too well. The previous afternoon he had been whipped with it, as a punishment for his slovenliness in not having replaced a broken shoelace. His flesh was still tender from the effects of this punishment; but the remembered sting of the rattan only intensified the ardour of his desire – that mysterious and uncertain desire which betrayed itself by an irrational wish to be mastered, scolded, shamed and whipped by his governess, and to touch and breathe the odour of every object belonging to her – above all, those objects consecrated to her immediate use.

He picked up the cane with a trembling hand, and pressed his lips to the end which had felt her grip, imagining he could still detect the warmth and scent of the strong hand which had held it.

Harriet Marwood, Governess

---

14. The equivalent of Sandhurst or West Point.

In its narrowest sense a cane is simply a stick. It has a number of practical uses: supporting plants where they grow, and the elderly or infirm as they move about. It may be split, knotted and woven into baskets, or even furniture, of pleasing appearance. A cane (as opposed to any other kind of stick) is made of one of the giant Asian grasses, bamboo or rattan, and has a slender, jointed stem. It will vary in flexibility from very little (the walking-stick or bean support), to a great deal (the fine canes woven into a chair back). It is an innocuous, cheap and useful material, whose only drawback is that it must be imported.

It has another use:

> The cane is the archetypal implement of English school discipline. Stroke for stroke, a good quality standard school cane probably administers the most intense sting of any instrument of correction and is greatly feared . . . With the cane every stroke must be clean, very hard and painfully effective. A caning is not a gentle or homely punishment. It is one of the most serious forms of discipline and should be treated as such.[15]

Single switches plucked from ordinary vegetation have always served as instruments of driving or punishment. But a switch has a short life and is cast away once its usefulness has finished. Not so the cane. Although there are many schoolboy legends in England about the best way to sabotage a cane and cause it to break mysteriously – a single human hair, properly pre-positioned on the victim's palm, is supposed to achieve this, though on what scientific principle has never been satisfactorily explained[16] – canes can, and do, last for years, being repaired as they fray, then trimmed, then bound again, until eventually the instrument is too short for use.

---

15. *The Female Disciplinary Manual.*
16. An incident of this type takes place in the famous mid-Victorian English schoolboy novel *Eric, or Little by Little*.

Durability is only one reason why the cane began to displace the birch in the early part of the nineteenth century, most notably in Britain, but also in Holland and other northern European countries. Like the strap, it has never really caught on in France, and although American SM practitioners now make use of it, it has seldom been part of the American disciplinary tradition. It was at the end of the eighteenth century, with the opening up of the great European trading empires in the Far East, notably the British and Dutch, that rattan, the quintessential cane-making material, first began to arrive in quantity. It was remarkably cheap – much cheaper than whalebone, which rivals it in most other ways – long-lasting and extraordinarily light and flexible: a punishment switch to outperform and outlast any splinter-prone bamboo or rude twig cut from the nearest hazel bush or birch tree. It came in a choice of grades, some thicker, heavier and less flexible, others thin and whip-like in their sinuosity; and of course it could be cut to any manageable length. And it was powerfully effective, capable of far harsher discipline even than the fabled birch.

Not least of the reasons for the general introduction of the cane was the growing suspicion that the baring of bottoms for punishment – until this point, a *sine qua non* of home and school discipline – might be considered indecent and an offence to sensibility.[17] The cane required no such prior condition for use.

He then selected his cane, a lithe four to five-footer, laying it for a few moments across the office desk, a flat-topped piece of furniture to the side of the fireplace. Next he ordered Albert to loosen his belt, and smartly pulling out the chap's shirt for him, he felt coldly underneath to make sure that there was nothing between trousers and skin – they didn't supply these young paupers with underclothes, I'd better add. Then he made the chap tighten his belt, then made

---

17. Another reaction was the introduction of the practice of chastising the palm – a much more dangerous theatre of operations, and far more painful.

him bend right down and touch his toes. Moloch then smoothed the shirt down on the chap's back, and now invited old Moses to come and do his usual part, the old man gripping the chap's head between his legs, and pressing down on the chap's back with his hands, and Moloch himself exerted some pressure as well to get the seat stretched at its very tightest.

'All as you wish it?' grunted the old man.

'Pretty much so,' Moloch grunted in return.

'Fifteen clean cuts, mind,' said the old man.

'I know you prefer 'em clean, sir, and I'll do m'best,' said Moloch.[18]

The above scene approaches the very limits of severity (though unlike Beatrice Fry, these are fictional characters). But even the traditional six of the best, less than half the above award, is no laughing matter, assuming the strokes have been delivered with optimum force. For despite its other acknowledged merits as an instrument of corporal punishment, the cane has one drawback: it is almost impossible to use with leniency. Up to a certain level of force, it simply falls across the target with little or no percussive or stinging effect. Not until it is swung with some determination does it achieve anything at all – and by then, it has already become painful: there is no middle way. Used with maximum force by a strong person, a heavy cane can be excruciating, even dangerous: it welts, and if the welts cross, it can wound. Some very dense varieties of rattan – so-called malacca, which is prominently jointed – or other similar materials, such as tamarind or palm-rib, can wound in any case; and in judicial canings conducted in some Asian countries like Singapore, they are intended to do so, horribly, from the very first stroke, and to leave permanent scars. Such brutalities have no place in this book, nor in any reasonable system of justice, even one willing to employ corporal punishment.

---

18. *The Blue Marble.*

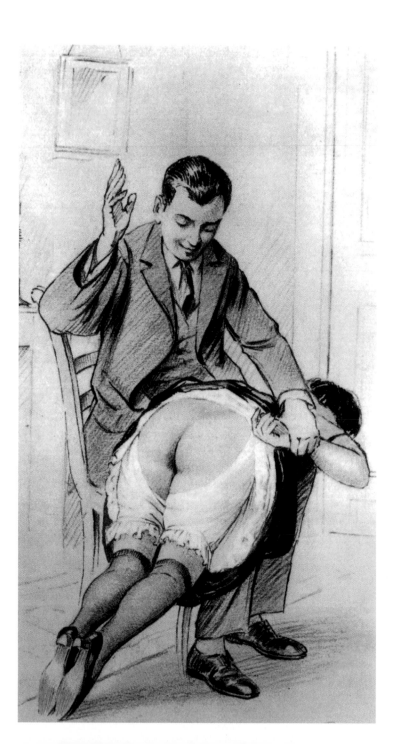

Let's BEAT *the* so-and-so *out of your* house-records!

together again in
M-G-M's
riotous comedy

WILLIAM POWELL
MYRNA LOY
in
"THE THIN MAN GOES HOME"

with GLORIA DeHAVEN
LUCILE WATSON · ANNE REVERE
HARRY DAVENPORT

The No-Nonsense Lover is a favourite archetype of the submissive female. 'Goaded or provoked, he will warn once—and then act. And it will hurt—but not too much: that would never do. For he is neither a bully nor an obsessive, and for him the flagellation is only nominally a punishment; its prime duty is to serve as a catharsis, its secondary purpose is aphrodisiac.' *[Chapter 9.]* The drawing *[facing page]* is an excellent example of a French erotic book illustration of the period 1910–30. *Above:* the film poster is in an even lighter vein—a rolled-up newspaper can't do a great deal of damage; while in the German drawing *[right]* the 'discipline' is being administered in the most voluptuous (and consentual) manner possible.

Domestic Discipline (1)

Upper: This 16th-century Italian copper-plate shows an unfaithful wife (horsed on the gardener's back) 'catching it' from the slipper-sole wielded by her irate, elderly husband (the decrepitude of whom doubtless explains the infidelity).

Lower: The 'Uncle from Hell' in full cry—this illustration is from the Marquis de Sade's *Thérèse Philosophe* (1st edition), and is fairly typical of the Marquis's œuvre. Nearly all de Sade's 'male leads' correspond to the Wicked Uncle archetype.

Domestic Discipline (2)
Above: Mama rules Papa (and the family) with an unashamed rod, as depicted in this 17th-century French satirical painting.

Below: These two late 19th-century German postcard images are droll examples of the same particular mode of Family Discipline.

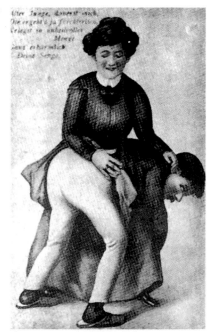

Male masochism:
There is such a
thing as a
masochistic
impulse, and it
can venture into
strange country, as
this terrifying
drawing (by
Planitz, *top left*),
shows. The
drawing [*lower
left*] is a 16th-
century depiction
of Aristotle at the mercy of
Phyllis; while the more
modern French drawing *c.*
1930 [*lower right*] attempts to
convey the genuinely
romantic feelings which may
be experienced by the male
submissive.

Flogging as a Judicial Penalty: Despite a widespread assumption that the (modern) Singapore implementation of judicial caning is a British legacy, the Chinese have always employed corporal punishment, with a cane, on the bare buttocks, to a ferocious degree, as this old print *(above)* confirms. Floggings were often fatal. These days they only wound (permanently). *Below:* An interested lady and gentleman inspect the Clerkenwell prison 'boys' pony' c. 1875.

Flagellation as Art, ancient and modern
Left: The Môther-archetype at work again, in this mediæval church wood-carving. *Below:* This bronze group with its egalitarian message, by an American sculptress, is called *Tables Turned*. A limited edition, it sells for $15,000 a copy.

It is therefore a formidable weapon, easily the most severe in English school tradition (in its day the birch was no less feared, but chiefly because of the shame attached to a birching). The cane has been a classroom prop from the beginning of the last century to very recent times, and in being finally banished from the classroom, it retreated only as far as the head's or housemaster's study, where it lurked in a cupboard ready for instant if private use. More reprehensibly, it was also issued to prefects in British public schools, and these youths were allowed to wield their canes on their juniors, nominally for disciplinary reasons. (The scenes in the films *If* and *Another Country* are vivid re-enactments of these events, half punitive, half bullying, wholly indefensible and barely credible to the non-British.)

The cane is a very precise weapon and its use must be learned. One way is on the job. Another is to get in a little practice beforehand.

There in the corner stood the cane. After a moment's hesitation he took hold of it and proceeded to examine it. It was both thicker and more springy than he had imagined. Altogether, in fact, it looked a brutally effective sort of instrument.

Then, idly at first, he began swishing with it. But that taught him nothing – except perhaps to avoid the dangerous backlash, the recoil. If he really wanted to experiment, he would have to hit something. A cushion possibly.

And why not a cushion? There was one, a red velvet one, on the settee in the corner. And, crossing the room with the cane tucked smartly under his arm, he picked it up and arranged the cushion carefully across the seat of one of the chairs. Then he removed his coat and rolled his sleeves up. He was engrossed, utterly engrossed, in this piece of practice by now. And he spat on his hand before attempting to get his grip right.

'Six of the best, I think we said,' he observed to the empty air above the chair. 'And if the treatment is not effective it can be repeated.'

'Six of the best!'

There was a classic ring about it, and he repeated the words, louder and more menacingly.

Then he began.

'One!'

Pause.

'Two!'

Pause.

'Three!'

He was breathing more heavily by now. And the veins in his forehead were beginning to pulsate. But he persisted.

'Four!'

It was just as he was about to deliver the fifth blow – the cane was raised and his teeth were clenched fast in readiness – when he heard somebody address him.[19]

So potent is the cane as a symbol of English school life that, like the schoolmaster's mortar-board, it serves as an 'instant graphic' for corporal punishment in its own right. However, it should be added that in England it has always been the tradition to bend one of the ends of a school cane into the famous curved handle, presumably so that it can be hung on a hook or cupboard rail. This effect may be achieved either by steaming or soaking. No other nation does this, and indeed, in England only in schools was the modification applied: naval or institutional canings were traditionally administered with longer, heavier, thicker, straight canes, sometimes with intricately bound handles.

THE BIRCH ROD

Cousin Daisy produced a bunch of twigs that I recognised as coming from the weeping birch outside the front door. I thought of her going out in her tweed suit and toque, perhaps

---

19. *Children of the Archbishop.*

this morning to pick these particular twigs, choosing them carefully for having already lost their leaves, and perhaps testing them against her own thigh. I wondered whether she had perhaps picked too many, and dispensed with a few, throwing them lightly aside on the grass, or whether she had thought her bunch too meagre, and so gone back for more.

'Pull down your drawers,' she interrupted my thoughts by saying, 'and kneel down.'

Daughters of Divinity

When historical writers talk about the 'rod', they mean the birch rod: a bundle of twigs from the birch tree (species *Betula*), gathered together at one end into a handle, with the other end left unbound to form a spray. That is the simplest definition. In fact almost infinite variety may be attained, and no birch will ever be exactly like another. There may be variance in the length, thickness and number of individual switches, the manner in which they are trimmed and bound and the freshness (or prior treatment, for example with salt-and-vinegar 'pickle') of the rod. It is not even necessary to use birch wood, since equivalent (though differing) effects may be achieved by using other kinds, such as hazel, willow, applewood, light rattan, broom or even heather shoots. Some birches are chosen from long, straight stems and stripped of all greenery and side twigs. These form slender rods with narrow, penetrating sprays. Others may be plucked more or less at random, with their natural bushiness left intact, like a besom broom, in order to achieve a wider spray and a more comprehensive stroke (though the air resistance will also be greater and the stroke necessarily less focused). Some are long and bulky and used in ceremonial mode; others are short, light and wispy and used across the knee. A birch may be put together very quickly, and with small ceremony, for instant use (provided the surroundings furnish the necessary raw materials): it is not strictly necessary to bind the handle of such an extempore rod. Others are 'put up' with enormous ritual (traditionally by the sinner in person, hence the expression 'to make a rod for one's own back') and may rival the most subtle Japanese flower arrangement for beauty and finish.

The 'wand of Venus' is certainly the most ancient – and elegised – of all rods of punishment, and used to be the symbol of corporal discipline, certainly in Europe, its original home. The menacing spray is seen, in many a mediæval woodcut, clutched in the fist of the dominie; later, it is also the wand of office of the village-school dame. It appears, again and again, in seventeenth- and eighteenth-century pictorial allegories of the Virgin and her predecessor, Venus (each uses one, with supreme old-world elegance, to chastise her boy child). The birch rod has a pedigree second to none, and is an elegant, feminine – even romantic – instrument. Moreover, despite its fearsome reputa-tion, it is not intrinsically severe, since to have any impact at all it must be used on the bare skin: even a single layer of clothing will render much of its effect null and void.

Nevertheless, despite its lineage and undeniable class, the birch is no longer ubiquitous. Thrifty professionals might well object to an instrument that is so much trouble to make and yet so short-lived in practice. Used with vigour, a birch will fray at the ends, and, sooner rather than later, disintegrate: the aftermath of a birching at one of the English public schools was a debris of twigs all over the floor of the punishment room. Many such schools employed a rod-maker, to ensure a continuing supply of birches (traditionally this task was given to the porter's wife, who might be unofficially named Mother Birch by the pupils for this reason), for the manufacture of a serviceable rod is no easy matter.

You must also understand how to choose the birch twigs; they should be full of sap and taken from a young tree, and the tips must be sharp as needles; the twigs ought not to be taken from a common birch broom, where the ends are cut off so that the tips are quite blunt, otherwise they may hit well enough, but there is no proper swish. Then you must know how to combine the thick with the thin and slender, and how they ought to be properly put together; they must be elastic and flexible, have reach and swing, so as to sing music in the air, be ready and willing for use, and come down in quick succession on the part to be visited until it soon becomes red all over. Again, the thickness of the rod is to be considered, that it may fit conveniently to the hand, nor should it be tied up too tightly, or else the rod will be like a stick and the twigs have no play. And do you also know, girls, how the broom-makers manage with old birch brooms to make them again soft and flexible? They boil them in water, and I used to do the same when a birch rod appeared to be used up.[20]

There was little grace or refinement, let alone any discernible sense of proportion, in the often ferocious birchings administered to naval cadets and juvenile criminals throughout the last and for some of the present century. The naval version combined the general flagellatory principles we have already seen in Beatrice Fry's approach (see chapter 10) with the considerable extra humiliation of the birch, administered publicly with terrific severity and full naval ceremonial (the Royal Navy has had great experience in arranging corporal punishments in an orderly and seamanlike manner). The prison or reform-school or police-cell version might be relatively more private, but was in no other way an improvement:

The room was about as bare as he had expected, and he at once noticed the donkey they would soon be riding, a sturdy tripod well furnished with straps, and two fearsome birch-rods, their twigs looking quite fresh from a soaking, propped against one of the donkey's legs. The screw who was apparently to do the job, a very stocky bloke with a fleshy face, was already waiting by the donkey, and after exchanging a word with him, Mutton-chops drew Albert and 924 up a couple of paces in front of him. A short, grim silence followed,

20. *Nell in Bridewell*, p. 94.

while Albert and the other chap stared at the donkey and the rods, and the two screws seemed to stare at each other, then appeared a stout, important-looking prison officer, woefully short in the legs for his position, whom Albert at once recognised as Ned's 'barrel of a bloke', he being followed by a tall young man in spectacles, ghastly thick spectacles they were, and he also had ghastly skin that looked like parchment, he being presumably a junior surgeon . . .

And now cold hands . . . stripped Albert of his prison trousers, and then lifted him on to the famous donkey, and strapped him down on it, till he knew he was a mere pair of bare round buttocks to those behind. But even at this delicate moment he retained some spirit – it was all in the game, wasn't it? But cry out he did at every stroke, though his cries were only cries of the moment, single cries of pain, for the twigs left a smarter pain than he had ever experienced before . . .[21]

But such are the variations in severity possible with this instrument that quite another approach is also possible:

Next day, when we were walking in the coppice, she said 'Let's get the twigs now for that birch. You choose them. It's for you, remember.' And we chose the twigs together. 'No, that's no good,' she'd say. 'They have to be flexible and springy. They musn't be too heavy. They've got to sting, remember, not to hurt, to cut, not bruise.' We collected about a dozen twigs. 'That'll make a very good birch,' she said. When we got back to the house, she took the twigs up into my room and hid them in a drawer under my shirts. That evening she brought up some ribbons. 'We'll make a pretty birch of it,' she said. And she tied up the twigs. She swished it through the air. 'This'll do,' she said.[22]

---

21. *The Blue Marble.*
22. *The Fatal Gift.*

How severe is the birch? Effects may vary from a mild pinkening of the skin to a lattice of shallow lacerations which bleeds profusely, if superficially, at the time, but heals, almost always without trace, within a few days. For many – perhaps most – people who practice flagellation, or are excited by its imagery, the shedding of blood represents the watershed of acceptability. Certainly it is as good a point as any to draw the line – not least because it is the moment at which the human body becomes vulnerable to a new range of possible infections, some of them deadly to life. It is nigh on impossible to do lasting physical damage with a birch, but it is certainly possible, given a little effort and perhaps more than one rod, temporarily to make it look and feel as if one has done so. As always this will depend on several factors: the weight and length of the component switches, the force with which they are wielded, the number of strokes (and the increased likelihood of crossing) and not least the resilience of the recipient's epidermis. Even without bleeding, the skin will be considerably stimulated by the lusty application of even a small birch; indeed, such is the physiological *raison d'être* of the birch rod's only 'respectable' employment: its application to the bare flesh by health-loving Nordics enjoying *après*-saunas in the age-old Baltic style.[23]

What I described earlier as the birch rod's romantic appeal derives from its feminine shape, the poignancy of its all-too-short life, and the uniqueness of each rod. These qualities are reflected in the lush ceremonies tradition has long attached to its employment. Personal recollection, erotic fiction, and that strange area where the one masquerades as the

---

23. I have taken part in one of these sessions. At the appropriate moment the fresh birch branches were produced and solemnly applied, to oneself and, with a certain amount of self-consciousness, to each other. It was all done in a manly, faintly jocular atmosphere; but all the same there was just a hint, a touch, a smidgeon of what-do-you-call-it, especially when one chap swatted another chap playfully across the behind while he was bent over, then rolled his eyes at him when he stood up.

other are bursting with examples of such exalted rituals.

Madame De Berros then clapped her hands, when two of the female attendants, who were always in waiting in the ante-room, came in through the folding doors and courtesied. 'Bring me a rod,' said madame to one of them. 'Prepare Miss B.,' she motioned to the other. The culprit scarcely even changed colour, and, seeming to know that all resistance would be in vain, resigned herself at once to her fate. The maid having brought in a long birch rod of very slender twigs, handed it to madame from a salver, with a courtesy, and then proceeded to aid her confrere in the unrobing. Having courtesied to madame, and kissed the rod – a cere-mony which was never omitted upon the occasion of a flagellation – one of the maids took her gently on her shoul-der, turning round at a little distance from madame. It being my first appearance at a flagellation, I felt a mixture of emotions which I cannot describe.

All being ready, madame, flinging back her arm, brought the rod down gently on the culprit, who at once uttered an exclamation as if she had been plunged in a cold bath. About a dozen stripes equally gentle followed, and then madame, as if warmed by the exercise, concluded in a way which brought the lady to tears. Being at length let down on an ottoman, her hands were released, when, after kneeling down and kissing the rod, Miss B. – retired with a profound courtesy, the attendant carrying her petticoats and robe into the ante-room.[24]

She placed herself on a high chair and her feet on a foot-stool, so as to make a broad lap. She desired me to lie across it well spread. I forgot to mention that each time upon being flogged by her (it was only twice) – perhaps to strike awe – she tied on a punishment apron of black satin. Her own

24. Letter to *The Englishwoman's Domestic Magazine*.

dress she lifted up in front, and tied the black apron over it, all in silence . . .[25]

These punishments are literally fantastic; and even some non-flagellants might find the second one enjoyable, whichever side of the black satin apron they prefer.

25. Ibid.

12

HAUTE COUTURE, COUTURE EN BAS

A Sweet disorder in the dress
Kindles in clothes a wantonness
Robert Herrick, *Delight in Disorder*

We have arrived at the outer reaches of the flagellatory experience, where minor themes, singular resonances, unexpected nuances, esoteric variations, eccentricities, digressions and strange oddments of equipment contribute in their various ways to the greater conception. Here flagellationism touches hands with several other well-charted and by no means mutually exclusive deviations, where most of the individual customisation of what might be otherwise a standard scenario takes place, and 'what was pervoise becomes pervoiser'.

Many of these flavours or touchstones are readily comprehensible even to 'civilians'. Key phrases or commands, even single words, may have genuinely heart-faltering impact. In many circles homogeneous materials like latex, rubber, plastic, leather and steel constitute an excitingly *de rigueur* dress code. Bondage – a risky pastime whose attractions are nevertheless by no means incomprehensible – may be a licensed part of some proceedings. To enable this and other refinements to be executed efficiently, specific items of furniture may be required: craftsman-built pillories, permanent and unashamed like Mrs

Berkeley's Horse[1] (and conversation pieces to get any party going); or cunningly collapsible whipping trestles which, when a door-bell unexpectedly rings, can convert to a sofa-bed·or birdcage in seconds flat – assuming that no patient is attached. Clothing of a deliberately humbling nature – an area of connoisseurship all its own, as we shall see – is often imposed on submissives, usually at their own wish and sometimes at their own request. Conversely, a dominant may wear an outfit whose sartorial message is no less unambivalent (in one form or another, 'I rule, OK?'). But however trivial any individual's added personal ingredient might appear to the uninitiated in the light of what else may be going on, its proper and timely fulfilment, execution or introduction may nevertheless be of vital importance to that individual. Such specialist curves do not fit into any of the broader trajectories discussed so far, yet should not be under-estimated or ignored, since a great many individual flagellants hold a number of these minor (and sometimes not so minor) preferences in common, to a greater or lesser degree. Properly tendencies rather than new scenarios, their combined influence shades a notable part of the general-purpose flagellant's fantasy landscape.

This is a bewildering country, less subject to rule by archetype and more individualistic, not to say anarchic. As a rough but by no means unfair rule of thumb, it may be guessed that the more frills and furbelows there are within an established flagellatory production, the more likely one is to find a male in the director's chair (probably nameplated 'False Submissive'). Much of this twilight zone is indeed concerned with specifically male fantasy. Uncoincidentally, it is also the moment in which the tastes of the two sexes, which thus far have been in generally harmonious accord, begin to diverge, for in general these are not areas of male sexuality which many women easily comprehend (or, comprehending, approve). Women are naturally wary of being

---

1. Mrs Teresa Berkeley, a notorious flagellant courtesan of the early nineteenth century, invented a special modular rack-cum-pillory which could be adjusted in an almost infinite number of ways to suit particular clients' tastes and physiognomies.

treated exclusively or even primarily as fetish objects, and undoubtedly there will be occasions when a woman discovers that flagellant practices with her partner, which she understands, have somehow diminished, in her view, into fetishistic, not to say quasi-masturbatory practices in which she finds herself effectively depersonalised and even disembodied. She cannot be expected to enjoy this situation, and many women do not: yet it remains as obsessively important as ever to the other party concerned. There is no obvious resolution to this problem once it has become an issue, and few ways back from the hurt that can ensue from the inevitable showdown. It can deteriorate with horrible rapidity into an outright collapse of the whole relationship, with resulting bitter resentment on both sides. Better to circumnavigate this and other calamities altogether by employing foresight, sensitivity, self-control and tact – in other words, love and kindness – at all times, even when the gift of complete understanding has not yet been bestowed.

FANCY DRESS

Pupils must be properly equipped with all the mandatory items on the Kit List. Items need not be new, but must be clean and neatly pressed. We may be able to assist those with problems acquiring kit. Badges must be properly attached where appropriate and all items clearly marked with the pupil's name.

Muir Academy Prospectus, 1993–94

A scenario with a script, actors, props and an abundance of goodwill still requires a suitable wardrobe if the production is to have the best chance of living up to expectations. Clothes maketh the deviant no less than anybody else, and no deviation is as much imbued with couture, both haute and the other kind, as flagellation. Careful costuming adds authenticity to any persona, and colour to any drama. It can aid the suspension of disbelief, at least for some of the people some of the time, and is one way in which the standing hierarchical values may immediately be defined; there are many other hidden codes, each with considerable symbolic force, which may be transmitted – all without a word being spoken.

Power-dressing is manifested at a logical level and works exactly the way one might expect. For example, a determined governess-*manquée* takes as much trouble as she can physically to invoke the archetype. She will emphasise those parts of her physical appearance that lend themselves to the desired image, and for which she has the clothes or accessories available, and suppress those parts of her which do not. She exchanges her normal, comfortable, unmenacing sweatshirt and denims for a severe and bossy outfit, certainly with a skirt (and a long skirt is better than a short skirt). She scrapes her hair back into a chignon and removes most of her make-up. She puts on a pair of sensible shoes, stitches an expression of chilly dignity on to her face, picks up her cane, and essays forth to do what must be done. She is dressed for the part, knows it, knows others will know it, and her confidence is high.

Couture en bas operates with no less sartorial variation. Most examples will be dictated by the scenario as a whole. Depending on overall context (and whether it is hers or her partner's fantasy which is being spoon-fed), a female submissive might expect to wear a schoolgirl's gymslip, or the short tunic of the slave girl, or the 'frou-frou' of a French Maid, or the tarty appurtenances of a teenage hooker. One or another of the various degrees of nakedness might be imposed. There are dozens of accepted themes and sub-themes, each of which offers different resonances, different degrees of submission. A schoolgirl costume implies immaturity but does not otherwise degrade. The slave-girl mini toga emphasises sexual submission rather than childishness. The teenage tart outfit stresses culpability, therefore eligibility for punishment (its submissiveness is derived from the wearer's moral disadvantage to the dominant). The various degrees of nakedness have always been 'shame states' in certain circumstances, and their unquestioning acceptance is a token of complete surrender.

The language of clothes operates on more than one level. Superficially, a dominant costume proclaims: 'I am powerful – you will submit.' On a deeper level, it adds: 'Behold the care I have taken over my appearance. This is evidence that I am taking trouble, that I am expert and dedicated, that I am in control – that with me you are safe.' In other words – and oddly enough in view of the superficially intimidating nature of the costume – its underlying message is: 'Trust me.'

Dressing down proclaims the opposite: 'I am weak – you have conquered. I trust you and will obey you. I place myself in your hands.' And just as the success of an authoritarian ensemble may reinforce the wearer's actual authority, so *couture en bas* of almost any form subverts self-esteem in accordance with the specific characteristic of the identified persona (by definition, there are no submissive archetypes). This can be longstanding (a uniform of some kind, a silver ankle ring, a placard reading SLATTERN; a dog-tag inscribed IF FOUND UNACCOMPANIED, SMACK AND SEND HOME); or – more immediate and devastating – the single expertly positioned stick of gelignite that brings the preposterous edifice of ego down in a ruinous heap.

'And now, Julian, you shall be deprived of your trousers. Take a long leave of them. When you will see them again, I do not know; they teach you all sorts of resistance and naughtiness and make you assume airs of ridiculous superiority which you do not possess. We must make a girl of you. Elise, make him stand up and take them off.' 'Oh, Mademoiselle! Oh, please do not before you and the girls. Oh, don't—' Elise, however, speedily unfastened the straps which kept me kneeling, but kept my elbows still confined, and busied herself in unfastening my buttons. Maidlike, she tore open all the front first, to my intense shame, and then fumbled round my waist with both hands at once, kneeling before me. I cannot describe what I felt at being close to a girl in this condition with her hands busy about me, the front of my principal garment opened and violated, and my person almost coming into actual contact with her swelling bosom as she proceeded with uncompromising promptitude and rapidity to unfasten my trousers, my governess and the three girls looking on with amusement. I myself felt like a fowl about to be roasted and was nearly stupefied with shame.[2]

In the above passage the change in status represented by the change in clothes is more thoroughgoing and complex still. Two motives operate: one, to impose 'shame discipline' of an ongoing sartorial kind on to a rebellious young male, in the above case by the simple expedient of confiscating his trousers; two, a later stage (still to come), actually to force the submissive to change sex, by imposing girl's clothing – 'We must make a girl of you.' Ostensibly, this is to 'feminise' him; objectively to improve his character by excising all trace of the rough, brutish male, by means of what today would be called crash assertion therapy or super-positive discrimination.

The same effect but to lesser degree is achieved by dressing the subordinate male in garments considerably more juvenile than those to which his real age might entitle him – a short-trousered ensemble of nearly any kind sharply reduces status and is the exact equivalent of the schoolgirl-submissive's gymslip and ankle socks.

Overall, these are displays of power on an angelic – or demonic – scale; authority so potent that submissives must even change sex or age to order.

There are several minor reasons why a submissive might be bidden to dress in an unusual or outlandish way. One at least is sharply, even lewdly, practical: to afford the dominant rapid and unencumbered access to those parts that are to be chastised, presumably within a scenario where chastisements are frequent and summary enough to justify the concomitant stylistic sacrifice. By partially preparing a submissive, well before he or she has done

---

2. *Gynecocracy.*

anything deserving of punishment, either by decreeing a specially revealing costume or by degrading an existing one, the dominant is displaying absolute certitude that something deserving of punishment will occur soon enough: a few prior preparations will save time and trouble later on. It is a message of ruthless implacability, and a self-fulfilling prophecy.

Another motive is openly whimsical: to afford the dominant some passing amusement. Ordering a submissive to dress and redress and dress again in a succession of humiliating costumes or combinations thereof is, in some circles, considered an entertaining way of passing a rainy afternoon.

BOY MEETS GIRL

Ever since I had been a boy, I had from time to time been besieged by queer fancies which at first I had laughed at, which afterwards at once fascinated and frightened me. I recognised in them a danger to my character, to my ambitions and an obstacle to the great career which lay before me. I had dreamed, in a word, of a world in which ladies, to punish me, dressed me as a girl in the most exquisite of frocks and high-heeled shoes, gloves and corsets and, then laughing at my pretensions to a career, kept me in bondage and subjection as a toy for their amusement. I had fought against these fancies because I felt them to be enervating, effeminate and likely to sap my will. I had ridiculed them as preposterous. Yet they seemed part of my nature, they returned – and now they were translated into fact, and being translated into fact fascinated and obsessed me with a force a thousand times stronger than ever.

Miss High Heels

Few male passions are as impenetrable to outsiders (many other males and nearly all females) as that in which a subordinate disciplinary role is combined with the enforced wearing of female dress – 'petticoating', as it is called in some quarters, a more accurate term than 'shame clothing' which, although it may indeed be the same thing, is not necessarily so. Other terms include sissifying and feminising. The former, an American word, contains overtones of contempt which may or may not be appropriate (but in any case are a stylistic intrusion); the second is more properly a description of one of the possible motives for this sanction – which, needless to say, is exclusive to the male submissive: there is no direct female equivalent.

The word 'sanction' is important because here it is the idea that the wearing of female dress is connected with punishment which distinguishes the activity from any other kind of transvestism. At the point where the two predilections meet either a transvestite undergoes discipline, or the transvestism is itself a discipline. If discipline is not present in some form, the activity is straightforward transvestism – or transsexuality, bisexuality, or androgyny – and does not concern us here.

This is a fantasy about which it is possible to be reasonably specific, since it so often appears to take a similar form in which it fulfils at least one of the requirements of true genre fiction. In the classic, novel-length version, a young(ish) male of blue blood but astonishing immaturity finds himself in the power of several females. Not all of them are older than he, though all are 'superior' and one is unquestionably superior to all: she is Cruella de Ville and Governess too, with high standards in all departments and punishments both severe and unusual for those who transgress. Before the end of chapter 1 our arrogant young narrator has already been protestingly debagged and probably thrashed as well. The next move is to pop him into a frock and thrash him again. And once more for luck, with a different frock. From now on he takes a relatively normal, subordinate part in the life of a household which appears to devote 90 per cent of its time to inflicting, accepting or discussing corporal punishment – except that he is now permanently dressed as a female, answers to a female name and is thrashed, as opportunity serves, exclusively by females, in exclusively female style.

Some written versions of this widespread fantasy, like *Gynecocracy* and *Miss High Heels*, press fearlessly on to the logical ends of their roads and conclude by presenting the narrator wholly reconciled to the idea of a permanent change of gender, willing even (gulp) to Have the Operation. In return for these sacrifices, it is understood that he will pass the remainder of his (probably short) life in a permanent state of hyper-submissive ecstasy. And the Bacchæ will inherit his money – a supremely happy ending. It is the story of the Year King in almost every basic detail.

Whatever particular form it may take, this is a 'kink' from which many women recoil. Some are understandably offended by the apparent notion that women's clothing is intrinsically shaming or degrading. Many simply cannot bear the sight of men in female dress. A few, determined for their own reasons to show that the whole enforced cross-dressing idea is a debauched masculine *idée fixe* for which no woman has ever borne any responsibility, journey down fantasy roads of their own.

The riddle remains of why [Victorian male flagellants] should go to the trouble of dreaming up elaborate fantasies involving girls and governesses instead of simply drawing on their own boyhood experiences. That it was actually the girl being beaten with whom they identified (rather than the governess) is suggested by the large number of flogging brothels that flourished during this period run by 'governesses' who were paid to administer vigorous 'discipline' to their clients. The sex of the characters in so many of these stories was often remarkably fluid, so that behind the figure of the girl – often called 'Willie' or 'Georgie' – there lurked an unmistakably masculine presence. What is more, according to Steven Marcus, who made an extended study of Victorian pornography in the 1960s, the extremely aggressive figure of the governess wielding her ever upright 'rod' was nothing more than a screen for the [male] teacher of the original public school scene. *The appeal of governess pornography seems to have been that it enabled its readers*

*to avoid any painful recognition of their own homosexual
desires by allowing them to transpose the fantasy of a public school flogging on to a more acceptable female cast.* That
the majority of these stories ostensibly involved a woman
beating a girl only confirms that it was the same-sex relationship which gave the scene its appeal.[3]

Here the analytical principle known as 'Occam's Banana'
('Hypotheses should be multiplied until political correctness is
achieved') may be seen at work. If psychosexual neuroses are
ineluctably based on personal experience – and a sustainable
abuse theory absolutely requires this – then the existence of
these fancies in such profusion can only mean that at least some
Victorian women in disciplinary authority over boys dressed
culprits in feminine 'shame clothing' in order to inflict humiliation; indeed, one might fairly conclude that very many women
did so. Since, however, this supposition violently contradicts
the feminist dialectic that almost all governesses were kindly,
gentle, underpaid, malnourished victims of a repressive system,
wholly incapable of such cruelty, it automatically follows that
such events never took place after all and are a malicious and
obscene libel by closet homosexuals.

Let us consider what evidence exists. Until at least mid-
Victorian times small boys were routinely dressed as girls until
they reached the age of about five or six (or even older, especially
in the middle years of the century). Then they would be
'breeched' – that is, ceremonially dressed in their first pair of
trousers. It was a pleasant family rite of passage in which the
symbolism was clear to all and resented by none.[4] Nevertheless

---

3. *The Victorian Governess*, pp. 137–38. The italics are mine.
4. The British upper classes still adhere to this practice so far as they are reasonably able: it has been noted by many commentators that small upper-class
boys are very often dressed in 'sissy', i.e., feminine, fashion until they are about
seven or even older. A real-life Little Lord Fauntleroy of the mid-nineteenth century might not have worn trousers at all – nor would it have been thought
extraordinary.

there must have been considerable expectancy on the part of the boy as the great day approached, and an initiation so devoutly wished for could easily be put to disciplinary use: that is, deferred, or even reversed, for bad behaviour or other reasons. Here is an example from the famous novel *The History of the Fairchild Family*, written in 1847 by Mrs Sherwood, and generally held to provide a lamentably accurate glimpse into early Victorian child-rearing practices.

> On the low seat between them was Henry, still wearing his petticoated jacket, for he was not eight years old, with a black girdle round his waist. Henry was to have a cloth jacket like a boy's jacket, made for him as soon as he reached the Grove; for his mamma thought he was old enough now for the change, but she wished him to look as young as he really was when he first made his appearance at their new home, for she knew the servants and people about would wish to flatter him and make a bustle about him as the future owner of the Grove; and he knew, that being but a little boy, he would be sure to do something silly if they flattered him much, and therefore the younger he looked the more excuse there would be for him.

A little later on it is made quite clear to Henry that the achievement of trousers is not an automatic right, but depends on his maturity and behaviour.

> 'Oh, Master Henry, Master Henry,' added John laughing, 'good Mrs Bunce makes a very baby of you, and if you were to stay in her house awhile you would never be fit to be put into jackets and trowsers: you must keep to your pinafores and frocks, for the others would in a day not be fit to be seen.'
>
> 'I am sure, John,' said Henry, very angry, 'I am sure, John, that you know nothing about it. Mrs Bunce is a very good woman, and she could not make a baby of me. I am too old to be made a baby of by her or anyone else.'

In these two passages we see pride coming before a fall, and the carrot already transmogrifying into the stick. A little boy recently breeched might just as easily be unbreeched – put back into frocks – should his behaviour be considered not, after all, mature enough to justify the dignity of such a garment. L.M. Montgomery has an incident of this type in *Anne of the Islands* – as a punishment for misbehaviour, a boy is made to wear his sister's pinafore – and we may also assume this to be the purpose of Miss Paraman's red calico petticoats, which the wearers had to sew themselves, veritable sanbenitos of the nursery and school-room.

There is a considerable body of reference to this particular disciplinary practice in the now-famous Victorian ladies' journals – *The Englishwoman's Domestic Magazine, Town Talk, Family Doctor*, and so on – which occasionally featured bodies of exotic correspondence on this and related subjects. The following example, which contains at least two distinct stages of *couture en bas*, is from the second journal named above, and has an unusually authentic ring about it, not least because the moral of the tale is unexpected.

I was a long time taught at home by the governess of my sisters, of whom one was a little older, the other younger by two years. I was idle – perhaps more so that I was delicate. She used for this to whip me very often and the whippings increased as I increased. I was between ten and eleven years of age at this time, and I used to fight for it, so that it was hard work for her and the maid of my sisters to manage it. One day I had been whipped as usual for a lesson in Geography (I remember it as if yesterday), and had fought hard, so that when the maid left I was not allowed to button up, but was made to stand with my trousers about my feet. I had thus stood for about half an hour when Miss Brock (she is dead now) demanded my lesson. I knew less about it than before. She said I should learn it, and sent me back to do so. I suppose she saw I did not look as if I was trying, and suddenly she went to the door, rang the upstairs bell, and came back. When the maid Jane came in, she said: 'Oh, Jane, I fear master N. will catch cold. Will you bring down some of Miss—'s (my eldest sister who was about my size) clothing? Bring frock and all.' The maid lingered a moment and went. In a very few minutes back she came with the dress on her arm and her hands full. I felt as if I would sooner be killed. The governess got up, and the maid having left her clothing on the table, all but the chemise, a most desperate fight began, which lasted amidst smacks and boxes on the ears, till tired out, the garment was put on all right. Stays were easy, but now came the fight again. The first petticoat I clutched hold of, and I think for ten minutes I held on, till at last that too was accomplished and I sat on the floor enthroned in flannel. They now easily accomplished the rest; shame overcame my courage, and I had no strength. My trousers were now entirely removed. I was made to stand up, under more slaps and thumpings and threatenings of birch, while my dressing was most leisurely completed with a stiff starched petticoat, a blue frock down nearly to my feet, stockings and sandal shoes. Then I was left in my place, with my book as before. At dinner I was forced to join them; I was kept at home while they were out walking; and not until I had repeated my lesson, after the usual bedtime, was I taken upstairs to be undressed. I know not if this punishment is more cruel than the birch; this I do know, that it put an end to it [the birch] at home. The mere threat of 'shall I send for some petticoats for you?' – always set me to work.

Beyond all doubt many – perhaps the majority – of these contributions were fantasies, in which, whatever the claimed gender of the correspondent, the hallmarks of masculine authorship may usually be detected. These subterfuges are therefore 'pornography'. Intended primarily to titillate, in themselves they prove nothing except the existence, in a highly developed form, of the fantasy itself. From this point on this remains a frequent sub-theme in the pockets of readers' letters on what today would be called fetish subjects – discipline, equestrianism, corsetry, lingerie – that appeared, every half-decade or so, in popular British magazines (*Photo Bits, Bits of Fun, London Life*), right up until the late 1950s and the first appearance of specialist magazines, which had the effect of hiving off such material into ghettoes all their own, where they currently remain.

Inventions many of these may be, in whole or part, but every now and again we get a glimpse of a solid reality behind the fantasy. The late Peter Lawford was dressed as a girl by his mother for reasons that appear to have been distinctly unmaternal. In 1962, Dirk Bannerman, a London schoolboy of eight, was a pupil at Drayton Park Primary School.

> One day I was called to the front of the assembly by the headmistress, Mrs Needham. She told me, in everybody's hearing, that I had broken a school rule in attending while wearing long trousers. I hadn't known before – nobody had said anything. My parents didn't know. She then summoned my older brother to the front and told him to take off my trousers. He didn't want to but he had to. I stood there miserably in front of the assembled school for about an hour in my shirt-tails. Then she let me go home and change. I'll never forget that day, or that woman, as long as I live.[5]

In 1979, fifty-two-year-old Mrs Sheila Primik, headmistress of Hebburn Quay Primary School, Hebburn-on-Tyne, was suspended for two weeks for forcibly dressing two six-year-old boys in girls' clothes – one in a dress, the other in a pinafore – and parading them in front of their mixed class as a punishment for repeatedly running into the girls' toilets. Mrs Primik was not attempting to satisfy some grotesque male requirement: she did it of her own accord, and was quite unrepentant, describing the reasons for her suspension as 'laughable'. She told a *Daily Telegraph*

---

5. Deposition made to the author.

reporter: 'They needed a shock. They kept going into the girls' toilets so I dressed them up and told them "You must want to be girls!"' The suspension angered local mothers, who organised a march and a petition in Mrs Primik's defence. One of these was the mother of one of the petticoated boys. Another told the *Telegraph*: 'I totally agree with what Mrs Primik did. She dressed them up to humiliate them and to stop them doing it again.'

The last report comes from the *Yorkshire Post,* 29 January 1991. Yet again it was a six-year-old peeping tom who was dealt with (sexual perversion in the male begins early). Luckily for him, the 'inhumane' sanction of smacking had just been abolished.

A teacher who forced a boy of six to wear a dress and hat because he sneaked into girls' toilets has been reprimanded by her education authority, it was revealed today.

She thought it would teach the boy a lesson after he was caught making his third foray within a few days to the toilets at Wildground infants' school in Dibden Purlieu, Hants.

But the boy's parents say he was humiliated and now does not want to go to school because of teasing from his class-mates.

A Hampshire County Council spokesman said yesterday: 'The matter has been investigated by the headteacher and the teacher concerned has been reprimanded.

'As far as the head is concerned there is no question of the teacher being suspended or sacked and the matter is now closed.'

Perhaps it is not such a fantasy after all.

Of course, a subordinate male may be required to wear female clothing in order to 'feminise' him rather than punish him. In many ways this may be seen as a practical application of the well-established theory that all human beings are mixtures of both genders. Since clothes certainly have power to condition attitudes and behaviour – the purpose of most uniforms – it is not entirely illogical to suppose that some males judged to possess an offensive surfeit of masculine failings (i.e., a deficiency of female qualities) might genuinely benefit from a dainty week or two in frocks.[6]

It is by no means an absolute requirement that a petticoated male dislike his new condition. If consent is present (the male maid, or the Muir Academy's boys-who-would-be-girls are good examples) most built-in penal motif vanishes. By now 'feminisation' is no longer an objective but an accomplished fact, of which the clothes are but a perfectly proper recognition. In other words, the disciplinary note is beginning to fade: we are at the threshold of 'straight' transvestism.

Whatever the motive, or mixture of motives, for petticoating, the fact remains, as has been stated, that many women instinctively dislike the practice and will have nothing to do with it, even in otherwise fairly baroque flagellant scenarios. There are two likely reasons. The first is æsthetic: with very few exceptions, adult males dressed in female clothes or juvenile garments, or both at once, are an intrinsically ludicrous sight. A paying customer is one thing; one's own lover or husband another matter entirely. The second is that many women do not greatly care for the idea that female dress 'shames' a male: without due consideration of the breeching/unbreeching theory, the logic of the comparison is obviously disadvantageous to females. But even when shame is not the motive, in the end the male half of the sketch will wish to be made to dress up as a female, at which point the supposedly dominant female may experience some misgivings. Only if she is able to see him as he sees himself can she properly enter into the spirit of things.

---

6. An extraordinary example of the longevity of this impulse was revealed some years ago with the discovery, by various newspapers, that in certain Labour-controlled school districts, particularly in London, a much-promoted reader for primary school pupils (seven- to eleven-year-olds), was a small book called *Bill's New Frock*, written by two feminist schoolteachers. The eponymous hero, aged about nine, wakes up one morning to find himself wearing a pretty frock instead of his trousers. Thereafter he finds himself treated as a 'mere girl' and discovers the inequities of modern patriarchal society from the front line etc., etc. Needless to say, the experience also refines and improves his own character.

13

THE RITE

*And now the former took a striking attitude, the harp
sounded a few notes, and she delivered a glorious recita-
tive, her majestic contralto filling the theatre as she
expressed her indignation and horror, her well-nigh disbelief in the testimony of her eyes, while she clasped her
hands, raised them in the air and dropped them to her
sides, rolling her eyes and shaking her head; an occasional interpolation from Mrs Barker's golden soprano
cut across her words, and then the two voices joined in a
sombre and stirring duet in which execrations were mingled with promises of punishment and invocations to the
spirit of birch.*

Aubrey Beardsley, *Under the Hill*

To take part in a ritual is to submit to forces outside oneself. These
forces may be atavistic – subtle procreationary dance rhythms
whose notation is stored deep within our genes – or they may be
rooted, more intellectually, in a sense of social obligation and an
awareness of precedent. Or they may have a distinctly practical
role, of enabling, enforcement and control. The aeroplane pilot's
pre-flight check has an obviously practical application, yet it also
bears many of the hallmarks of a submission ritual, a formal tip-
ping of the hand to the gods of flight in humble acknowledgement
that there are forces outside the pilot's self which are more powerful than he, and will slay him if he does not propitiate them.
Pre-flighting is more than a technical procedure and an absolute
legal requirement; it is a form of spiritual insurance, almost a religious rite. This sacerdotal aspect is deliberately inculcated into all

pilots from the moment they begin their training. What might otherwise have been perceived as a mere list of things to do has also become a mantra, a prayer for personal survival – and therefore it is much more likely to be executed with maximum thoroughness on every occasion, which is the real object.

Ceremony is a deliberate exaltation of ritual. By setting aside a special time and place, nominating participants, assigning roles, specifying clothes to be worn and words to be spoken, the ritual is brought forward into the light and elevated to the status of a rite. From this point onwards, depending on to what extent it is embellished in practice, it may take on a life and purpose of its own. Words are honed and polished into a mellifluous litany whose exact phrasing becomes all important. Costumes gradually become more and more specialised. Other trappings and aspects of the ceremony are refined. In due course the medium may become the message and in many cases the original purpose of the event will be semi-obscured in a blaze of pomp. In some examples (the Church of England springs to mind) the original meaning may even become deniable, or at least a subject for discussion; hardly surprising when one considers that adherents of all Christian denominations routinely practise symbolic cannibalism in the presence of a representation of an instrument of capital punishment – which is a grisly but, in its own terms, perfectly accurate way of describing the solemn and beautiful rite of Holy Communion.

S/M is the most liturgical of forms, sharing with Christianity a theatrical iconography of punishment and expiation: washing rituals, bondage, flagellation, body-piercing and symbolic torture. Like S/M, the economy of Christianity is the economy of conversion: the meek exalted, the high made low. Mortifying the flesh exalts one in the eyes of the Master. Through humility on earth, one stores up a surplus stock of spiritual value in heaven. Like Christianity, S/M performs the paradox of redemptive suffering, and like Christianity, it takes shape around the masochistic logic of transcendence through the mortification of the flesh: through self-abasement, the spirit finds release in an ecstasy of abandonment. In both S/M and Christianity, earthly desire exacts strict payment in an economy of penance and pleasure. In S/M, washing rituals and the pouring of water effect a baptismal cleansing and exoneration of guilt. These are purification rituals, a staged appropriation of Christian pageantry, stealing a delirious, fleshly advance on one's spiritual credit – a forbidden taste of what should properly be exaltation in the hereafter.[1]

In general, however, some trace of the original (ritual) purpose may be discerned from even the most lavishly rococo or bizarre ceremonies. Why Freemasons should be obliged to roll up one trouser leg to the knee on certain occasions is not widely understood, at least by the general public. This same general public may be hazy about the precise symbolic meaning of the orb and sceptre which a newly crowned sovereign of Great Britain will be required to hold, one in each hand, but the meaning of the crown itself is obvious. A witness who raises his right hand and swears to tell the truth may privately be intending to do nothing of the kind, but at least he is acknowledging (or, more properly, being obliged to acknowledge) that he *ought* to be telling the truth, and may fairly be penalised if he does not do so. The latter is a good example of ritual being used to compel behaviour: the subpoena (itself couched in ritually circumscribed terms) which brought the witness to the stand is an extension of the process, while the word 'subpoena' itself means 'under pain of'. A grimmer example of mandatory ritual is the ceremony that conventionally attends an execution; kinder, one might think, and certainly more logical, to have it over and done with as expediently as possible, but the gods of justice must have their due. A firing party closely resembles a human sacrifice in its

---

1. Anne McClintock: 'Maid to Order: Commercial S/M and Gender Power' in *Dirty Looks*.

forms, particularly the inexorable yet unhurried rhythm, one of whose purposes is to enable the sacrifice to control himself (also the reason for the blindfold and cigarette) and therefore 'consent': it is a very ancient idea that the gods are best pleased by the consenting sacrifice.

No form of sexuality is more ritualised than flagellation, and by definition its routines have a mandatory flavour, with a similar mixture of purposes both sacred (the consenting sacrifice) and profane (control, stage management). While actual ceremonies may vary widely from scenario to scenario, the underlying ritual remains the same, or nearly the same, in essence. Like any religious ceremony, theatrical production or symphony of music, these rites may be dissected into several component stages (acts or movements), each with its particular significance and unique role in the inculcation of atmosphere and the unfolding of plot. I have identified seven distinct stages of what may be called the proto-ritual:

1. Commission

The 'crime' – usually an error of commission or omission – takes place; needless to say, with every expectation of . . .

2. Detection

The Dominant 'detects' the error. This leads inexorably to . . .

3. Confrontation

The guilty party is faced with the evidence of fault. Past 'record' is invoked, judgement delivered and sentence passed.

4. Apprehension

A period of formal 'waiting for it'. Its purpose is to increase tension.

5. Preparation

The culprit is ordered to prepare (posture, clothing, etc.). Alternatively, and if the scenario is apposite, the dominant may forcibly lead the submissive to the place of punishment and personally make all ready.

6. Execution

The penalty is inflicted with the chosen rod.

7. Aftermath

The culprit is 'forgiven'. This may lead directly to more orthodox physical lovemaking.

Clearly not all scenarios conform rigidly to this template. For example, a dominant who decides to punish for no particular reason, or one so frivolous as to amount to whimsy, has no need for steps 1 and 2, and will begin at a (modified) step 3. Likewise, in the confessional scenario, steps 2 and 3 are combined. Some dominants may insert extra penalties (standing in the corner, 100 lines, washing up, no cigarettes for 24 hours) for step 7, either omitting the Aftermath altogether or postponing it until the completion of this extra penal stage. And in some cases where summary punishment is the appropriate mode, the entire routine will be reduced to steps 3 and 6 and the ceremony will therefore be cut to the bone. Many of these differences are scenario-specific, but there will also be many variations of style depending on individual taste and circumstances. Certainly they also offer tremendous opportunities for histrionic prowess, and variation: masters and mistresses of the dominant's craft may introduce ad libs at will, and as their skill allows.

> This waiting, even more painful than the whipping itself, was prolonged purposely. Any motive might be used as a pretext. Perhaps the birch rod which had been chosen was not suitable: it wasn't long enough, it didn't fit well to the hand, or again, not sufficiently sturdy, it might not fulfil its purpose. And then an infinite time was spent in looking through the drawer seeking a more suitable instrument. The perfidious flagellatress weighed each birch in turn, brandishing the implement at the end of her hand, whistling it through the air. And that terrifying music at once struck an echo into the heart of the unfortunate victim who started convulsively so far as the cord binding her hands allowed.[2]

Nonetheless, in its full panoply the flagellatory rite is a moral drama or Mystery Play: each of the seven fundamental stages marks a milestone in the progress from wrong to right. But here, unlike the often whimsical cruelties and partialities of the Olympian gods as depicted in the plays of the Greek dramatists, there is a sense of rectitude and balance – of salvation rather than downfall, powerfully expressed in the conceptual difference between punishment and torture. This is an undeniably moral note and one of the keys to the flagellant impulse.

As with all rites, there are intervals of greater and lesser intensity. While the moment of greatest focus is undoubtedly the actual punishment itself, the preceding stage, preparation, is of no less psychological weight within the overall event. Since it involves two important sub-components – posture and adjustment of clothing – it can also be seen as the most luxurious and considered of the seven stages.

---

2. *The Conjugal Whip.*

Posture – that is, the physical position adopted by or imposed upon the submissive in order to receive the punishment – is itself an area of some complexity, with several parameters to take into consideration. A submissive hauled summarily across the lap for a spanking is not given time to consent, nor is consent required. In other words, ceremony is temporarily at a discount. Ordering the same submissive to bend across the knee conveys a different tone, even though the eventual posture itself may be identical: it has become a rite.

A particular posture may be symbolic of the relationship as a whole: both bending over and kneeling offer the target in more or less the same way and at a similar angle of attack, but kneeling is more symbolically submissive. Leaving the grace notes of ritual aside for a moment, the choice of posture may also depend on simple physiognomy. Broadly speaking, the more acute the angle at which the submissive is bent – for example, when kneeling or touching the toes – the greater the physical pain, since the gluteal muscles are more tightly stretched and the nerve-endings are brought closer to the surface of the skin. On the other hand, a posture of this sort is almost *de rigueur* if the dominant wishes to apply punishment to the lower half of the seat (where, for many reasons, it is most effective). A particular posture may be ruled out simply because of the nature of the chosen rod: the over-the-knee position is only practicable when the implement is short enough. In any case this style of punishment is seldom severe, unless something like a riding crop is used, because the bending angle of the culprit is not very great (it can be made more acute by doubling the submissive across one thigh and pinning the legs with the other).

Bound up with posture is the question of restraint. Tying up a person before applying physical punishment is an act pregnant with dreadful connotation, the chief implication being that the forthcoming excoriation will be so severe that even the most submissive submissive cannot be depended upon to maintain the posture without help, much as he or she might prefer to. Restraints, of course, need not take the form of bonds.

Mr John . . . proceeded directly, as before, to get to the point, as briskly telling Dart ma[jor] that he was to be given a very sound birching, by order of the Doctor, for his gross effrontery and shameless behaviour, and inviting him to strip and kneel down on the block. Dart made something of a face, but behaved otherwise almost as meekly as his young brother, unfastening his waist-band himself and also slipping off his jacket and laying it over an arm of the chair, but letting the two Culvers, who seemed nothing loth, fin-ish the stripping of him, and they fairly soon had him kneeling on the block with his trousers down and his shirt rucked back, and presenting just his sturdy bottom to Mr J., who had by now taken the birch from Francis . . . When he saw that Culver ma had the chap firmly by the head and Culver mi[nor], on his knees, had him by the heels, he began to birch. . . .[3]

Most of the corporal punishments inflicted in the British public schools employed human 'holders' as a matter of course. For girls – who, perhaps even more than their brothers, might be expected to resist – still more threatening tactics might be employed:

> *'Now, now,' the Mistress mutters to the maids,*
> *'Pounce on her while she's stooping, quick ye jades!'*
> *A tip toe tripping lest the tread give note,*
> *Swiggins and Swipes securing waist and throat,*
> *Propel her to the block, where hand on skirt,*
> *They wait till 'Missis' has the means to hurt;*
> *Their clumsy fingers 'neath the linen slipping*
> *Make just the first preparatives to whipping.*
> *The slops slide down so swift no flesh is seen,*
> *The hands then shifting t'other side the screen*
> *Attempt untying – lo! to their surprise,*

---

3. *New Face at Repton Hall.*

> *The broad bow separates in hooks and eyes.*
> *Vainly the 'vulgar victim' vents abuse,*
> *Wriggles her rear and roars to be let loose.*
> *Vainly she slaps behind her, vainly twists,*
> *Two brawny arms are lock'd across her back;*
> *Fidgett advancing grapples both her wrists,*
> *Saluting first her cheeks with double smack;*
> *Then fixing firm her feet against the block,*
> *She leans in readiness for ruder shock.*[4]

An extraordinary range of postures and restraints was employed in British judicial birchings, as the 1938 Cadogan Report[5] makes clear:

> The method most commonly adopted is to bend the boy over a low bench or table. His hands, and sometimes his feet also, are held by police officers. This is done in order to ensure that he shall not move, for if he moved a stroke of the birch might fall on some more sensitive part of the body. This method, though probably the most common, is not universal. In some Police Forces one constable takes the boy on his back, drawing the boy's hands down over his shoulders; and another constable holds the boy's feet drawing his legs round the sides of the first constable; the first constable then leans forward, and the birch is applied by a third. We have also heard that in one Police Force the custom is for one constable to bend the boy over and hold his head between his knees, while a second officer administers the birch.

The report also noted that in one particular unnamed police district, the culprit – who might be a boy as young as eight – was

---

4. *Venus School-Mistress.*
5. Report of the Home Office Departmental Committee on Corporal Punishment (chairman: the Hon. E. Cadogan). This report was the eventual basis for the removal of judicial corporal punishment from the British statute books.

actually strapped to a frame.[6] While there is a certain logic in such a proceeding – nominally, to prevent the strokes landing in places other than the target – the overall effect is that of the torture chamber. Without the culprit being offered even the chance to accept his punishment submissively, all possible redemptive focus is removed. It is also an unbalanced punishment. Restraints may well serve to admit the infliction of greater than usual pain, but they also almost entirely remove the shaming component since the culprit has been overpowered by superior force.

The adjustment of clothing – assuming any is worn – is another area in which the urge to ritual may be given creative expression. It can also be of singular importance, and once again a comparison with orthodox lovemaking will show that this is so. Some of us particularly enjoy undressing our lovers, or being undressed by them, in slow, lingering stages. Others, more matter-of-fact in their approach, simply take their clothes off as quickly as possible. In the latter case garments are simply an impediment to the real business at hand; for the former group, their removal is a fundamental part of foreplay – and this is the entire point of striptease. Some garments possess clearly defined symbolic 'fetish' power in their own right, and the removal of these is especially charged with meaning.

The same rules apply to flagellatory transactions: to strip is one class of event; to be stripped is something rather different. Whether the culprit performs this task in person, or submits to having it done by the dominant, is another flavour in the overall experience.

She dragged me into her room. Laurence joined us there and laughing like us assisted in an epic struggle. I really wished to lose, though I put up a desperate resistance, not for the

6. See also Chapter 11. The outrageously severe judicial canings administered in Singapore also involve the victim being fastened to a stout wooden frame. Here there is no question of any person being able to accept the punishment without such a precaution, since its effects could hardly be more severe if the strokes were administered with a sword blade.

sake of appearances, but to make the game more interesting.

Madame Dulaure pushed me on to the bed and removed my skirt . . . she was sitting on my left and I was partly supported by one of her thighs. What joy! She was going to take my knickers down!

Her hand pulled on the elastic waistband. It was a delicious sensation to feel her hand busy at the top of my little tussore silk knickers. First she drew one side down, then the other, and finally pulled them down all round . . .

I realised she was deliberately refining the process, and that all the delays were really a sort of long exquisite caressing which her hands enjoyed as much as her eyes.[7]

For the dominant to prepare the target with his or her own hands while the culprit sprawls head-down is an extension of the summary, nursery approach, and conveys determination, ruthlessness and a desire to deprive the submissive of all dignity. Requiring the culprit to adjust his or her clothing before bending over introduces a different note; openly consensual, yet also obedient – a symbolic affirmation of the dominant's authority.

He turned half aside, and with trembling fingers, unfastened his braces, and unbuttoned his trousers, letting them slip down to his knees; and then he laid himself across the end of the sofa, with his hands resting on the floor at one side, and the tips of his toes on the other side, thus bringing his body into a curve with his bottom well raised up in a splendid position for receiving the rod. I could not understand why he had made so much fuss about letting down his trousers. It seemed very absurd.[8]

Another, often overlooked, aspect of the self-preparation process is the opportunities it affords for an articulate dominant to

---

7. *Paulette Trahié.*
8. *Frank and I.*

deploy those well-known phrases and code-words which enhance the experience for both parties. Here is this technique in perhaps its ultimate form (it should be made clear that the 'boy' referred to is a consenting adult male):

It will often be the case, however, that the nature of the pun-ishment requires that the culprit be commanded to prepare himself, at least in part. Some Governesses, I know, feel it necessary to give this command in the same tone a boatswain in the Navy might use to hail the masthead. I consider raising one's voice to give orders bad practice – unless an emergency looms and instant dominance is nec-essary – and when I tell a guilty boy to prepare himself for punishment I do so in a reasonable voice, and in a calm manner, thus:—

Now, [Surname], *you know why you are here. Go directly and stand by that chair by the wall.*

And when he has done so:—

Unfasten your trousers and let them down.

And when he has done so:—

Bend over the chair and hold the legs in front, with your face as close as possible to the seat. Keep your feet and knees together and your legs perfectly straight.

And when he has done so:—

I am now going to give you six strokes of the cane [or whatever punishment you have decreed]. *If you keep quite still and remain as quiet as you can it will soon be over. If you move, or attempt to get up, or speak without permission, I shall take down your drawers before continuing with the punishment. If you move or speak a second time we shall start again at the beginning. Do you understand?*[9]

There are other stylish extensions of the flagellation ceremony which were once very much in favour but today have fallen into

---

9. *A Guide to the Correction of Young Gentlemen.*

abeyance. One is to require the culprit to manufacture the rod in person, or, already noted with Mark Twain's Mrs Horr, at the very least to fetch it. Another is to make him or her actually ask for punishment.

'Now take the birch. Go to Lady Edith. Kneel down. Say, "Lady Edith, will you please punish me for the disgraceful exhibition of myself which I have just made, and for the insubordination to my mistress which rendered this discipline necessary, by birching my bare bottom as much as your Ladyship may think proper. And as I have been very naughty please do not fail to lay the strokes on as severely as you can."'[10]

The concomitant, which properly belongs in the Aftermath (stage 7), is to kiss the rod, standard practice in Tudor schoolrooms (the mandatory handshake after the prefects' beating in the film *Another Country* is an echo of this). Despite the modern connotations of added humiliation, its original purpose was reconciliatory and sacramental; an act of contrition and acceptance. It also sets the final seal on the dominant's dominance, and restores the hierarchy.

Mrs Wharton slapped the throbbing flesh about a dozen times, always without haste, in a fashion to vex the patient as much as possible, then she stood her on her feet and placed the warm palm which had done the slapping against the girl's mouth. This hand the latter kissed humbly. Once more she took Florence's crimson face between her two hands.

'Now,' she said, 'I reiterate my question; have you been well whipped?'

This time the girl's shivering was almost imperceptible, and Mrs Wharton had scarcely any cause to whip her anew. She murmured:

---

10. *The Petticoat Dominant.*

'Yes, Madame . . . I have been well whipped! . . .'

'Do you think it will be a warning to you not to fall back into your habitual faults?'

'Yes, Madame!'

'Very well. Ask my pardon!'

'Madame!' responded the girl, falling to her knees . . . 'I humbly beg your pardon . . . and I thank you very much . . . for having given me . . . a good . . . sound . . . whipping . . . It is for my good!'[11]

Finally, there is the question of publicity. Real punishments administered before witnesses were always intended to be particularly shaming and thereby more punitive. Consensual flagellatory events, however, are not real in this sense, suffering, when administered in public, from the usual connotations of debauchery always associated with exhibitionism and group sex. Nevertheless some rituals are completely satisfactory only when as many witnesses as possible are present – without an audience they would lose much of their point.

One day, in the course of a reception Claudia was giving, Edward dressed himself very sumptuously and his stupidity made him redouble the affectation in his way of walking. To punish him, Claudia took the young man by the ear and made him ask pardon of each of her guests. To mark the depths of his abasement, she made him kiss the tip of each guest's shoe . . .

Without taking her gloves off, Claudia completed the lesson by giving Edward a volley of blows on his fingers and palms and which drew tears and cries from him. Then, judging it necessary to go further in the way of severity, she sent a chambermaid to find the 'coffer'.

The coffer! This was a rectangular wooden box, painted white, which contained a complete assortment of the instruments

---

11. *Modern Slaves.*

used to teach impertinent young gentlemen the respect due to ladies.

Ranged in the order of their effect were birches made of broom, willow, rushes and birch. There were three martinets made of pigskin, a leather tapette, shaped like the sole of a shoe, a Scottish tawse, and an American paddle, inspired by the Japanese.

While the ladies passed the instruments from hand to hand to examine them more closely, Edward, his face full of apprehension and shame, pleaded with his terrible cousin, rubbing his tortured hands together, still on his knees in the middle of the implacable group.

Claudia dragged him to a sofa and stretched him over her. While Margaret joyfully came and held his wrists, Louisa held his ankles. Behind the back of the sofa, Diana leaned forward. She was well placed. In front and a little to the side, sitting on the white velvet carpet, Bess, the devotee, was ready to hand the different instruments in the box one after the other to Claudia.

This scene was one of the best composed in the film, and Monsieur Horace thought highly of it.

The subject was worth the trouble taken to get it right. The final shots were perfect. The removal of Edward's trousers was a double pleasure; for underneath the velvet shorts he wore, there was a pair of knickers made of lace which must have cost a fabulous sum . . .[12]

As far as I am able to compute, the above example covers nearly all the components of the flagellatory experience. Scenario, *dramatis personae*, rods, costumes, posture, preparation and ritual are all invoked and defined within the space of a very few paragraphs. It is a marvel of compression – and probably about as baroque as one can get, even in fantasy.

---

12. *Paulette Trahié.*

PART III

Flagellation and Society

14

LIKING IT

Don't want you to thank me
Just want you to spank me
Madonna, *'Hanky Panky'*

Most rational people would admit to the existence within themselves of feelings they would describe as cruel. Thereafter
definitions and responses vary, almost from individual to individual. For some, such impulses are satanic. Evidence of ancient
sin, fundamental impurity or, latterly, child abuse, they are con-
fessed only to be confronted, denounced and, if they cannot
wholly be eradicated, at the least subjected to control. No country or culture is free from awful memories of events when the
impulse to be cruel has been given free individual or collective
rein. It is the most terrible part of the human inheritance, with
which no compromise is possible, and we shall never rise above
our current condition until we find means of weeding it out.

Those who hold this viewpoint would say that they understand only too well the impulses which allow an individual to
derive pleasure of various kinds from the subjection and physical maltreatment, as they see it, of other individuals. The
contemplation of such activities may cause a part of themselves
to chime in recognition – a part they have already identified as
evil. Therefore those who do these things have not the same
degree of self-knowledge (or self-restraint); have surrendered to
an evil impulse; are acting in an evil manner; are evil. It is a logical viewpoint, if over-attributive, and it lies at the core of most
objections to active flagellation. The presence of consent at best

removes the coercive nature of the evil, but the unpleasant symbolism remains, and that too must be expunged.

But to feel as Rousseau or 'Florrie' did – to enjoy being at the losing end of a disciplinary confrontation, especially where this involves flagellation – is far less widely comprehended; and even if the cruelty label can hardly be made to stick, the activity is nonetheless seen as depraved if not actually demented, not only because it panders to the former, already condemned group, but because to derive pleasure or fulfilment from repression, humiliation and physical pain flies in the face of most rationalist thought. Did the great emancipators labour in vain in order to bring mankind a better, truer vision of himself and his place in the world? Are the noble struggles, the kindly conceptions, the soaring personal examples all to be muddied and subverted in order to incorporate an obvious and detestable neurosis within the compass of democratic human society?

Rousseau, as has been noted, was compelled by his own rationalism to detest these feelings within himself: he passed his life in hot, fevered imaginings and experienced continuous, wretched guilt. His desire to be chastised was itself at odds with the developing egalitarianism of the age. We may also suspect that his desire to submit to a *woman* clashed even more violently with a residual and still overwhelming patriarchalism, one of the very last items to be addressed on the rationalist agenda, which had barely been questioned in the early eighteenth century and is today still not eradicated, despite radical shifts in Western public opinion in the last twenty years or so. And it is true, if deplorable, that when that same unreconstructed public opinion contemplates the condition it calls masochism, it somehow finds it more understandable and tolerable in the female of the species; for it is both a credo of patriarchalism and a possible explanation for its long survival that women are more deferential, if not actually submissive, than men. Therefore, it seems less unexpected for masochism to take a female form; and when it does so, condemnation does not necessarily follow – except from one quarter. The negative pressures that modern feminist thought and influence exert on women in this respect are both intense and continuous. Whereas passive SM practices may be grudgingly allowed within a lesbian context, to wish to be dominated or chastised by a man is a fundamental betrayal of the prevailing ethos. (*Cosmo* girls are not spanked by their boyfriends, and God help the latter if they try.) It is therefore not unreasonable to guess that of all the basic combinations of gender, mode and sexual preference – male-heterosexual-dominant, male-homosexual-dominant, male-homosexual-submissive, male-heterosexual-submissive, female-heterosexual-dominant, female-homosexual-dominant, female-homosexual-submissive and female-heterosexual-submissive – it is the last category which is today the most likely to remain unfulfilled.

How rare is the genuine female submissive? To judge from the marketplace, rare enough:

> It is . . . commonly thought that men who pay for commercial S/M pay to indulge in the sadistic abuse of women. Yet the testimony of dominatrixes reveals precisely the opposite. By far the most common service paid for by men in heterosexual S/M is the extravagant display of submission. In most commercial B&D (bondage and discipline), men are the 'slaves', not women. As the dominatrix Lindi St Clair says, far from being the vicious unleashing of male dominance, S/M is typically 'the other way round'.[1]

But this is after all the marketplace, where the clientele is almost exclusively male: it is of small significance in assessing the proclivities of females en masse, and perhaps that is as it should be, since extrapolation from small quantities of data is a risky business. It may be worth noting, however, that the female editors of two prominent spanking magazines, one British, one American, are unashamedly passive in their tastes – and heterosexual:

---

1. Anne McClintock: 'Maid to Order: Commercial S/M and Gender Power' in *Dirty Looks*.

My favourite kind of spanking is given by a man that I like, respect, and enjoy being with. It should always be over the knee. I like it to begin on my skirt and to have the layers of clothing slowly pulled up and pulled down. I like a good deal of rubbing. I like touching with a spanking, being fingered. I like to be talked to, but it's not that important. I certainly don't like to be berated, scolded, or humiliated. 'You've been a bad girl' is okay . . .

There should be subtlety. I should always feel that the man cares for me, likes me a good deal.[2]

In other words, the author of the above passage (a false submissive if ever there was one) prefers the domestic discipline scenario, and her chosen partner is the archetype I have called the No-Nonsense Lover. It is a sensual exchange in which most of the deeper notes – of penitence, for example – are missing; though one may notice that a good deal of ritual is present: the carefully defined mode of undressing, for example, and the preferred posture.

Other female submissives prefer scenarios in which the overt sexuality of the transaction is replaced by more profound atmospheric feelings of submission, penitence and absolution. Here, as in 'Florrie's' fantasies, the ritual is exalted into a specific rite:

The sickness in one's stomach on the award of a punishment; the agony of anticipation at the prospect of the scorching sting of the tawse and searing bite of the cane; the knowledge that it is well-deserved, totally inescapable and absolutely necessary; the ensuing battle of mind over body during the punishment itself, in forcing oneself to accept the pain, in total obedience, without complaint and, above all, the overwhelmingly cleansing effect of severe corporal

2. Eve Howard, editor of *Stand Corrected* magazine (USA), quoted in *Different Loving*.

punishment, that leaves you feeling the debt is paid, the slate wiped clean.[3]

Such are the confusions and divisions even within the body of SM thought that one may fairly assume the writer of the first passage disapproves of, or at the least does not understand, the feelings expressed by the latter, and vice versa. Nevertheless, in the two quotations above we may identify two of the main strands of the flagellant experience: the wish to receive manageable pain in a gentle and overwhelmingly sexual context, and the desire to receive a much more severe chastisement, with sexuality all but extinguished, in an atmosphere that is both penitential and purgative. There are other differences: in the earlier example (even if one did not know it hailed from California) the displacement of democratic rule is clearly only temporary: the author is not only the editor of a successful magazine, but the owner and managing director of a sizeable company. The second quotation implies a permanent hierarchy. When severe pain is not only 'absolutely necessary' but 'totally inescapable', and the required response to it is 'total obedience' despite the 'agony of anticipation' – in other words, a major effort of will is required – then one cannot easily imagine the pecking order necessary to make such a scenario work disintegrating the moment the newly punished culprit stands up. The transition would simply be too abrupt.

But in both cases the subject appreciates the experience. Why?

As one might expect, there is a range of answers, none of which are mutually exclusive, and all of which represent shades of feeling associated with differing personalities. To take the most obvious first of all, many, perhaps most, passive flagellants enjoy being flagellated primarily because it excites them sensually. Much has been written, by the clinical school, about the physiological effects of corporal punishment on the buttocks, most of it

---

3. *Sweet Retribution.*

presumably accurate, and nearly all of it as informative as saying that a man enjoys making love to his wife because to place Organ A in proximity to her Organ B stimulates the release into his bloodstream of certain obscure chemical compounds, which excite his pleasure centres. Certainly the buttocks, in both sexes, are in close proximity to the sexual organs, and therefore to smack them may induce a state of secondary sexual excitement. But as we have seen, for most flagellants, including those who major on the physical sensations to the near-exclusion of other considerations, even the simple action of smacking has to be fully in context before any excitement ensues. Remove the context and both the sensuality and the concomitant excitement are also removed. The physical response is therefore coloured or pre-conditioned by other factors, and is indeed shown to be dependent on them. One curiosity of the purely sexual response, at least in males, is that the excitement which is said to be the direct result of the flagellation is, more often than not, deferred: the flagellant is far more likely to have an erection before or after the punishment – i.e. during an anticipatory or reflective stage – than while it is taking place.

It may be said that in cases where the sensual element is disproportionately, even grossly, to the fore, and most if not all context has disappeared, appetites have become so jaded that all factors other than personal gratification have become relegated to near-extinction. Surely this is evidence of a defect of general character rather than specific deviation? Most children prefer the cakes and jam to the bread and butter which precede them at tea, or they may prefer the fried potatoes to the spinach, but if they are permitted to consume the one without the other, they run the serious risk of confusing the subtle pleasures of the table with the untrammelled consumption of the richest possible foodstuffs – a misapprehension which can only too easily be extended into life as a whole. Greed is its own worst enemy, since it remorselessly excludes all items on the menu except those previously identified as affording the greatest pleasure for the minimum effort. In due course, even these will fail to satisfy, and so will be consumed in ever greater amounts, thereby accelerating the process.

It seems that we must therefore look to the nature of the context to explain why flagellants enjoy flagellation. Much of the present work has been devoted to context, and it will nonetheless by now, I hope, be obvious that, as a field of activity, it bears very close comparison indeed with orthodox lovemaking – a point I may have laboured, though I make no apologies for doing so, since I believe it to be a true signpost to understanding.

The exactitude of the parallel should offer food for thought, even to those predisposed to recoil or disapprove. The orthodox sex act remains, for perhaps 60 per cent of the human race, perhaps the most delectable of all experiences. And yet the way it is experienced is far from universal: no two sexual communions are ever the same, if only because no two people are the same. Thanks to the researches of Sir Richard Burton and others the Western arm of our species has long been aware of the enormous varieties of sexual interaction that have been dreamed up down the ages by (usually Oriental) experimenters. Love and sex can take astonishing forms – props, settings, scenarios, rituals, exotic clothing and third parties – and yet still remain fundamentally, if orgiastically, orthodox, in that the act is heterosexual and ultimately leads to the direct stimulation to orgasm of the sexual organs of either, both or all parties.

Yet perhaps it is because these 'Arabian Nights' confections are so fantastical that they are not taken seriously. Hard-bitten Western man, with his tabloid newspaper and his earring, is going to take some convincing that doing it upside down on a silk swing while covered from head to foot with sherbet is likely to be an improvement on what he already does, or has expectations of doing, with his nominated female. Nearly everyone has heard of the Arabian Nights, and naughty old-time foreign books, but their days as practical sex manuals, if they ever existed, are long over. Such fantasies cause small concern. They threaten nobody.

Homosexuality is another matter. Male homosexuals have long

held it as an article of faith that the most vicious reactions they experience from male heterosexuals are due to an unacknowledged chime within the aggressor – that they become the victims of a furious and savage rejection of a part of the aggressor's own self. Some homosexual theorists have extrapolated this (in my view) solid perception into the less sustainable position that 'nearly all of us are gay', 'six out of ten are gay', and so on. Of course, it all depends on what you mean by gay, but no matter what the percentages are, it is surely true that (1) a good many more men have homosexual inclinations than are prepared to admit it, even to themselves, and (2) it is the ones who will not admit it even to themselves who are most likely to be hostile, even aggressively so, to those who have not only admitted it, but delight in it.

Both homosexuality and flagellation are tiny shifts – each of a single parameter – from the basic model. Homosexual acts conform entirely to the orthodox pattern, with the sole modification that participants are of the same sex. Flagellation also conforms, as we have seen, in all but one clinical particular: indirect replacing direct stimulation of the sex organs.[4] In few fields other than sex would the difference of a single parameter in such a complex of interactions and contributory themes make such an almighty difference. Yet if one is at all disposed to see (even if one does not openly admit) how pleasure might be obtained from orthodox sex even in its most bizarre forms, then it is not easy to understand why other, relatively minor alterations to the universal script should automatically place those activities as a whole beyond the pale of acceptability.

---

4. However, direct stimulation may indeed follow the indirect stimulation, and frequently does so in the more sexually orientated scenarios. At this moment we must suppose that the activity has become orthodox.

15

DEMOCRACY
AND DISCIPLINE

'You'll have a revolt of your slaves if you're not careful,'
said the Queen.

'Oh, no,' said Cyril; 'you see they have votes – that
makes them safe not to revolt. It makes all the difference.
Father told me so.'

'What is this vote?' asked the Queen. 'Is it a charm?
What do they do with it?'

'I don't know,' said the harassed Cyril; 'it's just a vote,
that's all! They don't do anything particular with it.'

'I see,' said the Queen. 'A sort of plaything . . .'

E. Nesbit, *The Story of the Amulet*

A further explanation for an affinity towards disciplinary
pursuits may be found, as I have suggested elsewhere, in the
relentless egalitarianism of modern life behind the stalking-horse
of democracy.

In recent years conservatives have exulted in the fall of the
Soviet empire, hailing its collapse as the end of communism
and – less sapiently in my view – as the death of socialism. This
is about as accurate as the prediction, fifty years ago, that the
destruction of German Cæsarism obviously included the associated collapse of all conservative political thought. In both cases
the automatic linking between extreme political positions and
the 'next one along' on the left-wing/right-wing spectrometer
has proven to be unjustified. Capitalism has never ceased to

thrive, give or take a blip or two, its only remaining opponent now being its own record of rapacity, waste, greed and failure, rather than any ideological force. Communism, on the Soviet model, is not quite extinct – at the time of writing China, Cuba and North Korea retain systems of this general type – while socialism, or its slightly 'wetter' neighbour social democracy, is plainly alive and well in the upper echelons of the Council of Europe. Meanwhile, the former socialist radicals and members of the 'rainbow coalition'[1] have hived themselves off into the politically correct movement, where they are currently enjoying more success than ever they knew under the Banner of the Red Dawn.

All these political groupings would claim for themselves the label 'democratic'. This term simply means 'rule by the people', and over the two centuries since it first became a serious political force it has variously been interpreted in a bewildering number of ways, very few of which appear to add up to rule by the people except in the most diffuse possible sense. The deceits and outright chicanery which underpin so much Western legislative practice – no country whose system allows 'whipping in'[2] has any claim to be implementing democracy – is now better appreciated by Western electorates than ever before. Disillusion with the political process is rife. Democracy is no longer associated, as it was fifty years ago, with a noble ideal or crusade: it has become a brand of politics like any other, vaguer than most, which has not produced heaven on earth, nor is now thought likely to. It is even widely conceded today that some cultures may not take to democracy; are not suited to it. This argument is most commonly advanced in the case of Russia: it is being said that a people so accustomed to tyranny and authoritarianism simply cannot make any other

---

1. A term for ad hoc alliances between minority groupings which align themselves on the political left.
2. The enforced (by whips) voting by elected representatives along party lines under pain of penalty. This, surprisingly, is not a flagellatory metaphor, but a British fox-hunting term which refers to the marshalling of the hounds.

system work happily, and that the attempt to introduce one is a futile exercise which cannot succeed for reasons that are historic and cultural (since presumably they cannot be racial) but in any case inbuilt. In other words, that the democratic impulse is not, after all, universal and ineluctable, but a plant that can only flourish in certain soils and climates. Can the old conviction that all rival systems are worthless therefore be sustained?

Moreover, if one is forced to accept one kind of unexpected limitation on such a grand ideal, it is not unreasonable to postulate that it may have other deficiencies, hitherto largely unremarked so long as most eyes have been focused on external threats.

Generally speaking, the more apparent failings, many of which are acknowledged in at least some quarters, are held to show that modern society does not have enough democracy; that the representation system, the party system, the whipping system, patronage, outside interests, affiliations, the way in which votes are assessed, the allocation of the franchise itself and how often it may be exercised are no longer equitable or efficient tools for assessing the true will of the people (i.e., a majority of those allowed to exercise the franchise), especially in societies many times more populous than they were when such systems of representative democracy were first brought into being. Many on the political left – in both republics and constitutional monarchies – express such views regularly.

To knock democracy from the opposite direction – that is, to suggest that it may be fundamentally unnatural in some way and that perhaps we have too much of it – is a dangerous act. It was last done on an epic scale by the political movement known as fascism, and the subsequent implementation of the fascistic – or rather, German National Socialist – world picture of humanity graded into élites and not-so-élites involved such monstrous cruelty and persecution of innocents, even without the immensely destructive world war which was the recognition of the threat posed by National Socialism to the democracies, that to reawaken this particular dragon would be the height of irresponsibility, if not worse.[3]

I do not believe it is fascistic to propose that the newly perceived cultural limitations on democracy's spread suggest that limitations of other kinds might be found, if one nerves oneself to look closely enough: that many individuals, family groups and even entire communities within the democratic ambit might, like the Russians, conceivably be happier under arrangements substantially more authoritarian in style and tone. The frequent lament that nobody respects authority any more appears to be an index of this feeling; as does the strange survival, against all odds, of deeply hierarchical practices and institutions – schools, courts of law, the armed forces – within every society which has ever called itself democratic. Almost the first act of egalitarian revolutionary movements is to set up an executive authority with hierarchical characteristics. The more successful the revolutionary movement, the larger it will become, and the larger the executive will need to be: so the hierarchy will grow and stratify, and before too long – if the revolution runs true to precedent – the classic feudal power pyramid will be firmly in place (with those at its apex answerable, in theory, to the people; in other words, nobody). It will be argued that there is no necessary conflict between democracy and hierarchy, providing each tier of the hierarchy is elected by the one below (though no one in the West has ever suggested implementing such a rule in schools, law courts or the armed forces); but it cannot be disputed that, after all the franchise-withholding, positive discriminatory candidate-shortlisting, constituency-gerrymandering and first-past-the-post vote-counting, not to mention the iron grip of the party system

---

3. This is to ignore the earlier but no less ghastly atrocities perpetuated by the Soviet authorities on their own people in the 1920s and 1930s, this time in the name of Marxism-Leninism, a democratic creed of extreme egalitarianism in its original sense which had already reverted, after no more than ten years of power, into an old-style Czarist apparat with all the traditional tools of feudal repression already to hand, and – thanks to technology developed during the Great War – better armed than ever before. We might also remember Cambodia.

and the subsequent 'voting discipline', with constraints upon debate employed whenever a ruling party wishes to have its own way untrammelled, inevitably very little survives, at executive level, of what may once have been the people's will.

The standing justification for this is that the administration has the facts at its disposal, which the people cannot; that it commands the resources, which the people do not, and finally that it is a legally constituted management authority and must be allowed to manage without each and every decision being subjected to a mass vote, since otherwise its task would be impossible. In other words, that democracy is fine up to a point, after which it becomes incompatible with good government.

At this point the egalitarian democrat will start talking about accountability, which is not quite the same thing as democracy, though indeed it would have been entirely understood in the Middle Ages, when the monarch sat at the apex of the power pyramid but was fully 'accountable' to God. In this sense the fall of feudalism was a sign that the people were no longer content with God as guardian of their interests, a judgement which history appears to vindicate since so much of the feudal image – robber barons, the lot of the villein, *le droit de seigneur*, endless war, rapine and pillage – is almost too terrible to contemplate. It is sometimes forgotten, or overlooked, that the Middle Ages were horrible for many reasons which had little to do with the feudal system – the Black Death springs to mind[4] – and that despite its undoubted horrors feudalism's unbroken reign of roughly six centuries in western Europe (it lasted much longer in Russia) is nevertheless a rather better figure than can be claimed by any other political system to date, with the possible exception of Roman imperialism. For all its faults, it remains a role model for stability. Is democracy as safe for another 400 years?

---

4. It may be argued that the ruthless exercise of feudal powers – for example, by ordering city gates to be locked until the infection had moved on – saved many lives during the years of the Black Death. Cf. the spread of AIDS under the benign supervision of democracy.

And are all hierarchies necessarily as inflexible as they seem to be, after all? Even pecking orders may be subject to circumstances and conditions, as one of Havelock Ellis's lady correspondents suggested:

Submission to the man's will is still, and always must be, the prelude to pleasure, and the association of ideas will probably always produce this much misunderstood instinct. Now, I find, indirectly from other women and directly from my own experience, that, when the point in dispute is very important and the man exerts his authority, the desire to get one's own way completely obliterates the sexual feeling, while, conversely, in small things, the sexual feeling obliterates the desire to have one's own way. Where the two are nearly equal a conflict between them ensues, and I can stand aside and wonder which will get the best of it, though I encourage the sexual feeling when possible, as, if the other conquers, it leaves a sense of great mental irritation and physical discomfort. A man should command in small things, as in nine cases out of ten this will produce excitement. He should advise in large matters, or he may find either that he is unable to enforce his orders or that he produces a feeling of dislike and annoyance he was far from intending. Women imagine men must be stronger than themselves to excite their passion. I disagree. A passionate man has the best chance, for in him the primitive instincts are strong. The wish to subdue the female is one of them, and in small things he will exert his authority to make her feel his power, while she knows that on a question of real importance she has a good chance of getting her own way by working on his greater susceptibility.[5]

Let us suppose that in some mysterious manner the impulse towards hierarchical living is inbuilt in the human species, in

---

5. *Psychology of Sex*, II, p. 102.

the same way that many higher mammals, particularly dogs, appear to seek out and thereafter happily observe their place in a pecking order – this despite the fact that the same animals will freely co-operate in group activities such as hunting for food. Modern veterinary psychologists frequently point out that the absence of a clearly defined household hierarchy can cause neurosis in the otherwise well cared-for pet dog. Humans too are higher mammals and it is surely not illogical to suppose that we may profitably study those species most like our own in order to make observations about ourselves that might otherwise have remained hidden. To some extent this has been done already, but if any of the distinguished behaviourists who base conclusions on this kind of research have also produced recommendations that, for true happiness, all humans ought to grade themselves into a pecking order, then I have not encountered them. Other terms and concepts that have entered our consciousness this way, such as 'body language', 'mating dances', 'aggressive display' and 'territoriality', have been assimilated without hesitation, because they do not fundamentally threaten any of our most cherished precepts. The work of 'rogue' behaviourists such as Hans Eysenck has rather more inconsiderately drawn attention to the way different qualities, physiognomies and aptitudes are openly perceived and freely acknowledged – even, by breeders, promoted – in different breeds of the same higher-order animal; while even the possibility of equivalent fundamental differences across the human species is wholly deniable, to say the least. Contentious stuff indeed, so fraught a subject that it is plain that more than mere logical consideration is at work.

Openly to deduce supposed incompatibilities between the political system we call democracy and the fundamental sociology of the human animal can be similarly disadvantageous to the deducer. It is a shibboleth, not even to be approached.

If we do so nonetheless much of this odd passion for discipline is immediately explained. Clearly it is a passion which satisfies those who indulge in it. If satisfaction has taken place, then a need has been met. What is this need? In a flagellatory encounter, it might be a mere indirect stimulation of the sexual organs, but far more importantly it will be for a certain type of situation (context), with the physical component (which is, after all, not absolutely mandatory on every occasion) taking a symbolic and reinforcing rather than engendering role. And the nature of the situation which is found to be so satisfying? Something as unlike everyday life as can be; the most dramatic of all hierarchies – a disciplinary environment. A strange need, after two centuries of democracy: or perhaps not so strange after all.

16

PARADISE REGAINED

Except ye be converted, and become as little children, ye shall not enter into the kingdom of heaven.

Matthew 18: 3

The idea that childhood constitutes the happiest days of one's life is ancient and widespread, and surprisingly uncontaminated by most practical evidence. The ancient half-belief in a golden age – the Edenic or Arcadian idyll – is not just a communal or cultural vision. It is present within individuals too, a wistful longing for the childlike state, when (we tell ourselves) cares were few and easily healed, justice was simple and easy to understand, and responsibility – for oneself, for others – was still an unknown concept.

As we grow towards adulthood these happy states vanish or invert: cares become a multitude, and many of them are not healable at all; man-made justice appears to be at best spotty, and its complexities are wholly beyond all but a few specialists; divine justice is shown as a chimera, a placebo for the ignorant; and for most of us responsibility never ceases to be a burden – though one mitigated, for some, by the personal power that often goes hand in hand with it. 'Movers and shakers' accept the one as a condition of the other and are not, apparently, intimidated by either. But there is such a thing as stress, a word usually employed in connection with those occupations and vocations which are high-powered – responsible, dynamic, frequently event-driven. Police officers, combat soldiers, managing directors of giant companies, broadcasters, politicians – even

289

journalists – often pass their daily lives in conditions of such tension that other, less high-powered types would simply walk away in horror after taking a single glance; as many do. One might take a leaf out of the clinicians' book and describe such driven characters as self-evidently neurotic (movers and shakers can be uncomfortable to have around), but one must also admit that both society, which appears to prize such people more highly than the rest of us, and the deduced laws of evolution, which also favour them because they are the survivors, disagree with us. Yet the will for power, observed in isolation, is not a particularly attractive quality, while our admiration for those willing to accept more than their fair share of responsibility may later be qualified by a cool assessment of how they subsequently bear the burden. A tanker skipper asleep in his cabin with an empty bottle of Jack Daniels while his ship, laden with heavy crude, heads for a notorious reef not far from a world-famous bird colony, will not be judged to be discharging his exceptionally heavy responsibility in a proper manner. 'The Generalship of George Armstrong Custer' will never be on the syllabus at West Point.

Associated with power, responsibility and stress is ego, by which I mean the ability to exclude nearly all considerations except those of the self. Clearly a measure of ego is a survival quality; nevertheless those of us who possess it in super-abundance run the risk of being disliked as a consequence. All the same, a high opinion of one's own abilities may be an absolute pre-condition, within some individuals, for the acceptance of great responsibility. Beyond doubt the capacity to believe in oneself, even to the extent of being obnoxiously egotistical and self-centred, can yield valuable results. So large egos are tolerated, even admired, in the great – though we may notice that greatness is a condition of this tolerance, and not necessarily its product. For it is the particular fate of movers and shakers to be judged almost exclusively by their results, a burden the rest of us thankfully decline.

They accept it nonetheless, because with it comes power, and responsibility, and fulfilment of the needs of an unusually large ego – and stress, which they may well regard as a desirable stimulant. But stress accumulates: it builds beyond tolerable limits. The time-honoured ways to relieve it are to relax; to sit still; to take a holiday, with the added recommendation that the break should be as unlike everyday life as possible. The under-stimulated bank clerk actually wanting to experience stress may sign up for a frenetic tour of seventeen European capitals in three days flat, or he might join an adventure holiday or safari where he will enjoy at least the illusion that he is living in primitive and dangerous conditions. Conversely, the tycoon whose life is spent in hotel rooms or on executive jets, surrounded by fax machines, acolytes with mobile phones and a never-ending stream of decisions to be taken, may well prefer to lie on an exclusive beach somewhere and say and do absolutely nothing at all for as long as he possibly can. This may indeed relieve some of the stress (provided he can also put his business life entirely out of his mind), but the accumulated burden of who he is will receive no relief at all. The only way to ease that pressure is to *be* somebody else, someone as unlike his everyday self as possible, subordinate, utterly powerless, wholly innocent.

The ultimate version of this holiday from the self is, of course, a deliberate return to babyhood.

Male babyism holds up to society a scandalous, accusatory hybrid: not so much man-into-baby but man-*as*-baby, baby-*as*-man. Contradictions are exhibited but not resolved. In these scenes, men surrender deliriously to the memory of female power and their own helplessness in their mother's or nurse's arms. If men are socially tasked with upholding the burden of rational self-containment, perhaps in the baby-land of fem-dom [female domination] they can fleetingly relinquish their stolid control, surrendering responsibility and authority in an ecstatic release of power.[1]

---

1. 'Maid to Order' in *Dirty Looks*.

It is not too difficult to see how a stressed-out captain of industry might well find massive short-term vacational therapy in undergoing such an experience, nor is it at all hard to understand why he would rather die than have it generally known. But babyism (an essentially kinder word than the Freudian 'infantilism', one somehow feels), although a fascinating subject in its own right – several 'perversions' are here rolled into one – is not necessarily flagellationist (real babies are not smacked, at least one hopes they are not), though it is certainly strongly disciplinary. But infancy is an absolute condition of maximum helplessness and maximum innocence, whose essential discipline lies in restraint (the swaddling bands) and loss of all control (over movement, even bowel movement). Even to contemplate it is to be confronted with an extreme and, almost by definition, thinly peopled territory.

The next stage up from babyhood is childhood, and it is here, in one form or another, that most submissive flagellationists choose to locate their alter egos.

Childhood is an elastic term, conventionally referring to the window between infancy and early adulthood, a period of around a dozen years in which the human animal develops both physically and intellectually faster than at any other time of its life. On both counts, there is a great deal of difference between a child of six and one of sixteen – though both may find themselves referred to as children. A small child has only just begun to learn some of the harder lessons of life, and as a result will not be entrusted with much responsibility. He will be watched over, guarded, fed and even dressed by those in charge of him. His most intimate functions may still be under their direct supervision. His crimes almost by definition can rarely be called serious, though he may commit a great many less serious offences, from ignorance, forgetfulness and occasional deliberate naughtiness – which, in one of his age, will be dealt with in the knowledge that such manifestations of apparently bad behaviour may be nothing more sinister than a childlike seeking out of limits, a necessary requirement for his own personal sense of security. (This is not to say that a small child is not occasionally capable of real wickedness in the adult sense of the word, only that it is rare.)

By contrast, the older child is nearly an adult; in some legal senses, he may already be one – able to consent to sex and leave school to work. He is fully mobile and dressed in adult or near-adult fashion. He may already carry a considerable amount of responsibility, for himself and possibly even for others, and very few of the tasks he is routinely expected to accomplish will normally require assistance or supervision. He is, in fact, only just subordinate, only just a child; were he to be orphaned at this stage he would certainly survive. Significantly, he is by now judged capable of the entire panoply of human wickedness: any crime that may be committed by an adult may also be committed by a teenager. He is no longer in any particular special category of innocence. If any account is taken of his age at all it will manifest itself in the form of a slightly more lenient sentence than a fully fledged adult might reasonably expect to receive for the same offence, though even that is by no means certain.

The median age of childhood is between nine and fourteen: awkward hybrid territory for many, and full of paradox, since responsibility has already begun to be heaped on us, while our status is not greatly advanced over the six-year-old's (or so it seems). We are still wholly subordinate, very definitely children. 'They say come, and we cometh; they say go, and we goeth,' to paraphrase the centurion who boasted of his power to Jesus. We wear children's clothes but are expected to comport ourselves, when necessary, like miniature adults. We are sexually aware, but may not yet be sexually active. Even if we are (just), we may not legally consent to sex with an older person – the very fact of our age will be enough to convict the latter of, at best, unlawful carnal knowledge – though the same law peculiarly holds us capable of committing sexual crimes. And this is the time of one's life when one is under maximum repression – the physical constraints of babyhood, it now seems, were only slackened in order to expand and develop other disciplines which the adult world had ready and waiting, many of which are traditionally applied only to children of the middle age group. As adulthood approaches, these may be withdrawn stage by stage, but that is a long way off. In the meantime, if they want to get you, they can.

But this is also the time of one's life when one first realises how delicious it can be to be naughty in certain kinds of way. The joys of provocation and pursuit – and occasional, blissfully exciting capture – offer some of childhood's most ecstatic moments. 'Can't catch me!' (i.e., 'Please chase me!') is a traditional opening gambit. It is the possibility of being caught – and receiving retribution or penalty – which provides both the thrill and the point to childhood's wild hunts. But it would be no fun at all, only terrifying, were it not also perfectly well understood that the consequences of capture will be at least semi-playful. A moderate amount of discomfort and ignominy (a token spanking, being held upside down, having to pay a forfeit) is freely accepted under wild hunt rules; which nearly all children appear instinctively to grasp from their earliest days of personal mobility.

Above all, childhood is a stage of relative innocence. Being under discipline has a concomitant: one is self-evidently not fully responsible, otherwise imposed discipline would not be necessary. But if we are less responsible we are also less guilty. To a child passing through this stage of life 'first time around' it seems irksome beyond tolerance, weighted against him on all counts, and so he longs for adulthood. Later, as an adult, he may perceive in his vanished childhood the only time of his life he can ever remember not feeling used, begrimed, responsible, guilty. He sentimentalises it, idealises it; and, when the longing overpowers him, pays a discreet visit to a professional lady of his acquaintance, where he will freely exchange power for discipline. His submission purchases two hours of innocence, of freedom from the self. It will not be the same as the 'first time around' (if indeed there ever was one in quite these terms), but it may be enough to reawaken the longed-for sweet echoes. So – the truly important factor – the experience has a good chance of refreshing him spiritually. Whatever else it may do, and whatever a voyeur (or the *News of the World*) might think, the subject knows that among the cocktail of feelings he is experiencing are strong notes of an ineffable, wholly innocent joy – an ecstatic release of power indeed.

17

A SADOMASOCHISTIC
SOCIETY?

When all Italy was sullied with crimes of every kind, a certain sudden superstition, hitherto unknown in the world, first seized the inhabitants of Perusa, afterwards the Romans, and then almost all the nations of Italy. To such a degree were they affected with the fear of God, that noble as well as ignoble persons, young and old, even children five years of age, would go naked about the streets without any sense of shame, walking in public, two by two, in the manner of a solemn procession. Every one of them held in his hand a scourge, made of leather thongs, and with tears and groans they lashed themselves on their backs till the blood ran: all the while weeping and giving tokens of the same bitter affliction, as if they had really been spectators of the passions of our Saviour . . . and praying that He, who had been appeased by the repentance of so many sinners, would not disdain theirs.

Justin of Padua, *Chronicon Ursitius Basiliensis[1]*

Most of the Western world's great reforming movements came into being well over a century ago. They were founded by those who believed, with complete sincerity, that the condition of mankind was improvable in nearly all respects, and under that general banner they marched and agitated on behalf of emancipation,

---

1. Quoted in *HOR*, p. 102.

296

workers' rights, universal suffrage, universal compulsory education, a national health service and many other kindly causes, each intended to rectify injustice or alleviate hardship.

What may be termed the second wave of reform – which came later and is still very much in progress – addressed more specific issues, like animal welfare, the abolition of capital and corporal punishment, pacifism and racism. All of these have in common the wish to abolish or reduce a specific form of cruelty: vivisection and fox-hunting, the execution chamber, the rod, war itself. For an activity or practice generally to have been deemed cruel long ago became a *de facto* argument for its abolition. It has now become the chief demon. We still deplore injustice and hardship, but although nobody would claim perfection has been achieved a lot of the original objectives on these scores have largely been met. We no longer keep or trade in slaves (though our Middle-Eastern trading partners most certainly do); workers enjoy many rights (though not as many as they would like); everybody of eighteen years or over is allowed to vote (providing he is or she is not in prison); nearly all of us have attended school (whether we wished to or not); and most Western countries have a measure of public health care.

Cruelty is another matter. Quite clearly, it continues to flourish in many areas. Retreating from public life, like a malignant, incompressible tumour, it has popped up elsewhere. In recent years it has been spectacularly rediscovered in the workplace, the armed forces, and most of all the home. Yet while the original reformers were content to influence society as a whole (though by no means excluding legislation where appropriate), the second wave has from the first been determined to penetrate and police even individual family groupings in order to uncover – and, as they would claim, rectify – any cruelty they find taking place. Since their definition of cruelty carefully excludes anything they might themselves do in the task of rectification (dragging screaming, resisting children from their homes at 5am, for example, or forcibly administering tranquillising drugs to unco-operative children to induce them to allow their bottoms to be inspected for evidence of abuse[2]), and since these agencies are well armed with legal powers and restrained only by 'guidelines', it might even be thought possible that the overall incidence of cruelty has actually been increased by their activities. It takes a zealot to burn a heretic for his own good, but in all our history there has never been any shortage of zealots.

At the time of writing, incomprehensibly dreadful things are happening in a small, landlocked central African country; cruelty indeed, in so ferocious a form that it has horrified a world community well accustomed to atrocity. Endemic mutual dislike between two tribes obliged to share the same country we can comprehend – we have examples in our own backyard. The wish to acquire territory by displacing the other tribe we may deplore, but can also understand – many of the world's frontiers are made uneasy by potential or actual disputes arising from this cause. But the intent to murder the neighbouring population en masse is something almost beyond our comprehension, for even though our own culture group has also been blemished within living memory by similar ghastly impulses, massacres are somehow even more horrible when nearly every murder has been an individual, face-to-face affair. They are evidence of something much more dangerous than sadism – ravening, uncontrollable hatred.

Western society learned about Rwanda quite quickly because Western aid and news agencies made it their top priority to tell us. The aid organisations, appalled by human catastrophe on a scale exceeding all their experience, naturally wished to make urgent appeal to the world community for assistance and resources. In this they were helped by the world's TV companies, who – not for the first time but with less immediate effect than usual – succeeded in prodding their governments into some form of action. Yet while in the past most Western countries, either via government or mass fund-raising events, have been eager to lend

---

2. Both features of the notorious early 1980s Cleveland (north Britain) affair, in which dozens of children were removed from their homes and taken into care on the unsupported evidence of two pædiatricians.

a hand to the wretched of the earth, the response to the urgent appeals for Rwanda was, on the part of nearly all governments except the French (who in any case have a traditional interest in the region), distinguished by a significant hesitation to become involved. And yet the scenes from Rwanda were as distressing as any ever shown on television screens. It is almost as if, incredibly, such scenes are beginning to lose their power to appal us.

If human tragedy on a vast scale no longer has the ability to stimulate public compassion in the way that was so evident at the time of the concert for Bangladesh in 1970, or the remarkable Band Aid concerts of the last decade, then very little indeed can be said for the lasting efforts of those whose public mission has been to rid the world of cruelty during that same time. Or is it that for every small horror exposed and suppressed, dozens more, many of them almost inconceivably worse, are regularly brought to our attention, by those who seek out and trade in the news? By their own lights it is their duty: it is also self-evident that many of its consequences are useful. And after all, they do not commit the acts they report: they merely report them. Yet on the one hand, while the reformers and anti-cruelty lobbyists are busily seeking out new categories of cruelty and 'abuse' in all walks of life, even the humblest, in order to suppress them and 're-educate' their perpetrators away from such tendencies, on the other the news media undo all this sincere work by parading every night horror after horror across our retinas – sound-bitten, captioned and preceded by the standard 'health warnings' though they may be. It is a slightly appalling idea that the most horror most of us may experience in our lifetimes will be the vicarious kind brought to us by television and, to some lesser extent, the printed word.

We should not be surprised if a diet of mingled horror and scolding breeds strange and unwelcome impulses. How many times more cruel was made the punishment of Michael Fay, caned in Singapore in 1994 for vandalism, by his certain knowledge that half the Western world was luxuriating in his plight? Nor is television the only guilty party: in the winter of 1993 flooding in an American eastern seaboard city resulted in a young man being swept to his death in a swollen river. Nobody managed to rescue him – he was afterwards found drowned – but one individual had the presence of mind to take his picture as he went by downstream, still just alive, despair written on every line of his face. This dramatic photograph found its way, via the syndicates, even into the English quality press: the face of a boy in fear of death and about to die. Its effect on his relatives can only be imagined with difficulty, and the present writer does not hesitate to brand its publication as, at best, cruelly irresponsible; at worst something a good deal closer to 'sadism' than nearly all of the activities detailed in this book.

The press justification for all this is twofold: it is the public's right to know; and in any case the public demands it – look at the sales. The former claim is specious. There is no public right to intrude into private grief or humiliation. But the confession that the press feeds the public sadistic imagery because there is an existing appetite for it – in other words, that society is fundamentally sadistic in orientation – is interesting, because it directly opposes every single assumption of the social engineers.

It is also disingenuous. It is not often commented upon but true nonetheless that in all countries which have any form of media the latter never fail to play a major role in the judicio-punitive process. They would like a larger slice of the judicial process as well, and some successful moves have been made in this direction. For many convicted defendants, the sentence, whatever it may be, will certainly be made much harder to bear than the law as it stands may intend, simply by the fact, style and extent of press reportage. Once more, the press is simply 'doing its duty', reporting what it deems ought to be reported, but all the same its activities constitute a fundamental portion of the penalty itself. The destructive effect on the defendant (who may not, after all, be guilty) might be overwhelmingly greater than can possibly be desirable or remotely equitable because, and only because, of the publicity. To be humiliated in front of a courtroom, one's relatives, one's community, is one order of

penalty, and for some, bad enough – after all, it will be in addition to any penalty the court may impose. To have one's shame
noised abroad to an entire TV region or even a nation is a different matter entirely, and there are no laws or guidelines of any
sort to prevent the unjustified and excessive infliction of pain by
this means.[3] Famous persons pay for their fame by being more
badly treated than anyone else in this ongoing and increasingly
self-devouring *auto-da-fé* of private lives and reputations. The
higher the rank of the victim, the more rapidly society's protection appears to be withdrawn – not that the press will disdain to
maul and destroy humbler individuals given the chance and,
most importantly, the apparent justification to do so. For the
beast they are feeding so assiduously is becoming something of
a gourmand. Although any victim will do at a pinch, some – the
rarer kinds – are distinctly more delicious than others.

In late November 1993 two eleven-year-old schoolboys from
Liverpool, England, were found guilty of the murder of James
Bulger, aged four, and were sentenced to be detained at Her
Majesty's Pleasure, which is British law's way of saying 'until we
feel like letting you out'. This conveniently open-ended formula
is commonly employed whenever the courts desire to lock up a
child or young person for life, but do not wish to say so in as
many words, and it is usually a recognition that some very great
crime, perhaps even murder, has been committed. British law
holds that children as young as ten may be charged with this
most awful of all crimes, if there is reason to suppose they have
committed it, and must stand their trial in the manner of adults;
and if convicted, no less than an adult, they must expect to go to
prison for a very long time indeed.

There is no doubt that Robert Thompson and Jon Venables murdered the toddler James Bulger, having first abducted him from a

---

3. Malefactors guilty of some minor but shameful crime are often paraded on
TV news bulletins for no better reason than a shortage of competing stories. The
actual severity of their punishment is therefore affected by purely journalistic
considerations.

shopping centre, apparently for this specific purpose. They took him to a canal side – two ten-year-old boys, playing truant from school – and there slowly battered him to death with horrifying viciousness. I do not believe demonic possession was ever seriously mooted as a possible cause for this almost incredible behaviour, but if one were inclined to believe in such things, surely this is the form they would take? The entire affair was steeped in horror from start to finish; the wretched child suffered appallingly at the hands of his torturers before expiring under a shower of bricks, and the two ten-year-old random murderers made only the most futile efforts to conceal the crime and their involvement in it. It was as if they did not fully understand what it was they had done. A particularly damning piece of evidence was the video footage, from a security camera in the shopping precinct, of one of the boys coolly leading away the doomed infant.

The trial of these two boys and the media publicity attending it together constituted one of the most dreadful pieces of sadomasochistic theatre I can recall in my lifetime. Murder trials are always miserable and ghastly, of course, but the wholly different nature of these particular judicial proceedings was forcibly brought home by the posse of up to 100 media personnel from all over the world in constant attendance in and outside the court while the hearing was in progress. Unusually horrible though it was, it was not the crime that caused this attention, but the criminals.

True sadism ultimately requires a child victim. Here were three – one was already dead. It is very rare indeed that children are given over to the mob, but such, metaphorically, was the fate of the two homicidal eleven-year-olds. The assault of fists on the police van bringing them to court and the furious voices of heroic adult Liverpudlians baying for their blood had both flinching in terror even before they had entered the court. There, just like adults, they were seated in the great dock, each dwarfed by a large male social worker on his right-hand side. Facing them was the entire, intimidating panoply of a British court of law – wigs and solemnity underneath the arms of Her Majesty the Queen. There was no question of their age entitling them to give evidence by video; no consideration for their childhood whatever. Nothing except dozens of adults, bright lights, no hope, and hatred all around them.[4]

Had they been one year younger at the time they committed their crime they could not legally have been arraigned at all.[5]

But after all they *had* committed a horrifying crime, and presumably deserved everything they got. Such, one assumes, was the *Sun*'s justification for its revolting headline the morning after the verdict and sentence[6]; no doubt it was the reason why nearly all the 'quality' correspondents drew their readers' particular attention to the way the two boys wept while they were being sentenced. The grief when they parted from their parents for the last time before being taken away to prison for what will amount to life was also dwelt upon with lascivious enjoyment. Without exception the organs of public opinion pronounced agreement with the sentence[7]; everybody deplored the crime, though none

---

4. The German State Prosecutor has described these as 'barbaric proceedings'.
5. A key part of the prosecution case was whether or not the defendants knew the difference between right and wrong. The crucial 'expert opinion' – that they did indeed know – was provided by two Home Office-appointed child psychologists. Since it was upon this single ground that the conviction ultimately rested, one wonders (though the question was never put in court) precisely how the examination was conducted, and what indeed the validity of its proceedings. Was it made clear to the boys how definitive a 'wrong' answer might be? Were they warned in advance, advised of their rights, put on their guard? Again, one doubts it – and the definition of 'child psychologist' has in any case now openly been expanded to mean 'person who may cause you to be sent to prison if she doesn't like your answers'.
6. HOW DO YOU LIKE IT, YOU LITTLE BASTARDS? (allegedly quoted from the father of the murdered toddler). The *Sun* is the largest-selling daily newspaper in Britain.
7. By recent special order of the British Home Secretary, this has now been increased. The boys are to serve at least fifteen years in prison (in real terms, imprisonment for nearly twice as long as each boy has already been alive). They will be able to note the passing of the years because as they grow older, in contrast to all other prisoners, the régimes in which they are incarcerated will grow steadily harsher – like the open-ended sentence that is decided by the British Home Secretary rather than the trial judge, a peculiar disadvantage of being a child, rather than adult, criminal in modern Britain.

could say how it could have been foreseen or realistically prevented; all expressed the deepest sympathy for the parents of the
dead James Bulger, for whom the trial had been a wrenching
ordeal, and a few expressed some sympathy for the parents of the
two murderers. If the murderers themselves received any at all,
I did not detect it. Public hatred for these two was extraordinary,
even orgiastic; as if all the sins of every aggravating or wicked (or
undisciplined?) child had been heaped upon their two heads
and then discharged in a frenzy of execration.[8] Perhaps, in view
of their crime, what happened to them was just, but it was also,
in my view, disgustingly cruel. They were, after all, children.[9]

It is hard to share the view that much cruelty has been removed
from the world in the last century of unremitting effort. Even if
it has, we are now aware of so much more of it than before from
quarters that were never previously open to us that it makes little difference. Whether we like it or not, or even realise it, we are
constantly bathed in other people's misery, loss, pain, humiliation and destruction. We hear of their good fortune, too, but not
nearly as often, because – and it cannot be denied – bad news is
better 'news' than good news. One of the apparently universal
peculiarities of the human temperament is a particular fascination with others' misfortune: the world's cultures are awash with
Schadenfreude. The realistic and experienced newsman will
argue this position steadfastly, believing the evidence supports

8. The American vox-pop view of the Michael Fay affair was similarly and
weirdly callous, as if all the crimes ever committed by all vandals had been laid
upon Fay's charge.
9. In October 1994 three six-year-old Norwegian boys stripped and kicked a
five-year-old girl playmate into unconsciousness, and then left her to die in
freezing conditions. Since Norwegian law holds that no child under fourteen
can be tried for murder, no charges were preferred. The murdered child's
mother publicly forgave the boys and asked others to do the same. There were
no lynch mobs, no trials, no jail sentences, no media excoriation, even though
the age difference between the respective sets of murderous boys (Norwegian
and British) was no more than four years. At the time of writing no single media
commentator in Britain has pointed this out.

him. Cruelty, he will claim, is endemic and cannot be cured. Even if all television channels were shut down and all newspapers closed do we seriously imagine that people would cease being cruel to one another to the tiniest degree?

The social engineer is obliged to disagree – to take any other position would be to accept an intolerable postulate, namely that the enemy he has dedicated his life to fighting is unbeatable. The impulse to cruelty and other negative emotions like racialism, he argues, are not natural to mankind but corruptions of the human spirit brought about by want or deprivation in other areas – housing, employment, health, diet and above all education. (And disgustingly promulgated, he may add, by the gutter press.) Amend these, he says, and all else will right itself. In the meantime his organisation will continue to hunt down individual cruelties, while mounting parallel campaigns to condition public attitudes away from such impulses, enforcing this where possible with legislation. He concedes the task may be long and uphill but that is no reason not to attempt it.

I hold a position almost exactly between these two: that the impulse we call variously cruelty, sadism or *Schadenfreude* is grossly and wickedly over-stimulated by TV and printed news media for reasons that are almost entirely commercial, but that nonetheless in more modest quantities it is natural to the human species, quite possibly beneficial, and ultimately ineradicable. I believe that our present state of collective neurosis derives ultimately from the tension between those who wish to condition and suppress these tendencies out of existence and those who wish to promote them energetically, and that if we heard a lot less from both quarters we might begin to heal ourselves, though I admit it is an unlikely contingency.

In the meantime the two sides remain agreed on at least one thing: spankers are very depraved people.

18

'SOME ARE BORN DEVIANT . . .'

Society refuses to take seriously the notion of one person saying to another, 'I love, admire and trust you so much that to be dominated by you, punished by you, to be wholly under your control and at your mercy, would be a kind of Heaven' . . . But since these indeed are sometimes the very impulses that underpin serious affairs of the heart, across and between the sexes, those who experience romantic notions of this particular variety are forced to employ tremendous circumlocutions and stalking-games. And yet even so there inevitably comes the revelatory crux, the cards-on-the-table moment. The anticipated trauma of such admissions can prove an obstacle large enough to deter many from taking the step at all. So feelings become repressed and, in later life, a little bit pitiable – frustration makes a creepy obsession out of what was originally a generous and wholeheartedly affectionate impulse, not in the least bit strange providing one's definition of love is itself wide and generous enough.

The Queen of the Grove

The central objective of this book has been to deconstruct the flagellant experience in order to identify what I believe to be its essential keynotes – humanity, sensitivity and affection – thereby showing the activity as a whole in a rather better light than it has historically enjoyed. But before I could do so, I had first to identify and confront several existing negative preconceptions, the most significant of which concerns the true nature of the connection between childhood, discipline and flagellant sexuality.

Of a connection of some kind there can no longer be any doubt; that it is the same for everybody must be considered unlikely in the extreme. Most smacked toddlers do not grow up to be practising flagellants. Many of the latter were indeed never smacked as toddlers. Havelock Ellis believed that such impulses were, at root, congenital, and produced considerable research to support his contention that children have always played apparently spontaneous 'smacking games'. These he considered perfectly natural; that a taste for them should survive puberty and become a life's inheritance was, to him at least, neither extraordinary nor reprehensible, nor necessarily dependent on other influences. In this steady progress from infant to adult pervert no child abuse need take place (unless children may indeed 'abuse' other children), no crime requires to be committed, no duress employed. The entire process has been voluntary. Nevertheless deviation has been achieved.

I hope it is clear – not least because some people undeniably have had deviation thrust upon them – that this book emphatically does *not* advise readers to smack their naughty children. Those who would take such advice from a personally unknown third party, even if it were to be offered (which in this case it is not), would not be acting responsibly. Smack them if you would have done so anyway, and do not if you would not have done so anyway. Either way, there is as much likelihood, and probably no more, of causing lasting harm as there is in many other experiences to which you may subject your child, some of which he will clearly find unpleasant but which he must undergo because in your honest judgement they will do him good. You may turn out to have been wrong, but at least you will have been honest.

Of course children should and must not have any connection with anything remotely resembling adult sexuality. By this clause alone they are entirely excluded from the vast majority of what this book describes, and what 'sadomasochists' do. The child *image* is another matter: it preponderates throughout flagellant fantasy and, understandably enough, has contributed powerfully to the tacit assumption that flagellationists abuse children. A few certainly do, and should be condemned for it, but almost all do not, keeping their games both consensual and strictly adults-only, and in many cases identifying not with the chastising adult but the chastised child. Is it child abuse to pretend to be a child, in the mind's eye? Is it child abuse to pretend that another adult is a child?

If a malevolent and harmful connection with real children is shown to be not only unproven but unrequired, then adult flagellation, whatever else may be said of it, is revealed as, at the very least, an essentially harmless act. Any physical damage sustained is likely to be less grievous than many injuries which may be received on the sports field: in both cases the concept of consenting adults to which I subscribe removes moral onus from the damager. It is all too easy to think of 'lifestyle pursuits' which create a nuisance and involve a considerable amount of public danger – soccer, motor rallying/racing, the Tour de France, off-roading, motorcycle trials – but are tolerated by society nonetheless. Fox-hunting is tolerated by the law but increasingly disliked, and both legally and illegally obstructed by a large portion of the British citizenry. Boxing has a similarly 'mixed' status. And there are grotesque or silly activities – eating-record attempts, for example, or 'dwarf-tossing'. Dangerous, insensitive, cruel, violent, noisy, grossly intrusive, crass, unpleasant or simply tasteless though most of these are, none of their adherents individually attract the odium which commonly attaches to the sexual deviant – unless they turn out to be sexual deviants as well, in which case all bets are off.

But harmlessness is a feeble enough virtue. What if flagellation could be shown actually to *benefit* those who practise it, in the sense of fulfilling a need? Suspending judgement on the need itself for a moment, surely if its fulfilment brings happiness, pleasure, even ecstasy, as it so clearly can, then a case has been made for understanding why flagellationists flagellate or are flagellated: because they enjoy it so much. Things we enjoy doing are normally said to do us good – unless, of course, they are so awful that their happy fulfilment simply cannot be in the public interest.

Only the actual nature of flagellation itself prevents it from being classified as a bona fide form of therapy, since so far as I can see this is as accurate a definition as any. Of course it all rather depends on what you mean by therapy. There are practitioners of many kinds and grades of proficiency, and validity of discipline, who accept fees for probing more or less intimately (and responsibly) into the client's inner self, and even into his body. Drugs may be administered. In some cases these methods and their findings have come under heavy fire, but in no instance has a wayward psychotherapist yet been accused of anything other than negligence or irresponsibility. The ultimate validity of the therapy itself may well not be questioned at all.

One of public life's more 'Restoration drama' moments was provided a few years ago by the discovery that a professional dominatrix – a veritable 'Miss Whiplash' named Sarah Dale – was dwelling in and plying her trade from the basement flat of a building owned by the then newly appointed Chancellor of the Exchequer, Mr Norman Lamont. Informed of his tenant's line of work, the genuinely horrified politico duly shot the lady out into the night; but not before she'd bestowed several (one hopes remunerative) interviews upon the tabloids. Her claim that she was a 'sex therapist' was greeted with the usual haw-hawing, but to me at least it was blindingly obvious that this was *exactly* what she was – what all the Misses Whiplash are. Any definition of therapy I have ever read involves the client feeling better in some way, and without doubt client flagellationists feel a lot better after their flagellations. If they are dealing with an obsession planted within them as children, surely these are classically therapeutic transactions? And they pay for their sessions, which is also firmly within the tradition.

So in the last analysis it is what flagellants actually do, the actual need they appear to have, that prevents the subject taking its place in a long line of, at worst, mildly eccentric 'niche' activities. Most flagellants would settle for the level of public disapproval that attaches, say, to acupuncturists, or yogic flyers, or those who converse with plants.

What flagellants actually do is easily enough stated: they smack each other's bottoms. They do this in hundreds of different ways, but the important act – that which makes it flagellation and not some other activity – is the smacking of bottoms. From this simplest of transactions all else flows.

In order to make the bottom-smacking as 'real' as can be flagellants plunge themselves into a world gone by, perhaps one which never existed, in which all that is for them both sweet and sour about dominance, submission, childhood, discipline and sensuality is blended together into a pageant whose luxuriance or otherwise may depend on many circumstances, not least the partiality of the participants. At its best it is unquestionably an act of love: and even the act of love itself cannot claim more.

Finally, it is an intensely structured theatrical production, where little is what it seems and appearances may stand on their heads. The old grow young again; male becomes female; consent masquerades as non-consent; duress is actually the sweetest of communions; pain is wholly transmogrified into pleasure, and cruel punishment into the delightful caresses of a lover.

Might not the supposed depravity of the practice therefore also turn out to be the exact opposite?

SELECT
BIBLIOGRAPHY

(Abbreviations used in text or footnotes
are shown in **bold type**.)

Adams, **Richard** *The Day Gone By,* Hutchinson, London, 1990.

Anderson, **Verily** *Daughters of Divinity,* Rupert Hart-Davis, 1960.

Anonymous (attrib. Alice Kerr-Sutherland) *A Guide to the Correction of Young Gentlemen*, Delectus, London, 1992, 1994.

Anonymous (attrib. De Rhodes, Stanislas) (i) *Gynecocracy*, privately published, 1890; (ii) *The Petticoat Dominant,* Delectus, London, 1994; (iii) *The Yellow Room,* The Erotika Biblion, 1891.

Anonymous (attrib. Grassal, Georges) (i) *The Memoirs of Dolly Morton*, Carrington, Paris, 1899; (ii) *Frank and I,* Carrington, Paris, 1902.

Anonymous (attrib. Michaux) *Miss High Heels*, Blue Moon, 1988. (Originally published in 1931 by Groves and Michaux, Paris.)

Anonymous (attrib. Stock, St George H.) *The Romance of Chastisement*, William Dugdale, 1866, reprinted 1993 Delectus, London. Stock was a serving officer in an Anglo-Irish regiment: the influence of Algernon Swinburne is also detected, by some, in much of the prose.

Anonymous 'Madame Birchini's Dance', from *The Exhibition of Female Flagellants*, London, 1872.

Anonymous *The Romance of Lust*, Star, 1982.

Anson, **Margaret** *Recollections of the Use of the Rod*, privately printed in 1857, published in 1868 by J.C. Hotten, London. Actually by James G. Bertram (see **Cooper**).

Arden, **Noele** *Child of a System*, Quartet, London, 1979.

Beardsley, **Aubrey** *Under the Hill*. Originally published in *Savoy* magazine, 1897.

Bird, **John** *Percy Grainger*, Faber, London, 1982.

Blue Angel Nights, OBUS, Verlag, 1931.

Brame, **Gloria G.** & **William D.** & **Jacobs**, **Jon** *Different Loving: An Exploration of the World of Sexual Dominance and Submission*, Villard Books, New York, 1993.

Brinsley-Richards, **James** *Seven Years at Eton*, Bentley, 1883.

Cadiveç, **Edith** (i) *Confessions and Experiences*, Grove Press, New York, 1971. Originally published 1932 as *Bekentnisse and Erlebnisse*, probably written 1924–25. (ii) *Eros: The Meaning of My Life*, Grove Press, New York, 1969.

Collins, **Norman** *Children of the Archbishop*, Book Society, 1951 (originally published by William Collins).

Colman, **George** (**the Younger**) (i) *Squire Hardman*, Pastime Press, 1966. Actually written by John Glassco. (ii) *The Rodiad*: this savage though skilfully written poem, also attributed to Colman, was almost certainly the work of Richard Monckton Milnes, a friend of Swinburne's. It was first published in about 1876. False attributions and backdatings of this type are commonplace in most erotic fiction, but Colman has suffered more than most.

Cooper, **Rev**. **W.M.** (James G. Bertram) *An Illustrated History of the Rod*, Wordsworth Editions, 1988. (**HOR**)

D'Icy, **Jacques** (**Louis Malteste**) (i) *Monsieur Paulette (et ses Épouses)*, Orties Blanches, Paris, c. 1920; (ii) *Paulette Trahié* , Orties Blanches, Paris, c. 1929 (author's translations).

D'Olbert, **Gervas** *Chastisement Across the Ages*, Fortune Press, 1956.

De Granamour, **A.** (trans.) *The Conjugal Whip*, N.P. Inc., USA, 1969.

Dompierre, **Sophie** *Je Dresse Mon Mari*, Diachroniques, Paris,

1991 (author's translation).

Dreyfus, **Key** (ed.) *The Farthest North of Humanness: The Letters of Percy Grainger 1901-14*, Macmillan, London, 1985.

Ellis, **Havelock** *Studies in the Psychology of Sex,* Random House, New York, wartime edition, 1942. (**Psychology of Sex**)

Fitzmaurice, **G. Christiano** *A Lady's Sissy Maid*, Constance Enterprises, New Jersey, 1989.

Fleming, **Ian** *Doctor No*, The Book Club, 1958.

Forest, **Antonia** *The Player's Boy*, Faber & Faber, 1971.

Fowkes, **Aubrey** (i) *New Face at Repton Hall*, Fortune Press, 1965; (ii) *The Blue Marble*, Fortune Press, 1958.

Franklin, **Miles** *My Brilliant Career*, Virago Modern Classics, London, 1988.

Gambier Perry, **Major** *Annals of an Eton House*, John Murray, London, 1908.

Gathorne-Hardy, **Jonathan** *The Rise and Fall of the English Nanny*, Arrow, London, 1974.

Gibson, **Ian** *The English Vice*, Gerald Duckworth & Co., London, 1978. (**TEV**)

Gibson, **Pamela Church & Roma** (eds) *Dirty Looks: Women, Pornography, Power*, British Film Institute Publishing, London, 1993.

Godden, **Rumer** *The Battle of the Villa Fiorita*, Macmillan, London, 1963.

Grey, **Antony** *A Gallery of Nudes*, Star, 1967.

Henri, **E.J.**, **Professor** *Kiss of the Whip*.

Hughes, **Kathryn** *The Victorian Governess*, The Hambledon Press, 1993.

Isherwood, **Christopher** *Mr Norris Changes Trains*, Penguin Modern, London, 1969.

Kearney, **Patrick J.** *The Private Case*, Jay Landesman Ltd, London, 1989.

Langford, **David** *War in 2080*, Westbridge Books, 1979.

Lawrence, **D.H.** *The Rainbow*, Penguin, London, 1972.

LeFils, **Crebillon** *A Lady of Quality*, Brandon House, California, 1964.

Malatesta, Louise *The Queen of the Grove*, Chardmore Press, 1993.

Marshall, Arthur *Whimpering in the Rhododendrons*, Collins, London, 1982.

McNeill, Elizabeth *9½ Weeks*, Warner Books, 1992.

Montgomery, L.M. *Anne of Avonlea*, Penguin, London, 1975.

Moore, George *Héloise & Abélard*, Heinemann, 1939.

Morris, Ronald *The Captain's Lady*, Chatto & Windus, London, 1985.

Mosley, Leonard *Curzon: The End of an Epoch*, Longmans Green, 1961. (**Curzon**)

Reinhard, R. *Lenchen im Züchthause (Nell in Bridewell)*, Luxor Press, 1968. First published 1848 (F. Bielefeld, Karlsrühe); first English trans. 1900 (Carrington, Paris). (**Nell in Bridewell**)

Renton, Alice *Tyrant or Victim? A History of the British Governess*, Weidenfeld & Nicolson, London, 1991.

Richards, Frank (Charles Hamilton) *Billy Bunter of Greyfriars School*, Armada paperback, London, 1968.

Roquelaure, A.N. (Anne Rice) *Beauty's Release*, Warner Books, London, 1992.

Rose, Kenneth *Curzon: A Most Superior Person*, Weidenfeld & Nicolson, London, 1969. (**Curzon II**)

Sacher-Masoch, Leopold von *Venus in Furs*, J. Amslow, USA, 1960.

Saint Laure, Rose de *Two Flappers in Paris*, Grove Press, 1986.

Scott, George Ryley *Flagellation: The Story of Corporal Punishment*, Talliss, 1968.

Sellers, Terence *The Correct Sadist*, Temple Press, 1990.

Sheridan, Clare *Nuda Veritas*, Thornton Butterworth, London, 1927.

Underwood, Miles *Harriet Marwood, Governess*, Grove Press, New York, 1967. This novel has had at least three versions and three titles (including *The English Governess* and *Under the Birch*). The real author was a Canadian, John Glassco. (**HM**)

Various Authors *Sweet Retribution*, Alice Kerr-Sutherland Society Book Club, 1994.

Villefranche, **Anne-Marie** *Plaisir d'Amour*, Star, 1982.

Waugh, **Alec** (i) *The Fatal Gift*, W.H. Allen, 1973; (ii) *A Spy in the Family*, Granada, 1979.

Whitehorn, **Katherine** *How to Survive Children*, Eyre Methuen, London, 1975.

Wildfire Club, **The** (i) *When the Wind is Free: A Handbook for the Bonded Maidservant and Her Mistress*, Wildfire Club, 1992; (ii) *The Female Disciplinary Manual,* Wildfire Club, 1994.

Willows, **Claire** *Modern Slaves*, privately printed (USA), 1931.

INDEX

Proper names are listed by surname. Fictional characters are listed by most familiar usage (e.g. James Bond, Billy Bunter) with the name of the book quoted from following in parentheses. Noms-de-plume, pseudonyms and colloquialisms are shown within quotation marks. Films, TV programmes, books and other publication titles are listed in italics.

I have made no separate entry for *flagellation*, since this word and its derivatives may be regarded as *passim*.

SEX IN HISTORY

Reay Tannahill

'A shatteringly wide-ranging survey'
Sunday Times

Sex in History chronicles the pleasures – and the perils – of the flesh from the time of mankind's distant ancestors to the modern day; from a sexual act which was brief, crude and purposeful, to the myriad varieties of contemporary sexual mores.

Reay Tannahill's scholarly, yet accessible study surveys all manner of sexual practice, preference and position (the acrobatic 'wheelbarrow position', the strenuous 'hovering butterflies' position) and draws on sources as diverse as the *Admirable Discourses of the Plain Girl*, the *Exhibition of Female Flagellants*, *Important Matters of the Jade Chamber* and *The Romance of Chastisement*.

Whether writing on adrogyny, courtly love, flagellation or zoophilia, Turkish eunuchs, Greek dildoes, Taoist sex manuals or Japanese geisha girls, Reay Tannahill is consistently enlightening and entertaining.

'Level-headed . . . diligent, provocative and fascinating. The book is the most complete of its kind ever written'
Time

'Sanity on the subject of sex is all too rare; wit is in even shorter supply; and an engaging style is about as commonplace as eyebrows on an egg. Three cheers, therefore, for Reay Tannahill'
Washington Post

ABACUS
0 349 10486 7

ENCYCLOPEDIA OF UNUSUAL SEX PRACTICES

Brenda Love

Filled with more astonishing facts and fancies than most people could ever have imagined, the *Encyclopedia of Unusual Sex Practices* presents a unique guide to human sexual expression, ranging from the mildly kinky to the truly bizarre.

Carving a path through the mysteries of human behaviour, it records practices and beliefs from cultures world-wide throughout history, as well as from the author's extensive researches into contemporary sexual habits.

From Acrophilia (being sexually aroused by heights) to Zelophilia (being aroused by jealousy) via such arcane pursuits as furtling, nasophilia and felching, the *Encyclopedia of Unusual Sex Practices* contains information sometimes repellent, sometimes stimulating – but always absolutely fascinating.

'Those whose sex lives could do with spicing up but are not sure where to start need look no further'
GQ

'This is the kind of book which, once penetrated, is hard to extract oneself from'
Independent

ABACUS
0 349 10676 2

| ☐ Sex in History | Reay Tannahill | £6.99 |
| ☐ Encyclopedia of Unusual Sex Practices | Brenda Love | £12.99 |

Abacus now offers an exciting range of quality titles by both established and new authors. All of the books in this series are available from:

Little, Brown and Company (UK),
P.O. Box 11,
Falmouth,
Cornwall TR10 9EN.

Fax No: 01326 317444.
Telephone No: 01326 372400
E-mail: books@barni.avel.co.uk

Payments can be made as follows: cheque, postal order (payable to Little, Brown and Company) or by credit cards, Visa/Access.
Do not send cash or currency. UK customers and B.F.P.O. please allow £1.00 for postage and packing for the first book, plus 50p for the second book, plus 30p for each additional book up to a maximum charge of £3.00 (7 books plus). Overseas customers including Ireland, please allow £2.00 for the first book plus £1.00 for the second book, plus 50p for each additional book.

NAME (Block Letters) _____

ADDRESS _____

_____

_____

☐ I enclose my remittance for £ _____
☐ I wish to pay by Access/Visa Card

Number ⬚⬚⬚⬚⬚⬚⬚⬚⬚⬚⬚⬚⬚⬚⬚⬚

Card Expiry Date _____